EVALUATING CRIME REDUCTION INITIATIVES

Johannes Knutsson

and

Nick Tilley

Editors

Crime Prevention Studies
Volume 24

Criminal Justice Press
Monsey, NY, U.S.A.

Willan Publishing
Cullompton, Devon, U.K.

2009

© Copyright 2009 by
Criminal Justice Press.
All rights reserved.

Printed in the United States of America. No part of this book may be reproduced in any manner whatsoever without written permission, except for brief quotations embodied in critical articles and reviews. For information, contact Criminal Justice Press, division of Willow Tree Press Inc., P.O. Box 249, Monsey, NY 10952 U.S.A.

ISSN (series): 1065-7029.

ISBN-13 (cloth): 978-1-881798-82-8.

ISBN-10 (cloth): 1-881798-82-8.

ISBN-13 (paper): 978-1-881798-83-5.

ISBN-10 (paper): 1-881798-83-6.

Printed on acid-free and recycled paper.

CRIME PREVENTION STUDIES

Ronald V. Clarke, Series Editor

Crime Prevention Studies is an international book series dedicated to research on situational crime prevention and other initiatives to reduce opportunities for crime. Most volumes center on particular topics chosen by expert guest editors. The editors of each volume, in consultation with the series editor, commission the papers to be published and select peer reviewers.

* * *

Volume 1, edited by Ronald V. Clarke, 1993.

Volume 2, edited by Ronald V. Clarke, 1994.

Volume 3, edited by Ronald V. Clarke, 1994.

Volume 4, *Crime and Place*, edited by John E. Eck and David Weisburd, 1995.

Volume 5, *The Politics and Practice of Situational Crime Prevention*, edited by Ross Homel, 1996.

Volume 6, *Preventing Mass Transit Crime*, edited by Ronald V. Clarke, 1996.

Volume 7, *Policing for Prevention: Reducing Crime, Public Intoxication and Injury*, edited by Ross Homel, 1997.

Volume 8, *Crime Mapping and Crime Prevention*, edited by David Weisburd and J. Thomas McEwen, 1997.

Volume 9, *Civil Remedies and Crime Prevention*, edited by Lorraine Green Mazerolle and Jan Roehl, 1998.

Volume 10, *Surveillance of Public Space: CCTV, Street Lighting and Crime Prevention*, edited by Kate Painter and Nick Tilley, 1999.

Volume 11, *Illegal Drug Markets: From Research to Prevention Policy*, edited by Mangai Natarajan and Mike Hough, 2000.

Volume 12, *Repeat Victimization*, edited by Graham Farrell and Ken Pease, 2001.

Volume 13, *Analysis for Crime Prevention*, edited by Nick Tilley, 2002.

Volume 14, *Evaluation for Crime Prevention*, edited by Nick Tilley, 2002.

Volume 15, *Problem-oriented Policing: From Innovation to Mainstream*, edited by Johannes Knutsson, 2003.

Volume 16, *Theory for Practice in Situational Crime Prevention*, edited by Martha J. Smith and Derek B. Cornish, 2003.

Volume 17, *Understanding and Preventing Car Theft*, edited by Michael G. Maxfield and Ronald V. Clarke, 2004.

Volume 18, *Designing Out Crime from Products and Systems*, edited by Ronald V. Clarke and Graeme R. Newman, 2005.

Volume 19, *Situational Prevention of Child Sexual Abuse*, edited by Richard Wortley and Richard Smallbone, 2006.

Volume 20, *Putting Theory to Work: Implementing Situational Prevention and Problem-oriented Policing*, edited by Johannes Knutsson and Ronald V. Clarke, 2006.

Volume 21, *Imagination for Crime Prevention: Essays in Honour of Ken Pease*, edited by Graham Farrell, Kate J. Bowers, Shane D. Johnson and Michael Townsley, 2007.

Volume 22, *Surveying Crime in the 21st Century*, edited by Mike Hough and Mike Maxfield, 2007.

Volume 23, *Perspectives on Identity Theft*, edited by Megan M. McNally and Graeme R. Newman, 2008.

Volume 24, *Evaluating Crime Reduction Initiatives*, edited by Johannes Knutsson and Nick Tilley, 2009.

Volume 25, *Countering Terrorism through Situational Crime Prevention*, edited by Joshua D. Freilich and Graeme Newman, forthcoming 2009.

Volume 26, *From Research to Realisation: Designing Out Crime from Products*, edited by Paul Ekblom, 2010.

CONTENTS

continued

Acknowledgments

This book brings together papers that were first presented and discussed at a small meeting on evaluation of situational crime prevention and problem-oriented policing, which was held in May 2008 at Stavern, the Norwegian Justice Sector's Center for Training and Practice. We are grateful to the staff of the Center for making our stay a most enjoyable one. They made us very welcome, served delicious meals, and provided comfortable accommodation. We are also indebted to the Norwegian National Police Directorate and the Norwegian Police University College for funding the conference. Without their support this volume would not have been possible. Finally, we would like to thank the participants at the meeting not only for their contributions to this book, but also for the thoughtfulness of their comments on one another's earlier drafts.

Johannes Knutsson
Norwegian Police University College

Nick Tilley
Jill Dando Institute of Crime Science
University College London

FOREWORD

The effectiveness of differing methods of crime control is a key issue in many jurisdictions. Assessments of what is delivered are often undertaken by the police. The police are good at presenting promising results. Moreover they have well-developed routines for learning from experience. These circumstances may lead police managements to be content with their internal evaluations. They may therefore fail to involve external researchers who are competent to provide necessary quality controls.

Assessing what is good police work and what are workable measures can be technically demanding. The measures adopted and the measurements used are often rather short term and specific to the current situation: the measures prove effective there and then, but their scope in a wider perspective may be limited. They nevertheless give an air of efficiency and rigour. The exercise provides information that is sought after by the politicians, who draw up policies for policing and also set the budgets for police work.

This collection of articles includes interesting comments on the challenges that face those charged with looking into what works when it comes to reducing crime. All who work in the police service know that this is a complicated and difficult question. Statistics provide only part of the truth, and quality is hard to measure. In spite of this – or perhaps because of it – it is important that leaders within the police have the courage to ask for evaluation reports from competent bodies outside the police, rather than relying solely on internal judgements. Doing so will better secure both objectivity and quality. But, more importantly still, it will generate interesting and informed judgements on which preventive measures might be chosen.

Some of the results may be unwelcome. Not all measures work the way we hoped they would. On the other hand, robust findings on effectiveness and ineffectiveness give police leaders the necessary basis for future decisions. This is useful for decision-makers, and provides strong grounds for action. Furthermore, politicians and authorities can feel confident that money is wisely spent, in accordance with what both the police and the external research bodies know about which methods work and how.

A knowledge-based police service should rest on high quality evidence. To obtain this, it is necessary that the police and the research community work together in joint efforts to reduce crime. The will to be open, and the ability to listen, are always crucial as a basis for achieving better results, including those relating to reductions in crime. Independent evaluation should be a keyword for each and every serious leader in the police.

This book shows that the task of conducting qualified evaluations is complicated. It represents a challenge both to the police and to the researchers. In the first place, the police need to know what comprises a good evaluation and what it takes to conduct one. There seems to be some potential for improving police commissioning of evaluation reports. In the long run, more informative evaluation products will enhance the quality of police work. For their part, research bodies need to have not only the technical competence for conducting evaluations, but also insight into police work and the conditions under which it is performed. To achieve the required mutual understanding, the police and the research community need to develop more cooperative ways of working. We have made some headway, but there is still some distance to go. This is our present challenge.

Ingelin Killengreen
National Police Commissioner, Norway

INTRODUCTION

by

Johannes Knutsson
Norwegian Police University College

Nick Tilley
University College London

Evaluation has always played a central part in both situational crime prevention (SCP) and problem-oriented policing (POP). In the advance of situational crime prevention, where attempts to prevent crimes are made through opportunity reduction, evaluation has been a driving force. In POP, where tailor-made preventive measures designed to solve problems of crime or disorder are put into effect, evaluation is an integral part of the process, indicating whether the intended effect has or has not come about. There is a growing consensus, however, that much evaluation in crime prevention has been unsatisfactory, but there are also important debates over the best methods of effecting improvements. In what way can the effectiveness of crime preventive measures and programs be assessed systematically and rigorously? What types of evaluation will be most useful to policymakers and practitioners? What have we learned from past evaluations? These questions formed the starting point for the present volume.

The chapters both look backwards to what has been done so far by way of evaluation and forward to what might be done better in the future. The balance between retrospect and prospect varies. The early chapters, especially Knutsson's and Guerette's, focus mainly on what has been done to date. The later chapters, especially Henry's and Johnson's, focus mainly on what might fruitfully be added in the future. In varying ways, the

Crime Prevention Studies, volume 24 (2009), pp. 1–6.

chapters in between the aforementioned ones reflect on prevailing forms of evaluation and how they and their use might be improved (Braga & Bond; Eck & Madensen; Tilley).

The number of evaluations of situational crime prevention initiatives has grown very substantially since that approach was established in the late 1970s (Guerette). These programs use a variety of methods, but seem to provide compelling evidence of the effectiveness of prevention measures attuned to specific crime problems. A potential problem in discussing suites of past evaluations is, of course, publication bias – the well-known tendency for positive findings to be published rather than negative ones. Though this may, of course, be present in the case of situational crime prevention, it would appear more likely that the masses of situational measures routinely taken, for instance by businesses, simply remain unstudied and unreported. Moreover, the reasons for this have less to do with lack of resources or technical difficulties than with the self-evidence of success for these methods among businesses attempting to reduce their crime losses. Take, for example, the decision of a small retailer in a high crime neighbourhood to place high-value items behind the counter rather than on open display. This is clearly a situational measure, clearly makes the theft of those items practically impossible, and clearly in that sense deals effectively with that businesses's problem. The business itself is unlikely to be concerned with potential displacement of the offense to other merchants.

The very pervasiveness of situational means of preventing crime, and the lack of interest in them when they appear to be helping prevent crime – for example, requirements for employees to submit receipts to claim expenses; locking houses and cars to inhibit theft; not leaving valuables about where they might be picked up by strangers; having guards in art galleries and museums to deter thieves; producing banknotes whose forgery is difficult; and attaching dye-tags to high-value items aimed at youngsters in clothes shops so that their value is reduced if they are stolen – are seldom if ever formally evaluated because there is no interest in conducting the evaluation. Moreover, where evaluations are undertaken they can be carried out where measures are put in place unreflectively or where there is no relevant problem to address. A case in point is closed-circuit television (CCTV) in the U.K., for which there has been massive funding following upon widespread political and public support. This has led to widespread deployment of CCTV without the prior analysis of need or potential that is called for in situational crime prevention. Negative findings about effectiveness here may reflect mindless application rather than weaknesses in situational crime prevention as a whole or in the well-targeted use of CCTV in particular (Guerette). There is no reason to suppose that evaluations assess a representative sample of situational crime prevention interventions. There are, thus, various sources of selection bias affecting what is evaluated. On balance, these are likely to overlook the obviously effective measures and to home in on the more dubious approaches.

Situational crime prevention evaluations adopt a range of methods and these are reflected in the papers collected here. Though randomised control trials (or their close counterparts) may sometimes be possible (Braga & Bond; Guerette; Henry), many of the papers suggest that they are not always either necessary or ideal (Eck & Madensen; Henry; Tilley; Johnson). Particular problems relate to the fact that situational crime prevention initiatives tend often to be area-based, where the conditions needed for randomised control trials are especially difficult to create, though there are some examples where it is claimed that they are met satisfactorily (see Boruch et al., 2004). Randomized Controlled Trials (RCTs) – or even their close cousins, where some of the conventional conditions are breached – may sometimes be impossible, may sometimes yield invalid findings, and may sometimes be an inefficient methodology for advancing situational crime prevention theory, policy and practice. Other approaches may, thus, be more practicable or preferable in producing high quality findings. Suggestions include simulations (Johnson), examination of detailed expected outcome footprints (Eck & Madensen; Tilley), and regression discontinuity designs (Henry). There is certainly no reason to confine attention to evaluations that can be done or have been done using RCTs or their close equivalents, an approach that is emphasised in the Campbell Collaboration (see below). This book brings out well the fact that much has been and can continue to be learned from evaluation studies using different designs. This is not, though, to deny a place for RCTs when they are practicable and when critical discussion suggests that they will produce the most useful and valid findings for theory, policy and practice.

The papers brought together here bring out the practical difficulties that are faced in producing strong evaluation studies. Many situational crime prevention evaluations are methodologically inadequate, whatever particular approach is adopted (Knutsson). Where local evaluations are undertaken, for example of problem-oriented policing initiatives, this is especially liable to be the case (Knutsson). The schemes are often small and complicated and data are weak. And even where analysts are employed by the sponsoring agency, they are often not used in the evaluations and may lack the particular skills needed to produce findings that are capable of withstanding critical scrutiny (Knutsson). Moreover, crime prevention initiatives frequently encounter more or less serious implementation problems (Knutsson; Tilley). They are also characteristically introduced in complex settings where much else is going on in addition to the crime prevention activity, and in which offender, practitioner and policymaker stakeholders are liable to adapt their behaviour to one another (Henry; Tilley). Such implementation weaknesses and inherent complexity produce substantial challenges for the production of robust and useful evaluation findings. Thus, although as Guerette shows there are by now numerous studies that show the effectiveness of situational crime prevention initiatives, producing strong studies is more fraught with difficulties than might at first sight seem to be the case.

Evaluations serve varying purposes. Evaluations may be conducted in the interests of informing policy decisions: e.g., where should resources be allocated and which policies should be disseminated? (See mainly Braga & Bond; Johnson.) They may also be conducted to inform practitioners' and policymakers' decisions when faced with a new situation: e.g., what should we do to react to that change? (See mainly Guerette; Knutsson.) They may also be conducted in the interest of taking a field of applied knowledge forward: e.g., how do we develop, refine and test theory? (See mainly Eck & Madensen; Henry; Tilley.) The differing purposes of evaluation clearly overlap, but they may suggest the different standards, priorities and methods that are emphasised in the chapters that follow in this volume.

The problem of bias is clearly important in evaluation, and it can creep in, in many different ways. We have already mentioned some sources. Others that are discussed in this volume relate to temptations to accentuate the positive and to ignore the negative (Knutsson; Tilley). These temptations can come from scholars themselves, whose preferred theories or ideology may lead them to be selective in their analyses and in their choice of findings to report. The temptations can also derive from external pressures. In police services and government departments, for example, it will often be clear that those asking for the evaluation hope for and sometimes confidently expect positive findings. Both junior researchers within these organisations and external contractors can often be drawn into trying to present findings in the most favourable light possible.

It seems to us that there is a risk that experiments, in the sense of RCTs and their closest counterparts that compare apparently similar treatment and non-treatment cases or groups, will take on an unwarranted status as the unequivocal "gold standard" in evaluations. More seriously, they may thereby also be treated by potential users as well as members of the research community as the only methods that can produce dependable findings. Against this exclusivity, in addition to the points that emerge from many of the papers published in this volume, there is by now a massive and growing literature, both within and beyond the field of situational crime prevention, which shows this view to be untenable (see, for example, Cartwright, 2007; Berwick, 2007; Clarke and Cornish, 1972; Hollin, 2008; Pawson, 2006; Pawson and Tilley, 1997). It is likely that only the most rabid experimental enthusiasts would want to rule out other evaluation designs. Most, if not all, serious practitioners and theorists of experimentalism acknowledge that other methods are sometimes necessary in practice and can yield valid findings.

The Campbell Collaboration is the organisation most associated with experimentalism. Yet Donald Campbell, after whom the movement is named, stressed, "the obvious theoretical complexity of measures and the frequently plausible argument that the measured change was the result of irrelevant components of the complex" (1999, p. 167). He favoured "exploring multiple approaches to measuring 'the same thing' " (ibid.). He further averred that "all available measures have less than perfect validity, being systematically biased" (ibid.). His advice to "governmental science policy makers" was:

> Give up the notion of a single new evaluation designed to support a single administrative decision regarding expanding or curtailing a program. Substitute for this the development of a disputatious mutually monitoring, applied scientific community that will advise governmental decisions on specific programs from its general wisdom about research in the problem area. (Campbell, 1999, p. 169)

We agree. Multiple evaluations using multiple measurement methods and multiple designs with mutual checking and criticism are, we think, the approach that is most likely to contribute not only to well-reasoned advice, but also to progress in the fields of situational crime prevention and problem-oriented policing.

REFERENCES

Berwick, D. (2007). The science of improvement. *Journal of the American Medical Association,* 299, 1182–1184.

Boruch, R., May, H., Turner. H., Lavenberg, J., Petrosino, A., de Moya, D., Grimshaw, J., & Foley, E. (2004). Estimating the effects of interventions that are deployed in many places. *American Behavioral Scientist* 47, 608–33.

Campbell, D. (1999). Sociological epistemology. In D. Campbell & M. Jean Russo (Eds.), *Social Experimentation*. Thousand Oaks, CA: Sage.

Cartwright, N. (2007). *Hunting causes and using them*. Cambridge, UK: Cambridge University Press.

Clarke, R., & Cornish, D. (1972). *The controlled trial in institutional research: Paradigm or pitfall for penal evaluators*. Home Office Research Study 15. London: Her Majesty's Stationery Office.

Hollin, C. (2008). Evaluating offending behaviour programmes: Does randomization glister? *Criminology and Criminal Justice* 8(1), 89–106.

Pawson, R. (2006). *Evidence-based policy*. London: Sage.

Pawson, R., & Tilley, N. (1997). *Realistic evaluation*. London: Sage.

STANDARD OF EVALUATIONS IN PROBLEM-ORIENTED POLICING PROJECTS: GOOD ENOUGH?

by

Johannes Knutsson
Norwegian Police University College

Abstract: *In problem-oriented policing (POP), assessment is an integral part of the process in which the effectiveness of the implemented measures is judged. When the POP philosophy was introduced, more of the effort was put into disseminating it and explaining its merits, than to instruction about the more technical parts of the process, like evaluation. The POP approach attracted a lot of interest, and many police forces started to practice it as a strategy to prevent crime and disorder. Rather soon, evaluative examinations showed that the implementation was often frail and that the quality of the projects frequently was poor. This goes especially for the assessment phase, which is technically demanding. Given the skills of practitioners, in most cases police officers, and the circumstances in which projects are carried out, a higher degree of sophistication of the evaluations is not to be expected. Evaluations almost always have a one-group before-and-after design, which is often the only feasible one, and which is sufficient for many purposes. However, examination of a number of projects that represent best practice shows that there is*

Crime Prevention Studies, volume 24 (2009), pp. 7–28.

room for improvement. In order to achieve this, the police need to cooperate with academically trained analysts when practicing problem-oriented policing.

INTRODUCTION

In the last few years the term *evidence based* has become something of a catchphrase. It is often used in public debate about criminal justice policy, with the risk that the concept will be muddled, misunderstood and abused. The following definition is given in an easily accessible source (Wikipedia):

> **Evidence** in its broadest sense includes anything that is used to determine or demonstrate the truth of an assertion. Philosophically, evidence can include propositions which are presumed to be true used in support of other propositions that are presumed to be falsifiable. The term has specialized meanings when used with respect to specific fields, such as policy, scientific research, criminal investigations, and legal discourse.

In the field of crime prevention, the term "evidence based" has come to be associated with measures that are supported by scientific studies, often in the form of experiments. Here, a lively discussion of what kind of evidence is admissible has erupted. On the one hand, there are experimentalists who are reluctant to accept studies other than randomized controlled experiments[1] as admissible evidence, and on the other, a group who might be called pragmatists who display a more open attitude toward what is acceptable or not (Tilley, 2006). But even if there are some differences of opinion, both camps insist on evidence as a basis.

Looking back, evaluation studies played a major role in the creation of two related approaches to crime prevention that came into existence during the late 1970s and the beginning of the 1980s. Both are now well established and applied with good results, and furthermore, they continue to evolve as new experiences accumulate.

The main idea for one of these approaches, situational crime prevention, is to produce preventive effects by reducing opportunities for crime. Led by the Home Office in the U.K., but also to some extent by the National Council for Crime Prevention in Sweden, a number of evaluation studies of situational measures had shown their effectiveness (Clarke and Mayhew, 1980; Kühlhorn and Svensson, 1981). Similar findings were reported in the Netherlands (Willemse, 1994; Junger-Tas, 1993).

One reason for searching for new avenues for prevention was disappointment with the findings from research on the effects of correctional treatment. Results from a number of experiments had challenged the optimistic expectations that crimes effectively could be prevented by changing the personal dispositions of criminals.[2] To summarize: the results indicated that it was harder to alter the character of criminals and thereby change their behavioral tendencies, than to affect behavior by modifying the *situations* in which they acted and their perceptions of those circumstances.

The second approach, which will be highlighted in this chapter, is more of a philosophy about how police can conduct their business more efficiently with a clear focus on prevention. One of the motivating factors for the creation of this new way of thinking about and doing policing was the realization that conventional policing – the standard model – had not lived up to expectations of its preventive and safety-creating effects. To a large extent, the notion that old models of policing were failing and that fresh thinking was required had its roots in research, where evaluations had a central role. One of the most important studies in this connection was the Kansas City Preventive Patrol Experiment (Kelling et al., 1974). The study failed to find the assumed beneficial effects on crime and feelings of safety of patrolling in a randomized manner in marked police cars – an activity that took, and still takes, an enormous amount of police resources. This particular study has had – and still has – a massive influence in discussions of how policing should be carried out.

PROBLEM-ORIENTED POLICING

Instead of waiting for crimes or disturbances to take place and then responding to them, the police should first establish what caused people to call for the police. Concentrations of such incidents – signified as "problems" – were the starting point for the approach. Herman Goldstein, who created the philosophy, named it problem-oriented policing (POP; Goldstein, 1979). After carefully defining and describing the problem, an analysis of what caused it, or its preconditions, should be carried out. The next step in the process is to find and implement measures that would decrease or eliminate the problem. And last, but not least, an assessment of the effectiveness of the response should take place.

In this context, there are at least two distinctive and important features of the POP philosophy that should be pointed out. The first is that problem-oriented policing is a product of academics concerned with the quality and effectiveness of policing. The philosophy was offered to police organizations, which have a "practical" orientation and in many cases are unused to, and have little regard for academia, especially social sciences, from which POP emanates. How does an organization that to a large extent rests its practice on "tried experience" react to and accommodate a research-based approach?

The other distinctive feature of POP is the action-research model, in which evaluation plays an integral part. It is on this last step in this process that this paper will concentrate: assessment of the impact. We will discuss what should be the standard of these evaluations. Now that the POP philosophy has been practiced for several decades and experiences have been accumulating, has there been an improvement in the evaluation component? Admittedly there is a rather comprehensive literature dealing with the standard of problem-oriented policing and its implementation (Leigh et al., 1996; 1998; Read and Tilley, 2000; Clarke, 1998; 2002; Scott, 2000; Knutsson, 2003; Bullock et al., 2006; Knutsson and Clarke, 2006), but this specific step in the process has not been dealt with sufficiently.

EARLY DEVELOPMENT

The first and founding pieces of work on POP were mainly aimed at describing and arguing for the new approach. They discussed the inadequacy of conventional policing, advantages of the suggested alternative and how it was supposed to be practiced. Understandably the focus was mostly on the early phases of the process, with less detail on the follow-up (evaluation) step, although of course it was mentioned. In Goldstein's own words:

> A fully developed process for systematically addressing the problems that make up police business would call for more than the three steps just explored – defining the problem, researching it, and exploring alternatives. . . . for systematic analysis of substantive problems requires developing a capacity within the organization to collect and analyze data and to conduct evaluations of the effectiveness of police operations. (Goldstein, 1979, p. 25)

Even in a later more comprehensive work (Goldstein, 1990), this final phase is not given any more thoroughgoing consideration. However, Goldstein points out both the value and the necessity for the police to draw upon and to develop an evaluation competency of its own, to measure the effects of their efforts. Nevertheless, since evaluation is a complicated endeavor, the police also need to develop more productive relations with academia where this competence mainly resides (Goldstein, 1990, p. 49). External observers made the same judgment. To be able to carry out and to develop this form of policing, the police need access to qualified persons with research competence (Reiss, 1992).

Neither was the assessment phase given deeper deliberation in another of the other founding works from the latter part of the 1980s (Eck and Spelman, 1987). Their inquiry consists mainly of examples where the POP philosophy was tested by the police on different problems. In this publication, the process of carrying out problem-oriented policing was summarized with the acronym SARA, signifying *scanning*, *analysis*, *response* and *assessment*. SARA has almost become synonymous with problem-oriented policing. About the assessment phase, it was stated that, "This final stage provides feedback to the agency on how response works" (Eck and Spelman, 1987, p. 50). Those involved in the Eck and Spelman study had been introduced to elementary methods of evaluation, but since many of the projects used as examples had not reached that step at the time of writing the report, it was not possible to make a judgment about how well the evaluations were carried out. However, the authors pointed out that the ability of the police to conduct evaluations usually was very low, with the consequence that measures that did not work might continue to be used, and that measures that in fact were effective might be abandoned (Eck and Spelman, 1987, p. 101).

To conclude, it may be stated that what is required to conduct an assessment was not dealt with in any depth in these two early publications. This means that it was difficult for interested police officers, including their leaders, to understand what assessment really means and, above all, to learn how technically demanding it is. Even among academics, many were unfamiliar with evaluation methodology. This shortage of skill in evaluation meant that a precondition for good quality problem-oriented policing was not in place during early efforts at implementing it.

ESTABLISHING AND SUPPORTING PROBLEM-ORIENTED POLICING

Early experiences of implementing the POP philosophy made the proponents realize that there was a strong need to support police in their efforts to carry out problem-oriented policing. An important step was the creation of conferences devoted to the philosophy. Behind the meetings were different actors with insights into the approach and a strong belief in its effectiveness, but also an understanding of the complexity of practicing it. In the U.S., the conferences were first organized by the Police Executive Research Forum beginning in 1990. One of the recurring and important events of these conferences has come to be the announcement of winners of the Herman Goldstein Award. Those who had carried out POP projects were encouraged to submit projects to be judged. The idea was that problem-oriented policing would be supported by the power of good examples. The award has been in existence since 1993. During its first ten years, there were about 100 submissions on a yearly basis, but that has later decreased to about 50. Since 2004, the Center for Problem-Oriented Policing (see below) has taken over the responsibility for arranging the conference. In the U.K., starting in 1999, a similar conference – the Brit-POP – also includes a competition, the Tilley Award, as an important part of the meeting.

Instructions for Submissions

In the beginning, the instructions concerning the assessment step were rather meager. Those who wanted to submit projects to be considered for the Herman Goldstein Award were guided by the questions: "What was the goal of the problem-solving effort?. . . . [and] Was the goal accomplished?"

As a guide for describing the assessment phase in a project carried out according to the principles of problem-oriented policing, these questions provided little direction. It must be very difficult for practitioners, who are more or less without schooling in evaluation methods, to understand what is actually involved in developing convincing answers to the questions.

Probably as a response to the substandard quality of many assessments in the projects, the instructions have become much more elaborate, which could also partly explain the decrease in number of submissions. Nowadays, the instructions are given as a list of questions which, if answered, would give a good idea of what the assessment is about and what is required. Exactly the same development as to details in instructions is noticeable for the Tilley Award.

Later Development

Two institutions with important consequences for problem-oriented policing have been created during the first years of the 21st century – one in U.K. and the other in the U.S. At University College London, the Jill

Dando Institute of Crime Science has been established. Its task is described as follows:

> The UCL Jill Dando Institute of Crime Science is the first university department in the world devoted specifically to reducing crime. It does this through teaching, research, public policy analysis and by the dissemination of evidence-based information on crime reduction. (www.jdi.ucl.ac.uk)

The Dando Institute's publication entitled *Become a Problem-Solving Crime Analyst: In 55 Small Steps* (Clarke and Eck, 2003) has become a landmark. It comprises an easily digestible manual for conducting crime preventive projects, including their evaluation.[3] The manual has been very well received and has, for example, become the starting point for a course in problem-solving for crime analysts given by the institute.[4] Furthermore, the publication has become an international success and has so far been translated to more than ten foreign languages.

The Jill Dando Institute is not specifically devoted to supporting problem-oriented policing. However, that is the mission of the Center for Problem-Oriented Policing which has become the most important agent for disseminating the philosophy. The new information technology has been harnessed and the Internet has become the primary means of spreading information. Since 2002 there is a web site – *www.popcenter.org* – whose aim is to:

> . . . advance the concept and practice of problem-oriented policing in open and democratic societies. It does so by making readily accessible information about ways in which police can more effectively address specific crime and disorder problems. (www.popcenter.org/about/)

The site contains a lot of information that can be downloaded: literature, submissions to Herman Goldstein and Tilley Awards, guides about how to deal with different problems, discussions about analysis, and so forth. For the assessment step, there is a specific guide that became available in 2002 (Eck, 2002). The guide has been written for persons familiar with the SARA process, but who lack knowledge in evaluation methodology.

Over time, institutions and academics supporting problem-oriented policing have become increasingly clear in the disseminated information, focusing on areas needing attention in order to improve the practice. There is no doubt that this is a result of feedback from what has happened in the field. An interesting observation is that to a large extent the same persons who were active from the very beginning are still contributing.

IMPLEMENTING PROBLEM-ORIENTED POLICING

The main principle of problem-oriented policing is intuitive, attractive and simple to accept. The proposed philosophy was more or less immediately received with great interest by police, and also by administrative bodies responsible for the policing function. Many police forces soon tried to adopt and to practice it, not only in the U.S. but also in U.K. and several other countries.[5] Governmental and other organizations, like the Police Executive Research Forum and federal government's COPS office (Office of Community Oriented Policing Services) in the U.S., and the Home Office in U.K., supported the process. In Sweden, problem-oriented policing was one important element in a huge police reform in the mid-1990s under the auspices of the Swedish National Police Board.

It must be pointed out that no clearly defined recipe for how the actual work should be carried out was proposed, only some very basic principles. The lack of specificity makes a number of options possible when putting POP to practice. There are thus two issues to discuss: the success of the effort to implement the philosophy in the organization and the modes of practicing it.

As to the implementation, early experiences from U.K. were definitely not encouraging. The execution was usually frail. Often community police officers got the task of implementing POP principles. These officers by and large used conventional police methods and did little robust evaluation of their effectiveness. Since the assessment step is complicated to carry out, it is easy to understand why this was the weakest part of the implementation process (Leigh et al., 1996, 1998; Read and Tilley, 2000).

Even though there were no formal studies of the Swedish experience, it is fair to say that this has been probably the greatest failure in the history of problem-oriented policing implementation. About half of all Swedish police officers (around 8,000) were appointed as community police officers, who were instructed to focus on crime prevention and to employ the principles of problem-oriented policing. Since the National Police Board did not have a genuine understanding of the concept, and the police officers had little or no training and no adequate support, the endeavor was doomed to fail. According to my extensive contacts with Swedish police, very little problem-oriented policing was actually carried out, and POP fell into disrepute among many police officers and police leaders.

Norway started to implement problem-oriented policing rather late (during the first years of the 21st century) and could have learned the lesson from others. Yet there were still many barriers to overcome. Thomassen (2005) mentions five: (1) a feeble understanding of genuine problem-oriented policing, (2) lack of analytical capability, (3) lack of integration of the philosophy in the organization, (4) lack of incentive to carry out problem-oriented policing, and (5) barriers in the police culture, in which crime fighting has high status and crime prevention low prestige. Sollund (2008) has studied the effort to implement problem-oriented policing in the centre city district of Oslo with officers in first-line mode, and observed, just like Thomassen, considerable problems.

In Denmark, problem-oriented policing was introduced during the latter part of the 1990s, and was elevated in the 2007 police reform as the major model to be used for crime prevention. *Rigspolitiet* (the national police) has in its annual report claimed that local police to a large extent make use of problem-oriented policing. However, there seems to be a gross mismatch between that statement and the actual situation. A survey showed that half of the police districts had, in fact, not carried out any projects at all, or that they considered the quality too low to send them in for review. An examination of the projects the local police forces regarded as their best, showed that weaknesses were more the rule than the exception. The evaluations, if carried out at all, were altogether weak. This is evidenced by the fact that, when classified, the most frequent category was reported as "anecdotal evaluation," signifying "subjective impression of the outcome" (Hammerlich, 2007).

To conclude, there seem to be very few instances of force-wide, thoroughgoing and tangible implementation of problem-oriented policing. Given its record in receiving Tilley and Goldstein Awards, the police force that probably comes closest is the Lancashire Constabulary in Britain. But even in this instance there seem to be some barriers to a complete realization. For instance, the crime analysts who are employed by the force do not seem to be involved in the projects (Bullock et al., 2006).

Modes of Practicing Problem-Oriented Policing

Even if there are problems and disappointments when implementing the philosophy, POP has actually been practiced by many police officers, but more on an individual basis, often with successful results. There is an accumulating body of evidence suggesting that the philosophy is effective in preventing crime and disorder (Weisburd and Eck, 2004). When it comes to putting problem-oriented policing into effect, at least four different modes may be discerned with different advantages and disadvantages (Scott et al., 2008).

A common form of putting problem-oriented policing into practice has been to instruct first-line officers to work in a problem-oriented fashion. This has, for instance, been tried by some of the police forces in the U.K. and by the police in some districts in Norway. An advantage is that officers can deal with problems they are confronted with in their daily work. A considerable risk is that the work will be superficial and disturbed by ordinary routine tasks. In many cases it is doubtful whether it is proper problem-oriented policing that is conducted. Clarke (1998) characterizes it as problem solving, meaning that officers take care of small, easily defined problems, that do not require either substantial analysis or complex responses, and where the assessment is easy or unnecessary since the outcome is so evident.

Another variant is to encourage police officers assigned to community policing or to crime prevention units to engage in problem-oriented policing. In Sweden, for example, officers who were assigned to carry out community policing were instructed to practice problem-oriented policing. This approach makes it possible for the officers to concentrate on their task, to dig more deeply into the problems, and to work in a genuinely problem-oriented fashion. On the other hand, there may be difficulties in demarcating problem-oriented policing from the citizen-contact activities that are usually important in community policing and traditional crime prevention.[6]

A third type of implementation is to create specialized units tasked to undertake problem-oriented work. A strength of this method might be that the officers will be able to develop a greater understanding of and competence to practice the principles of problem-oriented policing. There is, on the other hand, a risk that they might start to use conventional police tactics to solve the problems.

Finally, the fourth mode of practice is to create or to strengthen crime analysis units, giving them competence in and responsibility for supporting problem-oriented policing. This model most closely resembles Goldstein's original suggestion. An advantage is that they may also take on large-scale problems, but might on the other hand miss smaller local ones. This model is open to different organizational solutions. One approach is for the crime analysis unit to carry out the whole process, while another is for the analysts to support officers doing the actual tasks in the POP projects.

A variant related to the last approach is to involve researchers in specific problem-oriented policing projects, assisting the police. An advantage is, of course, the input of outside competence, but it is likely that support will only be given for limited periods of time.

Figure 1. Mode of Practice and Analytic Rigor in Problem-Oriented Policing Projects.

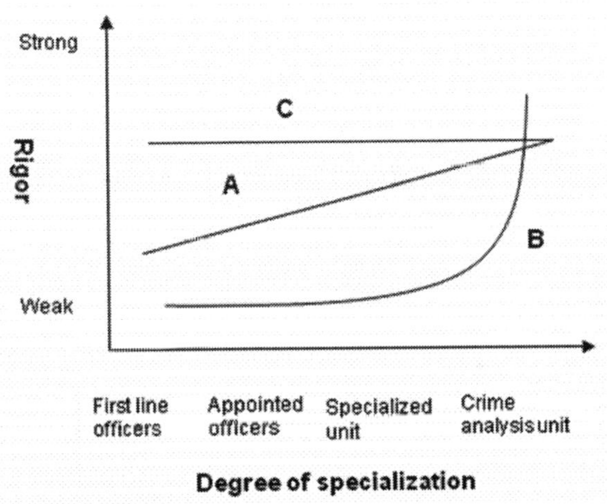

These different modes can be seen to fall on a scale of increasing specialization and competence of the involved personnel. How might the mode of implementation influence performance and quality of the assessments? There are a number of possibilities. The following discussion assumes that personnel with academic training in relevant subjects – in this case evaluation methods are the critical knowledge area – are only found in the crime analysis unit mode.

It is possible to discern at least three hypothetical associations between implementation mode and quality of performance. If there is a clear connection between increased experience and training in problem-oriented policing (assuming the personnel really are trained), the quality of the projects and of the assessments ought to increase according to the degree of specialization, resulting in a linear relationship, as illustrated by line A in Figure 1.

Since evaluations are technically demanding, requiring qualified persons to do them in an adequate manner, the result would instead be a qualitative shift, resulting in an inverted L-curve, shown by line B.

However, there is also a third alternative, assuming differentiation of tasks. According to this alternative, analysts in crime analysis units provide support to police officers, especially with the more analytically demanding tasks such as the assessment phase, irrespective of how the police officers are organized. This would result in evaluations of adequate quality, independent of mode, as illustrated by line C.

Given the experiences to date from the practice of problem-oriented policing, the most likely relationship is expressed by curve B and line C.

EVALUATION DESIGNS IN PROBLEM-ORIENTED POLICING PROJECTS

For two practical reasons the most common design in the assessment of problem-oriented policing projects will be the one-group pretest-posttest design (Campbell and Stanley, 1966). The first has to do with the competence and perspective of practitioners, and the second with what is feasible.

Competence and Perspective

Seen from the police perspective, the motive for engaging in a problem-oriented endeavor is that they want to eliminate or decrease a problem. However, what slightly complicates matters is that they also want credit for the achievement. Positive confirming evidence, whatever its quality is welcome, but negative findings are, as a rule, unwanted and often neglected. The positive value of negative outcomes–i.e., to be able to rule out a measure as ineffective–is not appreciated. The last remark points to a rather undeveloped attitude in the police organization to the function of evaluations.

Even in police corps with rather high standards, like the Norwegian and the Swedish forces, the level of sophistication on the issue of evaluations is still fairly, if not to say, very low. In a strategic document produced by the National Norwegian Police Directorate from 2007, the need for evaluations is stressed. But it is also stated that evaluations should not be carried out in such a complicated manner that “external competence” is needed, after which follows a list of what an evaluation should accomplish (Politidirektoratet, 2007). There does not seem to be a realization that thorough and well designed evaluations have to be used, precisely in order to reach the stated goals.

This, in my opinion, points to a main barrier when new knowledge-intense procedures or schemes are introduced into the police organization. There is an almost xenophobic reluctance to employ or make use of persons without a police background. When a philosophy like problem-oriented policing is implemented, there is thus no academic tradition to connect to–there is a very low initial baseline.

For the police, before-and-after designs have a strong intuitive appeal, in comparing the initial unwanted situation with the one after the measures have been put into effect. For them it will provide an answer to their straightforward question, "Did our problem disappear or decrease?" If it did, it is then assumed that it was because of the police response and accordingly that the police were successful. That the latter requires a demonstration of a causal link between the response measure and the effect that a simple comparison cannot accomplish is far beyond most police officers. The limitations of this particular design, which some scholars consider inadequate and uninterpretable, are of no concern, primarily because police officers know little or nothing about the strengths and weaknesses of different designs.

Feasibility

The second reason that the single group before–and-after design is most commonly used pertains to the options which are realistically available. I will do a little circumvention when discussing this particular issue.

Sherman (2007) argues that to increase the possibility of catching strong treatment effects in randomized controlled experiments, it could be a good strategy to focus on the "worst" cases, those with a prognosis for causing most harm. When problem-oriented policing is considered, at least two remarks are in order. The first is that on the whole, the "worst cases" are the starting point for problem-oriented policing projects; in many instances these are local concentrations of crimes or disturbances. The second remark has to do with the availability of eligible cases. Under the not too risky assumption that places with these properties–"worst" cases–are located in the tails of normal distributions, there will by definition be (relatively) few of them. In fact, in many instances, especially in smaller societies–including whole nations like the Nordic countries–there will only be one or very few such distinct places. The consequence is that it is more or less impossible to find similar areas, let alone to find enough of them for random assignment to experimental groups and controls. Even to get quasi-experimental designs with matched control groups is simply in many, if not most cases, not possible.

But in the rare instances where it is possible to conduct random assignment, it is very unlikely that the police, in a problem-oriented project, would choose such a design. Restrictions in time and resources–expressed in monetary terms as well as in academic competence–would most likely block that alternative. The primary concern of police is to get rid of problems, not to produce solid evaluations and to test the effectiveness of programs. Besides, the refinement of skills in evaluation methodology within the police organization is usually not sophisticated enough that they might see controlled experiments as an option at all.

Where controlled experiments have been employed in connection with what is stated to be problem-oriented policing, it is doubtful whether they can be classified as regular problem-oriented policing projects (see, e.g., Sherman, 1992). It is probably more sensible to look upon them as academic research projects, even if there is a clear policing aspect to them, and even if they have been carried out according to the formula of problem-oriented policing. Such projects can of course be very valuable for the POP philosophy, providing important input.

To go back to Sherman (and experimental criminology), an implication of the argument is that meta-analysis methodology[7] cannot be an adequate method to evaluate the philosophy of problem-oriented policing: for one thing, projects with strong designs that fulfill the requirements to be included in meta-analysis (randomized controlled experiments) are not representative of problem-oriented projects. Assessments with weaker designs using matched controls will also be rare. Given the diversity in types of problems and the quality of the assessments, data will in addition often not be reported in a way that makes them amenable for more advanced statistical analyses. Thus, researchers evaluating the philosophy using meta-analysis methodology (see Weisburd et al., 2007) will end up with very biased samples.[8]

In the problem-oriented policing guide for police entitled *Assessing Responses to Problems: An Introductory Guide for Police Problem Solvers*, the author (John Eck) explains and instructs in a straightforward and accessible way how to go about conducting assessments in problem-oriented policing projects. It is easy to agree with the pragmatic view that a weak design will suffice to document an eventual decrease of the problem. But if the police consider using the particular response in other situations, it is necessary to go into the issue of causality and try to exclude rival explanations for the decline (Eck, 2002a, b, 2006).

Ultimately the critical question will be, "How much uncertainty is acceptable?" But this uncertainty has to be balanced according to the claims that are made. The issue is thus to navigate between the Scylla of the police organization's willingness to accept any evidence (sometimes absence of evidence and even counterevidence) as an indication of success, and the Charybdis of the scientific rigor demanded by academics.

In the view of "experimentalists," as manifested in the Maryland Scientific Methods Scale, evaluations using single group before-and-after designs are considered inadequate and uninterpretable (Sherman et al., 1997; Welsh and Farrington, 2006). This attitude is in stark contrast to the view of pragmatists with a more open attitude, who insist that it is possible to decrease threats to internal validity by different means like adding qualitative evidence, using time-series data, investigating possible alternative hypotheses or being guided by a precise theory (see Pawson and Tilley,1997; Eck, 2002b; 2006; Tilley, 2006).

The conclusion will then be that in the choice of design for assessments, for the most part those in charge of the projects will have to make do with what is attainable, which to a large extent will be the one group pretest-posttest design. But given circumstances and purposes, it is both fruitful and possible to see assessments in problem-oriented policing projects along a continuum: from "fast and dirty" evaluations that in some cases might be justifiable, to more proper assessments, and on to ambitious evaluations that possibly will satisfy researchers specializing in evaluation methodology, even if the designs are not randomized controlled experiments (see Shadish et al., 2002, pp. 499-504).

QUALITY OF PROBLEM-ORIENTED PROJECTS

Even if genuine force-wide implementation so far is rare, weak, or nonexistent, many problem-oriented policing projects have in fact been carried out. Of these, some have been submitted to the Herman Goldstein or the Tilley Awards.[9] From the outset, several hundred projects have now been judged. In a couple of studies, samples of these submissions have been inspected.

Since the projects have been considered good enough to be critically examined in the award process by those who submitted them, they might be considered to represent "best practice." And if the examination consists only of the projects that received awards, it is definitively an indication of best practice.

An early inspection was carried out of all Herman Goldstein Award submissions from 1995, in total 88. It showed that only 30 fulfilled the criteria for problem-oriented policing projects. Of the four steps in the

SARA process, the assessment phase was judged to be the weakest. In about a third of the submissions, there was no formal evaluation at all. In 18 of the submissions, the design involved before-and-after measurements, and in two of the submissions time-series data were used. None of the 20 submissions had control groups, and no real investigation of possible displacement was carried out. A major conclusion was that the police need considerable support to undertake the assessment step (Clarke, 1998, 2002).

Scott (2000) has examined the best Goldstein Award submissions from 1993 to 1999, altogether 100 entries. Compared to the Clarke study, Scott's focus was on best practice. Despite this fact, there was agreement by Scott concerning the assessments, that submissions lacked quality.

As to the situation in U.K., Bullock et al. (2006) examined a sample of Tilley Award submissions (150 of 503 submissions from 1994 to 2005). Those who were engaged in the projects had in two-thirds of the cases also carried out the evaluation. However, in some of the cases formal evaluations were nonexistent; the explanation for a number of projects was that they had not come that far in the process. Only 1% of the assessments had been conducted by external evaluators. Where evaluations had been completed, in most cases they consisted of a comparison of data from a pre-implementation period to a post-implementation period. In general, more space was devoted to the analysis than the assessment step. Bullock et al. (2006) also made a judgment of the overall strength of the presented arguments. For about a third they were considered convincing, for 44% not at all convincing, and for 13% partly convincing. In 10% of the cases data or other information was missing. The conclusion was that, on the whole, the assessments were weak with no improvement over time.

To get a up-to-date impression of the state of problem-oriented policing projects, of the designs used and of the standard of the assessments, I examined all winners and runners-up in the Herman Goldstein Award between 2002 and 2007, altogether 34 projects. This sample thus amounts to "best practice." The variability of the problems taken on is striking. They included problems of crime and disorder created by particular pubs, motels or night clubs, traffic congestion close to a school when parents leave and pick up their children, feelings of uneasiness and insecurity created by kerb-crawlers looking for prostitutes, drug dealing in neighborhoods, operations of illegal taxicabs in city centers, crimes committed by prolific drug-dependent offenders, underaged drinking, domestic violence against females, robberies with immigrants as victims, accidents in traffic causing injuries and deaths among immigrant farm laborers, just to mention a few. The size of the affected areas ranges from a few blocks around a pub, motel or night club, to entire city centers and neighborhoods, to statewide problems.

The creativity shown in responses is impressive, ranging from a single measure to whole packages. For example, nightclubs have been closed, safety measures in and around them have been put in place, and, obedience to drinking regulations has been checked. Traffic has been diverted to make illegal taxicab driving more difficult. There are even examples of focused deterrence in combination with increased social services for prolific drug-dependent offenders. To decrease vandalism and breaking and entering, and to improve living standards for residents, houses have been torn down and others repaired in combination with rules for and checks on tenants. Parks have been changed according to Crime Prevention through Environmental Design (CPTED) principles, and locks installed in storage facilities. Social pressure has been systematically applied to make drug sellers move out of an area, to mention just a few of the responses.

One observation concerns the content of the assessment. In instructions on how to carry out evaluations it is usually pointed out that first a process evaluation has to be conducted to check whether or not the measures have been implemented in a proper manner. But since the SARA process has usually been followed, this particular issue is most often dealt with in the response phase. The results are mostly presented in the form of a narrative describing how the concerned partners acted and reacted, and which measures were put into effect. Thus, in most cases, the assessment phase solely concerns the impact of the response.

As could be expected, the dominant design was the one-group pretest-posttest design–in fact it had been used in all of the projects in this sample. Judged according to their face value, the evaluations were acceptable–which, since we are discussing award-winning projects, was to be expected. When making statements about the face value the question put is not, "What about the internal validity? How have the threats been dealt with?," but rather "When reading the presentation of the project, do I accept that this is a credible account of what occurred–including the claims of effects of the measures?"

Another related issue is the format of the presentations, which often lack rigor. The matter here is to some extent one of language and formulation. But of greater importance are the data used and the way they are presented, quite often with flaws.

This leads to a further observation. In only a few of the projects were researchers or other persons with academic backgrounds engaged in the projects. It occurred in just four of the cases, with four more possible (the information given is not clear enough). This leaves police officers as solely responsible for at least 26 of the projects. In many instances the police officers themselves, most of whom are not used to and trained in an academic format, are the authors. Most importantly, they are not used to analyzing even simple data and to presenting results. A recurring reflection when reading the presentations is that it in many instances it would not have taken much effort to tighten the case–a few more data points or a few checks would have decreased some of the uncertainty.

CONCLUSION

The answer to the straightforward question, "Is the standard of assessment in problem-oriented projects good enough?" is probably "No!" The quality of the average problem-oriented policing project–if such an entity exists–is unknown, but in all likelihood it is at a minimum questionable. Even for projects that have won awards, questions may be raised. The answer for those projects will perhaps depend on who is asked. A practically experienced pragmatist might very well say, "Yes, their success claims are pretty persuasive," but a conventional academic versed in orthodox methodological principles is likely to say "No," or at least to raise serious doubts.

There is only one way of improving the standard of evaluation in problem-oriented policing. When the philosophy was first presented in the late 1970s, it was pointed out that the police need to improve their analytical competence to be able to perform better. This statement has been repeated again and again (Goldstein, 1979, 1990, 2003). The police have to make use of, and to employ persons with proper competence. To be fair, the universities have not been very good at producing academics with the skills and attitudes the police need. Analysts with adequate training are not an off-the-shelf commodity. This just underlines the need to evolve the relationships between police and academia.

Address correspondence to: Johannes Knutsson, Norwegian Police University College, Pb 5027 Majorstua, 0301 Oslo, Norway; e-mail: johannes.knutsson@phs.no

Acknowledgments: I am grateful to those at the meeting for their comments and suggestions. I am also indebted to Nick Tilley and Gunnar Thomassen for reading through and correcting a later draft and to Shane Johnson for assistance in formulating some definitions.

NOTES

1. In a randomized controlled trial, to ensure that the two groups – experimental and control – are comparable they are allocated to conditions by means of randomization. As well as equating the groups on a range of variables (measured and unmeasured), this procedure also ensures that eventual differences in outcomes cannot be attributed to biases in the allocation process.
2. One of the most influential studies was the compilation *The Effectiveness of Correctional Treatment: A Survey of Treatment Valuation Studies* (Lipton et al., 1975), where one of the contributing authors, Robert Martinson, got the nickname "Nothing works Martinson."
3. The U.S. version consists of 60 steps (Clarke and Eck, 2005).
4. On a yearly basis about 100-200 persons, most often crime analysts, have attended the course, beginning in 2004.
5. See Scott, 2000, pp. 36-44, for a thoroughgoing description.
6. A basic idea in community policing is to engage the local community in the effort to prevent crime and disorder. The focus is often the contact in itself. In problem-oriented policing, a response could be to engage the local community to solve a problem, but the specific response is guided by the analysis and not the notion that the community should be involved.
7. In a meta-analysis, the typical approach involves computing a standardized measure of effect size for a series of evaluations, and then summarizing the results to produce a single (weighted) value to indicate whether an intervention has the intended effect or not.
8. In the study altogether seven studies are included in the metaanalysis, of which three have persons as units. The finding is not unexpected, but this type of unit is very rare in problem-oriented policing projects.
9. Or both. Many of the award-winning projects in the Tilley Award have also been submitted to the Herman Goldstein Award.

REFERENCES

Bullock, K., Erol, R., & Tilley, N. (2006). *Problem-oriented policing and partnerships. Implementing an evidence based approach to crime reduction*. Cullompton, UK: Willan Publishing.

Campbell, D., & Stanley, J. (1966). *Experimental and quasi-experimental designs for research*. Chicago: Rand McNally.

Clarke, R. V. (1998). Defining police strategies: Problem-solving, problem-oriented policing and community-oriented policing. In T. O'Connor Shelley & A.C. Grant (Eds.), *Problem-oriented policing: Crime-specific problems, critical issues and making POP work*. Washington, DC: Police Executive Research Forum.

Clarke, R. V. (2002). Problem-oriented policing, case studies. Report to the U. S. Department of Justice. Document 193801. Available at: www.popcenter.org/Library/RecommendedReadings/POP-SCP-Clarke.pdf

Clarke, R. V., & Eck, J. (2003). *Become a problem-solving crime analyst: In 55 small steps*. London: Jill Dando Institute of Crime Science.

Clarke, R. V., & Eck, J. (2003). *Crime analysis for problem solvers. In 60 small steps*. COPS office. Office of Community Oriented Policing Services. Available at: http://www.popcenter.org/library/reading/PDFs/60Steps.pdf

Clarke, R. V., & Mayhew, P. (1980). *Designing out crime*. London: Her Majesty's Stationery Office.

Eck, J. (2002a). *Assessing responses to problems: An introductory guide for police problem-solvers*. Problem-oriented guides for police. Problem-solving tools series. Guide no. 1. Office of Community Oriented Policing Services. Available at: http://www.popcenter.org/tools/pdfs/AssessingResponsesToProblems. pdf

Eck, J. (2002b). Learning from experience in problem-oriented policing and situational prevention: The positive functions of weak evaluations and the negative functions of strong ones. In N. Tilley (Ed.), *Crime Prevention Studies* (Vol. 14, pp. 93–117). Monsey, NY and Cullompton, Devon, UK: Criminal Justice Press and Willan Publishing.

Eck, J. (2006). When is a bologna sandwich better than sex? A defense of small-n case study evaluations. *Journal of Experimental Criminology*, *2*, 345–362.

Eck, J., & Spelman, W. (1987). *Problem-solving. Problem-oriented policing in Newport News*. Police Executive Research Forum/National Institute of Justice. Washington, DC: Police Executive Research Forum.

Goldstein, H. (1979). Improving policing: A problem-oriented approach. *Crime & Delinquency*, *25*, 234–258.

Goldstein, H. (1990). *Problem-oriented policing*. New York: McGraw Hill.

Goldstein, H. (2003). On further developing problem-oriented policing: The most critical need, the major impediments and a proposal. In J. Knutsson (Ed.), *Problem-oriented policing: From innovation to mainstream*. Crime Prevention Studies (Vol. 15, pp. 13–48). Monsey, NY and Cullompton, UK: Criminal Justice Press and Willan Publishing.

Hammerich, M. (2007). *Problemorientert politiarbeide– Når tjenesten tilladet det. Avgangsprojekt*. Diplomuddannelsen i Kriminologi. Köbenhavns Universitet.

Junger-Tas, J. (1993). Policy evaluation research in criminal justice. *Studies on Crime & Crime Prevention*, 2, 7–20.

Kelling, G., Pate, T., Dieckman, D. & Brown, C. (1974). *The Kansas City Preventive Patrol Experiment: A technical report*. Washington, DC: Police Foundation.

Knutsson, J. (Ed.). (2003). *Problem-oriented policing: From innovation to mainstream*. Crime Prevention Studies (Vol. 15). Monsey, NY and Cullompton, Devon, UK: Criminal Justice Press and Willan Publishing.

Kühlhorn, E., & Svensson, B. (Eds.). (1981) *Crime prevention*. Swedish National Council for Crime Prevention. Report No 9. Stockholm: Liber förlag.

Leigh, A., Read, T., & Tilley, N. (1996). *Problem-oriented policing. Brit pop*. Crime Detection and Prevention series, paper 75. London: Home Office.

Leigh, A., Read, T., & Tilley, N. (1998). *Brit pop II. Problem–oriented policing in practice*. Police research series paper 93. London: Home Office.

Lipton, D.S., Martinson, R., & Wilks, J. (1975). *The effectiveness of correctional treatment: A survey of treatment valuation studies*. New York: Praeger Press.

Pawson, R., & Tilley, N. (1997). *Realistic evaluation*. London: Sage.

Politidirektoratet. (2007). *Nasjonal strategi for etterretning og anlayse*. POD publikasjon 2007/5.

Read, T., & Tilley, N. (2000). *Not rocket science? Problem-solving and crime reduction*. Crime reduction research series paper 6. London: Home Office.

Reiss, A. J. (1992). Police organization in the 20th century. In M. Tonry & N. Morris (Eds.), *Modern policing*. Chicago: University of Chicago Press.

Scott, M.S. (2000). *Problem-oriented policing. Reflections on the first 20 years*. Washington, DC: U.S. Department of Justice, Office of Community Oriented Policing Services.

Scott, M., Eck, J., Knutsson, J., & Goldstein, H. (2008). Problem-oriented policing and environmental criminology. In R. Wortley & L. Mazerolle (Eds.), *Environmental criminology and crime analysis* (pp. 221–246). Cullompton, Devon, UK: Willan Publishing.

Shadish, W. R., Cook, T. D., & Campbell, D. T. (2002). *Experimental and quasi-experimental designs for generalized causal inference*. Boston: Houghton Mifflin.

Sherman, L. (1992). Attacking crime: Police and crime control. In M. Tonry & N. Morris (Eds.), *Modern policing*. Crime and Justice (Vol. 15, pp. 159–230). Chicago: University of Chicago Press.

Sherman, L. (2007). The power few: Experimental criminology and the reduction of harm. *Journal of Experimental Criminology*, 3, 299–321.

Sherman, L. W., Gottfredson, D. C., MacKenzie, D. L., Eck, J. E., Reuter, P., & Bushway, S. D. (Eds.). (1997). *Preventing crime: What works, what doesn't, what's promising*. Washington, DC: National Institute of Justice. Available at: http://www.ncjrs.gov/works/wholedoc.htm

Sollund, R. (2008). The implementation of problem-oriented policing in Oslo, Norway: Not without problems? In K. T. Froeling (Ed.), *Criminology research focus* (pp. 175–193). New York: Nova Science Publishers.

Thomassen, G. (2005). *Implementering av Problemorientert Politiarbeid. Noen Sentrale Utfordringar*. Available on pp. 218-223 at: http://www.nsfk.org/downloads/seminarreports/researchsem_no47.pdf

Tilley, N. (2006). Knowing and doing: Guidance and good practice. In J. Knutsson & R. V. Clarke (Eds.), *Putting theory to work: Implementing situational prevention and problem-oriented policing*. Crime Prevention Studies (Vol. 20, pp.

217–252). Monsey, NY and Cullompton, UK: Criminal Justice Press and Willan Publishing.

Weisburd, D., & Eck, J. (2004). What can police do to reduce crime, disorder, and fear? *Annals of the American Academy of Political and Social Science*, 593, 42–65.

Weisburd, D., Eck, J., Hinkle, J., & Telep, C. (2007). *Does problem-oriented policing reduce crime and disorder? A systematic review.* Campbell collaborative annual meeting. University of Maryland, College Park, Maryland.

Welsh, B. C., & Farrington, D. P. (2006). Evidence-based crime prevention. In B. C. Welsh & D. P. Farrington (Eds.), *Preventing crime: What works for children, offenders, victims, and places* (pp. 1–20). Dordrecht, Netherlands: Springer.

Willemse, H. M. (1994). Developments in Dutch prevention. In R. V. Clarke (Ed.), *Crime prevention studies* (Vol. 2, pp. 33–48). Monsey, NY: Criminal Justice Press.

THE PULL, PUSH, AND EXPANSION OF SITUATIONAL CRIME PREVENTION EVALUATION: AN APPRAISAL OF THIRTY-SEVEN YEARS OF RESEARCH

by

Rob T. Guerette
Florida International University

Abstract: *Over the past three decades increased attention has been placed on the prevention of crime through opportunity reduction. At the same time, researchers have embarked on the task of determining the impact of opportunity-reduction measures on the levels of crime and fear of crime within communities. While the focus of this research agenda is clear, less certain is the appropriate methodology that should be used in reaching usable findings. This paper discusses the current demands facing situational crime prevention (SCP) evaluation methods within the context of a pull toward randomized experimentation, the push toward scientific realism, and the expansion of developing technical issues such as crime displacement, diffusion and anticipatory benefits, among others. It undertakes an appraisal of the current body*

Crime Prevention Studies, volume 24 (2009), pp. 29–58.

of SCP evaluation methods by examining over 200 evaluations of SCP efforts carried out from 1970 to 2007. It reviews the types of methodologies employed, reports on the conclusions of these studies, and discusses the implications for future SCP evaluation.

INTRODUCTION

The focus on preventing crime through opportunity reduction that emerged over the last several decades represented a clear departure from conventional criminological thought. Previously, mainstream thinking about criminality, and ways of preventing it, were largely directed at understanding and altering the deviant propensities of individual offenders. Opportunity-reduction measures, most notably those of situational crime prevention (SCP), instead began to focus on altering the environmental landscape in such a way that it is no longer an attractive host for crime behavior. The assumption behind this is a pragmatic one: that it is easier to alter environmental conditions than individual behavioral tendencies.

Within this opportunity-reduction approach, much attention has been paid to trying to determine the effectiveness of these types of situational interventions. Though the objective of this research has been clear, there have been much different views regarding the most suitable methods for determining their impact. This methodological debate revolves, at least partly, around the applicability of conventional methods tailored to the individual level to evaluate place and system-based interventions.

The methods used to evaluate SCP are simultaneously being pulled, pushed, and expanded. The "pull" is toward more systematic use of randomized field trials (Farrington 2003a, 2003b; Sherman, 2000; Weisburd, 2003). Historically considered the "gold standard" of research, randomized experimentation is thought ideal because it has the highest possible internal validity, making conclusions about the impact of the treatment effect on an outcome most certain (Cook and Campbell, 1979). Because of this greater certainty, it has been claimed that there is a moral imperative to use randomized experiments, resulting from the obligation of researchers to provide valid answers to questions about effective interventions (Weisburd, 2003).

The "push" is toward greater reliance on pragmatic methods of evaluation, which is associated with scientific realism. This approach questions the utility of randomized designs, and instead places greater value on research that pays attention to how various mechanisms of change operate in the variety of contexts in which prevention schemes might be conducted (Clarke, 2004; Eck, 2002; Pawson and Tilley, 1997), as well as the soundness of the theoretical guidance used in formulating the intervention (Clarke, 2005; Eck, 2005).

The expansion of acceptable SCP evaluation designs results from several unique issues that arise in assessing situational interventions. These include: crime displacement (the relocation of crime to other places, times, tactics, targets, offenses, or offenders as a result of an intervention); diffusion of crime control benefits (the reduction of crime in other times or places not targeted by an intervention); anticipatory benefit effects (the reduction of crime in advance of the actual implementation of an intervention); greater use of cost-benefit analysis; and longer follow-up periods.

While there have been general assertions about the current status of SCP evaluation methods and calls for their improvement, no systematic appraisal of those used has been undertaken. Given the demands on SCP evaluation methods and the crucial importance of determining effective crime reduction practice (Tilley 2002), it makes sense to examine the existing body of SCP evaluation methods to determine what further developments are needed. This paper seeks to do that, and it is divided into three parts. The first part discusses in more detail the pull, push, and expansion facing SCP evaluation. The second part presents a descriptive review of evaluations of situational crime prevention from 1970 to the present. It reports on various qualities of the research designs used, the environment where the intervention was evaluated, and overall conclusions. The third part discusses these findings in relation to needed methodological refinements for future SCP evaluation.

I. THE PULL, PUSH AND EXPANSION OF SCP EVALUATION

The Pull - Randomized Experimentation

Situational crime prevention evaluation is being pulled toward more widespread use of randomized experimental designs, with the intention of identifying "best practices" in crime prevention (Dunford, 2000; Farrington 2003a, 2003b; Farrington and Welsh, 2006; Feder and Boruch, 2000; Sherman, 2000). To promote the use of randomized experiments in criminology, the Academy of Experimental Criminology (http://www.crim.

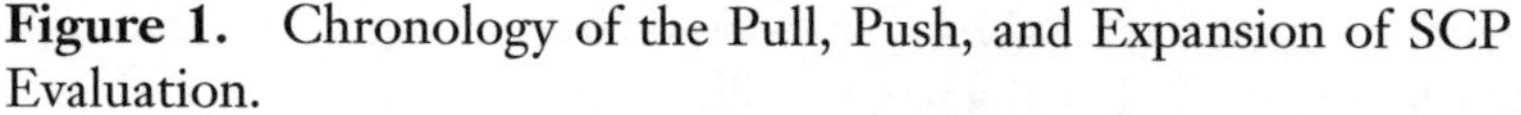

Figure 1. Chronology of the Pull, Push, and Expansion of SCP Evaluation.

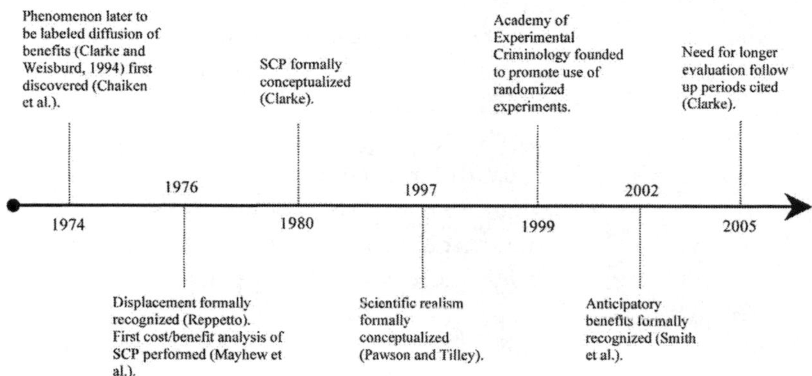
Phenomenon later to be labeled diffusion of benefits (Clarke and Weisburd, 1994) first discovered (Chaiken et al.).
SCP formally conceptualized (Clarke).
Academy of Experimental Criminology founded to promote use of randomized experiments.
Need for longer evaluation follow up periods cited (Clarke).
1974
1976
1980
1997
1999
2002
2005
Displacement formally recognized (Reppetto). First cost/benefit analysis of SCP performed (Mayhew et al.).
Scientific realism formally conceptualized (Pawson and Tilley).
Anticipatory benefits formally recognized (Smith et al.).

upenn.edu/aec/) was formed in 1999 (see Figure 1). While this call has been made for determining effective practice among all forms of crime prevention (e.g., schools, families, communities, etc.), it also includes evaluation of situational-based interventions, but it is also here that it may face the greatest difficulty.

The benefit of randomized experiments is that they ensure equivalency in comparisons between those individuals assigned to the treatment and comparison groups. The process of random assignment removes selection bias on all possible measured and unmeasured variables that might stand to influence the outcome variable. The equivalency of groups means that the researcher can be certain that it was in fact the intervention that caused the observed effect and not some third intervening variable: thus, it is high on internal validity. From the conventional perspective, randomized experiments are viewed as superior to quasi-experimental designs,[1] which do not use random assignment. Alternatives include matched groups or the use of statistical controls to account for possible group differences, although they do not reach the level of internal validity achieved by randomized experiments.

The appropriateness of increased reliance on randomized experiments has met with several criticisms. In a Home Office report entitled, *The Controlled Trial in Institutional Research: Paradigm or Pitfall for Penal Evaluators?* Clarke and Cornish (1972) submit that "the additional certainty which experimental methods are supposed to be able to provide over correlational methods is either unattainable or not worth the extra costs involved." They identify several objections to randomized experiments stemming from their own research and that of other earlier randomized experiments funded by the Home Office (Farrington, 2003a). These include:

1) *Ethical concerns* – offenders in an experiment may get no treatment or the wrong treatment;
2) *Intrusiveness* – the administration of randomized experiments in organizational settings severely disrupts proper functioning;
3) *Limited conclusions* – they might be able to explain *what* happened in an intervention (i.e., there was or was not an effect), but they are unable to explain *how* or *why* it happened;
4) *Poor external validity* – whether the same results would be found at other settings and environments is uncertain (e.g., the usefulness of findings is severely limited by their inability to be generalized);
5) *Hawthorne effect* – it is often not possible to administer double-blind experimentation, thus one cannot rule out reactivity;
6) *Heterogeneity* – it is often difficult to ensure that treatments are administered similarly and equally; and,
7) *Other options* – there are other available methods that are less intrusive and cost less which provide sufficient determinations of effectiveness, such as matched groups.

In the evaluation of situational interventions, perhaps the strongest claim against the use of randomized experiments stems from poor external validity. While randomized experiments may provide the best way to rule out third intervening variables, their controlled nature means that these experiments are unable to determine whether the same result would be achieved in different settings. This is important for SCP because the varieties of possible situations are so numerous that any specific situational technique or package thereof may prove effective in one time and place but not another. In response to such concerns, Farrington (2000) and Weisburd and Taxman (2000) have called for the use of multi-site designs and the replication of randomized experiments in different places.

Yet, the repeated evaluation of the same situational technique in different times and places to determine promising practice may not be appropriate. This is because SCP (and its sibling, problem-oriented policing) place great emphasis on the *process* of determining suitable interventions that are tailored to the nature of the specific crime problem. Thus, the interventions used need to be problem-led rather than universally applied to all places and times. Whether SCP interventions are successful is largely determined by the context in which they are implemented. What works in some place(s) will not work in others. Eck (2002) articulates this point concisely where he argues that sound situational focused intervention and their evaluation should be based on theory. He writes:

> . . . place-focused programs should be based on this set of theories [routine activity and situational crime prevention]. The theories do not dictate specific actions, but provide a framework for the creation of context relevant interventions. In this example, the answer to the question, "what works?" to prevent crime at places is "routine activity theory and situational crime prevention." The answer is not, CCTV, lighting, locks, management screening of prospective tenants, nuisance abatement, street redesign or any other particular measure. These are tools that might work in some circumstances but probably do not work in every circumstance. (citing Clarke, 1997)

This implies that the unguided, uniform implementation and evaluation of any SCP technique across time and place, and any resulting conclusion about a measure's overall effectiveness, could result in a Type II error, or rather, a false conclusion about the technique's ineffectiveness if it is not based on a thorough understanding of the problem and its context.

The Push - Scientific Realism

Situational crime prevention evaluation is also being pushed toward the more applied research method of scientific realism. Scientific realism seeks to understand how generic causal mechanisms operate in specific contexts (Pawson and Tilley, 1997; see Figure 1). In this sense it bridges nomothetic and idiographic approaches to explanation because it exhibits elements of both (Maxfield and Babbie, 2008).[2] It places emphasis on very specific questions within specific times and places, while also being concerned with more general causal relationships.

The "context" is made up of four settings: social, temporal, physical, and legal (Brantingham and Brantingham, 1993). Eck (2002) elaborates the importance of context in relation to causal mechanisms, introducing the concept of context sensitivity. Context sensitivity refers to the variability of intervention effectiveness as determined by differing social, temporal, and physical settings. The amount of context sensitivity is determined by the variation of effectiveness. The greater the context sensitivity, the more variation there will be in the effectiveness of a mechanism across contexts. The scientific realism approach not only anticipates, but expects there to be different outcomes of intervention effectiveness in relation to the times and places in which they operate. Taking great lengths to ensure internal validity of an intervention through randomized experimentation, then, is of marginal use from this perspective.

The scientific realism approach also places emphasis on understanding the how and why of intervention effectiveness, which randomized experiments do not provide (Clarke and Cornish, 1972). Determining this requires understanding of the social and behavioral mechanisms at work. It also requires that interventions be based on well defined theories, something that has been stressed by many (Eck, 2006; Farrington, 2006; Harrell, 2006).

Eck (2002) differentiates between large claim and small claim interventions. Large claim interventions, like DARE (Drug Abuse Resistance Education) or juvenile boot camps, assume context insensitivity. That is because they are espoused to work uniformly across all settings. Because of this they are more suited for randomized experimental evaluation. Small claim interventions are those tailored to a specific and small context. These do not make any claims of effectiveness beyond the specific intervention and context applied. Situational crime prevention efforts are usually small scale and, if done properly, context specific (Eck 2002).

Like randomized experiments, findings from scientific realist evaluations are limited in their generalizability. The high contextual dependence of the scientific realism approach means that they do not universally apply, nor are they intended to. Instead, this approach calls for the accumulation of results from a large number of small scale studies rather than trying to generalize from a small number of large scale evaluations. In other words, the aim of scientific realism is to catalogue the variety of situations where an intervention works and does not work. For instance, Baumer, Maxfield, and Mendelsohn (1993) found that home-based electronic monitoring worked differently for convicted adults, convicted juveniles, and pretrial adults. Rather than concluding that electronic monitoring is only partially effective, the scientific realism approach makes note of this and acknowledges its usefulness for these different contexts.

The Expansion - Developing Concepts and Technical Issues

The scope of SCP evaluation is being expanded with the introduction and refinement of the concepts of displacement, diffusion, and anticipatory benefits as well as the technical issues of longer follow-up periods and greater use of cost-benefit analysis (see Figure 1). These conceptual and technical expansions are different from the pull and push on SCP evaluation because they remain important regardless of whether a researcher employs a randomized experimental design or follows the model of scientific realism. They also present the need to move beyond simple (or not so simple, as it were) determinations of whether an intervention produced a meaningful decline in the number or rate of crime. If any SCP evaluation is to be adequate, it must accommodate these concepts and issues when relevant and possible.

Crime Displacement

Displacement is the relocation of crime from one place, time, target, offense, tactic or offender to another as a result of some crime prevention initiative. The first and most common form of displacement recognized by those studying situationally based efforts was spatial displacement (Eck, 1993). Reppetto (1976) expanded the original concept, and now there are a total of six possible forms of displacement routinely acknowledged, which include: temporal (offenders change the time at which they commit crime); spatial (offenders switch from targets in one location to targets in another location); target (offenders change from one type of target to another target type); tactical (offenders alter the methods used to carry out crime); offense (offenders switch from one form of crime to another); and offender (new offenders replace old offenders who have been removed or who have desisted from crime).[3]

Displacement is generally viewed as a negative consequence of SCP efforts, but even when displacement does occur it can still provide some benefit. Current thinking on crime displacement suggests that less harmful or "benign" displacement could occur in several ways (Barr and Pease, 1990; Bowers and Johnson, 2003; Eck, 1993; Guerette and Bowers, forthcoming):

1. The *severity* of the displaced crime can be less (such as the shift to petty thefts rather than robbery).

2. The *impact* of the displaced crime could be less in three ways:
   a. The redistribution of concentrated crime across a bigger pool of *victims* (i.e., relocating victimization from a small group of repeat victims to a larger pool of victims).
   b. The transference of crime away from more *vulnerable groups* of the population (e.g., children and the elderly).
   c. The relocation of crime to *places* where the community impact is less harmful. This could take two forms:
      i. The *relocation* of a street drug or prostitution market from a residential area to a remote area would produce less community harm, such as fear of crime or less residential and business decay.
      ii. The *dispersion* of the same volume of crime to a larger area where the harm is less concentrated.

3. The *volume* of crime could be less (e.g., the target area may experience a reduction of 100 crimes post intervention, whereas the displacement of crime only resulted in an increase in comparison area of say 50 crimes post intervention. Thus, there are still 50 fewer crimes).

At worst, displacement can lead to more harmful consequences. This occurs when there is a shift to more serious offenses or to offenses which have more serious consequences (Barr and Pease, 1990). Referred to as "malign" displacement, it involves any situation where the relocation of crime made matters worse. This could be an increase in the volume of crime at the relocated area, the concentration of crime to a smaller group of victims, the relocation of crime to places where it has greater impact on the community, or the relocation of crime to more vulnerable groups of the population. Only when the benefits of any crime prevention initiative are outweighed by the harm and/or volume of displaced crime can the prevention effort be found ineffective (see Guerette and Bowers, forthcoming). For this reason, any SCP evaluation would need to weigh the costs of crime displacement against the benefits achieved by the intervention.

Diffusion of Crime Control Benefits

The opposite of displacement is the phenomenon of diffusion of crime control benefits. Crime diffusion is the reverse of displacement: it entails the reduction of crime (or other improvements) in areas that were close to targeted crime prevention efforts, even though they were not targeted by the intervention itself. Though less recognized than displacement, the diffusion phenomenon has been observed by many (Bowers and Johnson, 2003; Chaiken, Lawless, and Stevenson, 1974a, b; Green, 1995; Miethe, 1991; Weisburd et al., 2006; Weisburd and Green, 1995). Early findings of diffusion effects referred to them in a variety of ways, including the "bonus effect," the "halo effect," the "free-rider effect," and the "multiplier effect."

In cases where any degree of diffusion is observed, the benefit of any treatment effects experienced in the targeted area are amplified, since improvements were gained without expending resources in those areas. This is important for the evaluation of SCP. Failure to consider diffusion could result in a conclusion that only marginal gains were made, whereas when diffusion was observed, more favorable conclusions on effectiveness would follow.

Anticipatory Benefits

Anticipatory benefits occur when there is a reduction in crime (or other outcome measure) prior to the actual implementation of an intervention. This effect may be produced in a variety of ways (see Smith, Clarke, and Pease, 2002), but it is generally believed to be a consequence of the altered perceptions among offenders regarding the change of circumstances. Of the three concepts, anticipatory benefits is perhaps the least known but it is significant nonetheless, having been noted in roughly one out of four study site evaluations in a previous review (Smith et al., 2002). It is important for evaluations of SCP to take into account the presence of anticipatory benefits when determining treatment effects. Failure to do so could lead to misleading conclusions. Actual treatment effect sizes will be deflated when conducting pre-post tests, unless adjustments are made for anticipatory-benefit effects. Thus, failure to do so could result in a Type II error (false negative), leading the researcher to conclude that the prevention measures did not result in a significant reduction in crime, when it in fact did.

Incorporation of displacement, diffusion, and anticipatory benefits in SCP evaluations has several implications for methodology. Taking account of spatial displacement and diffusion requires that a minimum of two comparison areas be used in addition to the treatment area. One comprises a "buffer area" to identify possible displacement or diffusion effects, and the other a "control area" to estimate treatment effects. The control area should be similar to the treatment area and at a distance from it so that it is not influenced in any way by the intervention. The selection of the buffer area should meet three criteria: (1) it should be adjacent to the treatment area; (2) it should be comparable in size; and (3) it should be free of contamination from other treatment areas. Each of these requirements is guided by theory.[4] To identify possible anticipatory benefits, time-series data are required in order to observe any premature reduction in crime.

Cost-Benefit Analysis and Longer Follow-up Periods

The two most notable technical issues requiring the expansion of SCP evaluation are greater use of cost-benefit analysis and the use of longer follow-up periods after an intervention is in place. The call for more widespread use of cost-benefit analysis is not particular to SCP evaluations, but is part of a general trend in the evaluation of all crime prevention initiatives and other government-funded programs. For instance, the U.S. Government Reporting and Performance Act (GPRA) calls for established outcome measures for all federally funded programs in order to determine the "return on investment," and the federal National Institute of Justice specifies that it gives priority to grant proposals which include cost-benefit analysis (NIJ, 2008). Similarly, Washington State has required that all state funded programs be evaluated based on cost-benefit analysis. Though this is a general trend, it is equally relevant for SCP if the usefulness of the approach is to be justified.

There have also been claims that evaluation follow-up periods are too short. Clarke (2005) claims that, with the exception of one long-term study, most evaluations of SCP have studied outcomes for only one or two years. Longer follow-up periods would allow for assessments of criminal adaptation.

Randomized experimentation, scientific realism and the developing concepts and technical issues just discussed differ in terms of what they mean for desirable SCP evaluation. Yet, what they have in common is that they all seem to imply greater complexity. One question that arises is whether any single research approach can or should try to sufficiently accommodate altogether the pull, push and expansion that SCP evaluation currently faces. The following section takes a closer look at the current body of SCP evaluation methods to see where it is now and what this might mean for the future.

II. APPRAISAL OF SCP EVALUATION METHODS

Search Strategy

The search for evaluation studies of situational crime prevention began with a thesaurus of terms, which included the various types of situational crime prevention measures (e.g., closed-circuit television, target hardening, lighting, etc.). These terms were used in searching the following databases: *Criminal Justice Abstracts*, *National Criminal Justice Reference Service* (NCJRS), *Sociological Abstracts*, Google, *Google Scholar*, *CINCH* (an Australian Database), and *Academic Search Premier*. In addition, the most relevant crime prevention journals were searched in their entirety. These included: *Security Journal*, *Crime Prevention and Community Safety: An International Journal*, and the various volumes of *Crime Prevention Studies*. The numerous crime prevention reports issued by the Home Office were reviewed, and the literature searches performed for the various Center for Problem-Oriented Policing guides provided an additional resource.

Bibliographies and reviews of publications addressing specific crime prevention techniques were searched and included the following: Clark (2002), Cozens, Saville and Hillier (2005), Deisman (2003), Farrington and Welsh (2002), Nicholson (1995), Nieto (1997), Poyner (1993), Smith, Clarke, and Pease (2002), Welsh and Farrington (2004), Welsh and Farrington (2003), Welsh and Farrington (2002), and Welsh and Farrington (1999).

A similar search was made for documents relating to the displacement effect in crime prevention programs. This included a search of the bibliographies on the topic, as well as a thorough search of *Criminal Justice Abstracts* and the *National Criminal Justice Reference Service* databases. For documents that reviewed the displacement literature, the following were particularly useful: Barr and Pease (1990), Bowers and Johnson (2003), Brantingham and Brantingham (2003), Clarke and Weisburd (1994), Eck (1993), Hesseling (1994), and Reppetto (1976). Both published and unpublished reports that were written in English were included. If unpublished reports were not readily available, an effort was made to secure them from the individual authors, or to borrow them from another library. From this search, 261 articles were retrieved.

Inclusion and Coding

Each of these 261 articles was then assessed and included in the analyses using the following conditions:

1. It was written in English.
2. It was published as either a journal article; government report; organizational report or book (including book chapters).
3. The article reported an evaluation of a crime prevention effort that was predominantly or exclusively a situational intervention. In some cases the crime prevention effort also included dispositional interventions but the situational intervention(s) were predominant.
4. The situational techniques employed in the intervention could be classified using Cornish and Clarke's (2003) listing of 25 situational crime prevention techniques.
5. Studies which involved targeted police tactics were not included (even though they could have been classified as "strengthening formal surveillance"). Studies which involved a prominent use of situational measures and also involved targeted police efforts were included.
6. The evaluation used some quantitative measure of crime.
7. The article reported original research findings. Systematic reviews or other meta-analyses of prevention projects themselves were not included, though articles which reported on several case studies were included. In cases where the same project was reported in two different publications (e.g., in a government report and in a journal article), only the manuscript with the most detailed information was included.

The net result of this assessment produced 206 studies used in the review.

Results

In the majority of studies. the situational crime prevention interventions were found effective. These are reported in Table 1. Specifically, of the 206 SCP evaluations reviewed, three out of four (75%, n = 154) concluded that the intervention was effective overall. Twelve percent (n = 24) concluded that the situational intervention was not effective, while 6% (n = 12) reported mixed findings, and 8% (n = 16) of the study outcomes were inconclusive.

Table 2 presents the distribution of general research designs used in the evaluation of SCP. The most common design used was a before-after with some comparison at 38% (n = 78), followed by a simple before-after with no comparison at 27% (n = 56). The next most common type was

Table 1: Conclusions of Situational Crime Prevention Evaluations

N = 206	Frequency (%)*
Effective	154 (75%)
Not effective	24 (12%)
Mixed findings	12 (6%)
Inconclusive	16 (8%)

* Percent does not equal 100 due to rounding.

Table 2: Distribution of Research Designs in SCP Evaluations

N = 206	Observed Frequency* (%)**
Before-after w/ comparison	78 (38%)
Before-after***	56 (27%)
Time Series	44 (21%)
Time Series w/ comparison	24 (12%)
Before-after w/ buffer and comparison	15 (7%)
Cross-sectional	9 (4%)
Cross-sectional w/ comparison	7 (3%)
Before-after w/ Randomized control	6 (3%)
After	2 (1%)
After w/ comparison	3 (1%)

*Frequency does not equal sample N of 206 since many studies used multiple designs (e.g., time series and a before-after with comparisons).
**Percent computed using study N of 206 as denominator.
***Three of these entailed a before-after with removed intervention.

the use of a time series (21%, n = 44) followed by a time series with comparison at 12% (n = 24). Cross-sectional only and cross-sectional with comparison designs were used in 4 and 3% of the studies, respectively (n = 9, cross-sectional; n = 7, cross-sectional with comparison). The least common design was a simple after test and after with comparison, each comprising only 1% (n = 2, no comparison; n = 3, with comparison).

Of the 206 studies reviewed, only 15 studies (7%) had a treatment, buffer and a comparison area, thus allowing for determination of overall treatment effects in relation to displacement and diffusion effects. Finally, just 3% of studies (n = 6) included in the review used a randomized experimental design. All but one of the randomized experiments had been conducted since 1993. Additionally, all of the randomized evaluations concluded that the situational intervention was effective (see Appendix for more detail on these).

The distribution of situational crime prevention techniques used across the evaluations is presented in Table 3. While the SCP techniques were coded using Cornish and Clarke's (2003) 25 categories, they also provide a way of cataloguing the types of mechanisms that might be used in the accumulation of knowledge under the scientific realism approach. Of the five conceptual categories (effort, risk, reward, provocation and excuses), techniques that have been devised to increase the effort and the risk have been evaluated most commonly. Of the techniques to increase the effort, target hardening was the most common (24%), followed by access control (18%), and the deflection of offenders (7%). Within the "increase effort" category, screening of exits and controlling weapons or tools were the least commonly use at 2% each. Within the category of methods to increase the risk, strengthening formal surveillance was by far the most common (44%), followed by techniques to assist natural surveillance and extend guardianship (28% and 22%, respectively). The use of place managers was evaluated in 8% of the 206 evaluations, while techniques to reduce anonymity were evaluated in only 3%.

Of the techniques designed to reduce the rewards of offending, proportions evaluating property identification and denial of benefits were about the same, at 7 and 8%, respectively. These were followed by removing targets and disrupting markets: each was assessed in 3% of the 206 evaluations. The technique of concealing targets was not evaluated. The reducing provocations category of situational measures was only recently added to the SCP approach (Cornish and Clarke, 2003), so it is not surprising that it was the least evaluated among the five conceptual categories. Within this category, avoiding disputes was most common (2%), followed by techniques to reduce frustrations and stress and those to reduce emotional arousal, each at 1%. Techniques to neutralize peer pressure and discourage imitation were not evaluated in any of the 206 studies. Finally, within the category of removing excuses, alerting of conscience was most common (4%), followed by the controlling of drugs and alcohol and rule setting, each at 2%. Posting instructions and assisting compliance were each evaluated in about 1% of the sample.

Table 3: Distribution of SCP Techniques Assessed in Evaluations

N = 206	Frequency* (%)**
Increase Effort	
Harden targets	50 (24%)
Control access	37 (18%)
Deflect offenders	13 (7%)
Screen exits	4 (2%)
Control weapons/tools	6 (2%)
Increase Risk	
Strengthen formal surveillance	90 (44%)
Assist natural surveillance	57 (28%)
Extend guardianship	46 (22%)
Use place managers	15 (8%)
Reduce anonymity	6 (3%)
Reduce Rewards	
Deny benefits	15 (8%)
Identify property	13 (7%)
Remove targets	5 (3%)
Disrupt markets	5 (3%)
Conceal targets	0 (0%)
Reduce Provocations	
Avoid disputes	3 (2%)
Reduce frustrations and stress	1 (<1%)
Reduce emotional arousal	1 (<1%)
Neutralize peer pressure	0 (0%)
Discourage imitation	0 (0%)
Remove Excuses	
Alert conscience	8 (4%)
Set rules	3 (2%)
Control drugs and alcohol	3 (2%)
Assist compliance	2 (1%)
Post instructions	1 (<1%)

*Does not equal study sample n of 206 since many studies assessed more than one SCP technique.

**Does not equal 100 due to rounding. Percentages derived using number of studies (N = 206) as denominator.

Table 4: Environment of Situational Crime Prevention Measures Evaluated

N = 206	Frequency (%)*
Residential	61 (30%)
Public ways	50 (24%)
Transport	36 (17%)
Retail	25 (12%)
Multiple	18 (9%)
Human Service	7 (3%)
Recreational	5 (2%)
Industrial	1 (<1%)
Offices	1 (<1%)
Open/transitional	0 (0%)
Agricultural	0 (0%)

* Does not equal 100 due to rounding.

Table 4 presents the distribution of environments where the situational interventions were implemented. The coding for environments was based on Eck and Clarke's (2003) 11 categories. These categories are not totally representative of the context, but they do represent one dimension. The most common types of environment where SCP measures were evaluated were residential (30%, n = 61), followed by public ways (24%, n = 50), transport (17%, n = 36) and retail (12%, n = 25). Nine percent (n = 18) performed an evaluation of interventions applied in multiple settings. The least common environments of SCP evaluations were industrial and offices (each <1%, n = 1), educational (1%, n = 2), recreational (2%, n = 5), and human service (3%, n = 7). No SCP interventions were evaluated in agricultural or open/transitional environments.

The extent to which displacement, diffusion, and anticipatory benefits were examined among the SCP evaluations is shown in Table 5. Of the 206 evaluations of SCP measures, 102 specifically examined or presented data which allowed for determination of displacement effects. Among these 102 examinations, the most common form of displacement was spatial (77%), followed by target (28%), offense (15%), and tactical (10%). Temporal forms of displacement were examined in only 5% of the 102 displacement studies and none of the studies examined for perpetrator

Table 5: Examinations of Displacement, Diffusion, and Anticipatory Benefits

Type	Displacement n = 102 (50%) Frequency (%)*	Diffusion of Benefit n = 84 (41%) Frequency (%)*	Anticipatory Benefit n = 47 (23%) Frequency (%)
Temporal	5 (5%)	1 (1%)	n/a
Spatial	77 (77%)	79 (94%)	n/a
Target	27 (27%)	4 (5%)	n/a
Tactical	10 (10%)	—	n/a
Offense	15 (15%)	—	n/a
Perpetrator	—	—	n/a
Total	134**	84	47

* Percent of those studies examining displacement or diffusion (e.g. for displacement denominator n = 102; for diffusion denominator n = 84).
**Does not equal study n of 102 as a result of several studies examining multiply forms of displacement. Thus, the unit of analysis is the number of times the various forms of displacement were investigated.

displacement. Several studies examined multiple forms of displacement, such as spatial, offense, and target, for example. Because of this, while there were 102 studies which examined displacement, there were 134 different types or instances of displacement studied.

Eighty-four (84) studies examined or presented data which allowed for determination of diffusion-of-benefit effects. Spatial diffusion was most frequently examined (94%), followed by target (5%) and temporal (1%). None of the studies inquired as to whether or not tactical, offense, or perpetrator diffusion took place. Lastly, anticipatory benefits were examined or examinable in just less than 1 in 4 studies (23%, n = 47).[5]

Table 6 provides the proportion of SCP evaluations that either computed or presented data, which allowed for some level of cost-benefit calculation of the intervention(s). Altogether, 39% of the studies included this in the evaluation (n = 79). Twenty-two percent (n = 45) actually made cost-benefit computations, while another 17% (n = 34) presented data that would allow for some determination of cost of the intervention in relation to the benefit gained. The large majority of the evaluations did not include any sort of cost-to-benefit determination of the SCP intervention being evaluated (62%, n = 127).

Table 6: Proportion of Studies Providing Cost/loss Data

N = 206	Frequency (%)*
Computed	45 (22%)
Allowed for	34 (17%)
No	127 (62%)

* Percent does not equal 100 due to rounding.

Table 7: Distribution of Post-Intervention Evaluation Periods (in months)

N = 206	Observed Frequency (%)
< 12 months	49 (24%)
12 to 24 months	91 (44%)
25 to 36 months	17 (8%)
37 to 48 months	5 (2%)
> 48 months	12 (6%)
Various	18 (9%)
Undeterminable	3 (2%)
Not applicable	11 (5%)

Mean = 22; Mode = 12; Std. Dev. = 31

The distributions of post-intervention follow-up periods are reported in calendar months in Table 7. On the aggregate, the average length of follow-up was just under 2 years (mean = 22 months), while the mode was 1 year (12 months). The standard deviation was 31 months. Categorically, 24% (n = 49) of the designs had follow-up periods less than 12 months, 44% (n = 91) had follow-up periods between 12 to 24 months, 8% (n = 17) were 25 to 36 months long, just 2% (n = 5) were 37 to 48 months, and 6% (n = 12) had follow-up periods greater than 48 months. Nine percent (n = 18) of the studies had various follow-up periods. In 2% (n = 3) of the studies the follow-up period was not reported and in 5% (n = 11) it was not applicable.

III. IMPLICATIONS FOR FUTURE SCP EVALUATION

The findings reported here suggest several implications for future SCP evaluations. First, only 6 of the 206 studies reviewed used a randomized experimental design, but the conclusion from each study was uniformly the same. That is, the situational intervention was found effective (see Appendix). Though Weisburd, Lum, and Petrosino (2001) found in a review of a variety of criminal justice interventions that non-randomized designs were more likely to result in a false positive than were randomized experiments, the conclusions of the six SCP randomized evaluations here have some convergent validity with those of the non-randomized SCP evaluations. The conclusions from the randomized evaluations are generally consistent with the majority conclusion of the non-randomized studies, where three out of four (75%) reported that the situational intervention was effective.

If the findings from SCP randomized evaluations are the same as those derived from non-randomized designs, one is left to wonder whether the added trouble, cost and intrusiveness of randomized experimental research in field and organizational settings are warranted. As Eck (2002) suggests, the answer to this question may be different for evaluations of large-scale, large-claim interventions where contextual sensitivity is low than it is for small-scale, small-claim interventions. Randomization may be better suited for the former rather than the latter. But even for large-scale randomized evaluations of SCP, the result could only tell us that the *process* of SCP is a viable solution. It could not say that any specific intervention or package of situational measures is universally effective across all places, systems or times.

Second, the restricted distribution of environmental contexts in which SCP interventions have been evaluated means that those pushing toward scientific realism have a long way to go. The classifications examined here only partially assess the multiple dimensions of context, but even on this one dimension they are disproportionately clustered among just four environments: residential, public ways, transport, and to a lesser extent retail venues. Comparatively little is known about the effectiveness of SCP interventions in recreational, human service, or educational environments, and virtually nothing is known about how SCP interventions operate in agricultural, industrial, office or open/transitional environments. The environments catalogued here most closely represent the physical part of context, and also implicate the social processes that take place there, but the remaining temporal, and legal dimensions identified by Brantingham and

Brantingham (1993) remain mostly unassessed. Similarly, much remains to be known about the effectiveness of the variety of mechanisms, at least those 25 identified by the SCP approach. The majority of evaluations have assessed just two (increased effort and increased risk) of the possible five conceptual categories of mechanisms.

Third, the limited incorporation of displacement, diffusion and anticipatory benefits in the evaluations suggests that future research has much to do to accommodate these recent conceptual expansions. This incorporation is needed on two fronts. For all three of these concepts, the first front entails the routine incorporation of displacement, diffusion, and anticipatory benefit effects into the research design. These incorporations should not be carried out as peripheral assessments (as noted by Weisburd et al., 2006, for the study of displacement), but should be central to determining overall intervention effectiveness. This is because the overall outcome of any SCP intervention can be either amplified or eroded by their presence and the complete impact of the intervention cannot be determined unless their effects are measured against any gains achieved by the intervention.

For the incorporation of spatial displacement and diffusion, this means that research designs should incorporate no less than three areas: one treatment area, one buffer, and one control. Of the 206 evaluations reviewed, only 15 (7%) included this in the design, thus allowing for inspection of treatment effects in relation to displacement or diffusion. The selection of areas should also be guided by theories on displacement, which require that buffer areas be close or adjacent to treatment areas, that they are proportionate in size, and that they are free from contamination from other nearby interventions. The selected control area should also be immune from any influence of the intervention being studied. Few of these 15 studies were able to meet all of these criteria. To measure anticipatory benefits requires making adjustments in the form of "reverse lags," which appropriately assign reductions observed prior to the formal implementation of an intervention to the post-intervention mean. For research design this means using both time series and before-after comparisons. While several of the studies reviewed used multiple designs such as these, none adjusted for the premature effects of the intervention.

The second front relevant for measuring displacement and diffusion deals with more systematic assessment of their various dimensions. The vast majority of displacement and diffusion of benefits inspections in our sample involved measuring of spatial effects (77% for displacement, 94%

for diffusion). Comparatively less is known about the extent of temporal, target, tactical, offense, or perpetrator forms of displacement or diffusion. The recent introduction of the weighted displacement quotient (WDQ) and the total net effect (TNE) developed by Bowers and Johnson (2003) gives us a tool for determining overall effects in light of displacement and diffusion, but it has thus far been mostly applied to spatial forms. Future research should follow the lead of Bowers, Johnson, and Hirschfield (2003) and use these methods to assess the other forms of displacement/diffusion or develop adaptations thereof. Another aspect of this second front is the need for more complete exploration of the various attributes of displacement/diffusion within each of the six forms. The discussion in section one identified several forms of displacement within the three classifications of severity, impact, and volume. Few examinations of displacement and diffusion have explored or tried to measure the myriad of ways displacement might behave.

Fourth, a minority of studies included computations of cost-benefit analysis and fewer provided monetary figures that would allow for such computations, but together the picture is not altogether depressing. These two categories combined revealed that 39% of the studies included monetary data. Though this is less than half, it does at least approach the halfway point. Even so, future studies will need to include monetary costs more routinely if SCP measures are to be adequately assessed, particularly as governments funding these schemes yield to increased pressures to validate the outcomes of their expenditures. Finally, the analysis of follow-up periods confirms the need to study SCP intervention effects for longer periods. This will be easier for aggregated, retrospective studies. For prospective, small-scale SCP evaluations this may be more challenging since data are often produced or collected specifically for the evaluation. With time, organizational priorities and interests will shift and resources will likely diminish, making protracted evaluation periods less feasible.

This appraisal also raises another question. Can or should any one evaluation accommodate altogether the pull, push, and expansion facing SCP evaluation? In other words, should it be expected that an evaluation of SCP accommodate random assignment, isolation of the mechanism and cataloguing of context, the variety of displacement and diffusion effects, anticipatory benefit effects, cost-benefit analysis and lengthy follow-up periods simultaneously? This will certainly be constrained by access to organizations, their information and the resources for collecting and analyzing data, all of which might be outside the scope of the researcher regardless of the best intentions. Given the oppositional stance of randomization versus scientific realism, it seems unlikely that the pull and the push will work together, but this doesn't mean that they could not do so (Knaap, Leeuw, Bogaerts, Nijssen, 2008). More likely is that in any given evaluation either the pull of randomization or the push of scientific realism will prevail. In the end, we might find that the more important need is to develop research designs and methods which accommodate the conceptual and technical expansions regardless of whether that is within a randomized experiment or a scientific realism approach.

Address correspondence to: Rob T. Guerette, Ph.D., School of International & Public Affairs, Florida International University, University Park PCA 366B, 11200 SW 8th Street, Miami, FL 33199; e-mail: guerette@fiu.edu

Acknowledgments: The author thanks the Center for Problem-Oriented Policing, which provided support for part of this research, and Phyllis Schultze, librarian of the Don M. Gottfredson Library at the School of Criminal Justice, Rutgers University at Newark, for facilitating the search of the literature.

NOTES

1. Quasi-experimental designs resemble experimental designs in the sense that they may have "pre" and "post" measures and comparison groups. However, they differ in that they do not use random assignment.
2. Idiographic explanations seek to understand exhaustively the many causes of what happened in a particular instance. They are limited in the scope of the understanding to that instance. Nomothetic explanations seek to explain a class of situations or events rather than just one incident or case. They identify the few strongest explanations for the class of events and settle for a partial understanding rather than an exhaustive one.
3. For more on this see Reppetto (1976).
4. See Bowers and Johnson (2003), and Guerette and Bowers (forthcoming) for more discussion on this.

5. It might be noted that the only other existing review of anticipatory benefits (Smith et al., 2002) revealed a similar proportion, but a different number. There it was found that of 142 evaluations there were 211 inspections and 52 which analyzed anticipatory benefit. The present study included all of the 142 evaluations reviewed by Smith et al. (2002), plus an additional 64 for a total of 206. The seeming discrepancy is the result of different levels of analysis. The Smith review reported on the number of inspections within the 142 evaluations, whereas here the unit of analysis was the number of evaluations rather than the number of inspections within these evaluations. Thus, if any study had more than one assessment of anticipatory benefit, it was coded as 1.

REFERENCES

Barr, R., & Pease, K. (1990). Crime placement, displacement and deflection. In M. Tonry & N. Morris (Eds.), *Crime and justice: A review of research* (Vol. 12, pp. 277–318). Chicago: University of Chicago Press.

Baumer, T. L., Maxfield, M. G., & Mendelsohn, R. I. (1993). A comparative analysis of three electronically monitored home detention programs. *Justice Quarterly*, *10*, 121–142.

Bowers, K., & Johnson, S. (2003). Measuring the geographical displacement and diffusion of benefit effects of crime prevention activity. *Journal of Quantitative Criminology 19*(3), 275–301.

Bowers, K., Johnson, S., & Hirschfield, A. (2003). *Pushing back the boundaries: New techniques for assessing the impact of burglary schemes.* The Home Office Research, Development, and Statistics Directorate, Online Report 24/03.

Braga, A., Weisburd, D., Waring, E., Mazerolle, L., Spelman, W., & Gajewski, F. (1999). Problem-oriented policing in violent crime places: A randomized controlled experiment. *Criminology 37*(3), 541–580.

Brantingham, P. J., & Brantingham, P. L. (2003). Anticipating the displacement of crime using the principles of environmental criminology. In M. Smith & D. Cornish (Eds.), *Theory for practice in situational crime prevention. Crime prevention studies* (Vol. 16, pp. 119–148). Monsey, NY and Cullompton, UK: Criminal Justice Press and Willan Publishing.

Brantingham, P. L., & Brantingham, P. J. (1993). Environment, routine, and situation: Toward a pattern theory of crime. In R. V. Clarke & M. Felson (Eds.), *Routine activity and rational choice. Advances in criminological theory* (Vol. 5, pp. 259–382). New Brunswick, NJ: Transaction Publishers.

Chaiken, J., Lawless, M., & Stevenson, K. (1974a). *The impact of police activity on crime: Robberies on the New York City subway system.* New York: New York City Rand Institute.

Chaiken, J., Lawless, M., & Stevenson, K. (1974b). The impact of police activity on crime. *Urban Analysis 3*, 173–205.

Clark, B. A. J. (2002). *Outdoor lighting and crime, part 1: Little or no benefit*. Victoria, Australia: Astronomical Society of Victoria.

Clark, B. A. J. (2002). *Outdoor lighting and crime, part 2: Coupled growth*. Victoria, Australia: Astronomical Society of Victoria.

Clarke, R. V. (1980) Situational crime prevention: Theory and practice. *British Journal of Criminology*, *20*,, 136–47.

Clarke, R. V. (Ed.). (1997). *Situational crime prevention: Successful case studies* (2nd ed.). Monsey, NY: Criminal Justice Press.

Clarke, R. V. (2004). Technology, criminology and crime science. *European Journal on Criminal Policy and Research*, *10*(1), 55–63.

Clarke, R. V. (2005). Seven misconceptions of situational crime prevention. In N. Tilley (Ed.), *Handbook of crime prevention and community safety* (pp. 41–72). Cullompton, Devon, UK: Willan Press.

Clarke, R. V. & Cornish, D. B. (1972). *The Controlled Trial in institutional research: Paradigm or pitfall for penal evaluators?* Home Office Research Study No. 16. London: Her Majesty's Stationery Office.

Clarke, R. V., & Weisburd, D. (1994). Diffusion of crime control benefits: Observations on the reverse of displacement. In R. V. Clarke (Ed.), *Crime prevention studies* (Vol. 2). Monsey, NY: Criminal Justice Press.

Cook, T. D., & Campbell, D. T. (1979). *Quasi-experimentation: Design and analysis issues for field settings*. Chicago: Rand McNally.

Cornish, D., & Clarke, R. V. (2003). Opportunities, precipitators and criminal decisions: A reply to Wortley's critique of situational crime prevention. In M. Smith & D.B. Cornish (Eds.), *Theory for situational crime prevention. Crime prevention studies* (Vol. 16, pp. 41–96). Monsey, NY and Cullompton, Devon, UK: Criminal Justice Press.

Cozens, P. M., Saville, G., & Hillier, D. (2005). Crime prevention through environmental design (CPTED): A review and modern bibliography. *Property Management*, *23*(5), 328–356.

Deisman, W. (2003). *CCTV Literature review and bibliography*. Ottawa: Research and Evaluation Branch, Community, Contract and Aboriginal Policing Services Directorate, Royal Canadian Mounted Police.

Dunford, F. W. (2000). Determining program success: The importance of employing experimental research designs. *Crime & Delinquency*, *46*(3), 425–434.

Eck, J. (1993). The threat of crime displacement. *Criminal Justice Abstracts* *25*(3), 527–546.

Eck, J. (1998). Preventing crime by controlling drug dealing on private rental property. *Security Journal 11*, 37–43.

Eck, J. (2002). Learning from experience in problem-oriented policing and situational prevention: The positive functions of weak evaluations and the negative functions of strong ones. In N. Tilley (Ed.), *Crime prevention studies* (Vol. 14, pp. 93–117). Monsey, NY and Cullompton, Devon, UK: Criminal Justice Press and Willan Publishing.

Eck, J. (2005). Evaluation for lesson learning. In N.Tilley (Ed.), Handbook of crime prevention and community safety (pp. 699–733). Cullompton, Devon, UK: Willan Press.

Eck, J., & R. V. Clarke (2003). Classifying common police problems: A routine activity approach. In M. Smith & D. Cornish (Eds.), *Crime prevention studies* (Vol. 16, pp. 7–40). Monsey, NY and Cullompton, Devon, UK: Criminal Justice Press and Willan Publishing.

Farrington, D. (2006). Methodological quality and the evaluation of anti-crime programs. *Journal of Experimental Criminology*, *2*(3), 329–337.

Farrington, D. (2003a). A short history of randomized experiments in criminology: A meager feast. *Evaluation Review*, *27*(3), 218–227.

Farrington, D. P. (2003b). British randomized experiments on crime and justice. In (Eds.), *Annals of the American Academy of Political and Social Science*, Misleading evidence and evidence-led policy: Making social science more experimental (Vol. 589, pp. 150–167).

Farrington, D., Bowen, S., Buckle, A., Burns-Howell, T., Burrows, J., & Speed, M. (1993). An experiment on the prevention of shoplifting. *Crime Prevention Studies*, *1*, 93–119.

Farrington, D., & Welsh, B. (2006). A half century of randomized experiments on crime and justice. *Crime and justice* (Vol. 34, pp. 34–55). Chicago: University of Chicago Press.

Farrington, D., & Welsh, B. (2002, August). *Effects of improved street lighting on crime: A systematic review*. Home Office Research, Development and Statistics Directorate, Research Study 251.

Farrington, D. (2000). Explaining and preventing crime: The globalization of knowledge– The American Society of Criminology 1999 presidential address. *Criminology*, *38*(1), 1–24.

Feder, L., & Boruch, R. (2000). Need for experiments in criminal justice settings. *Crime & Delinquency*, *46*(3), 291–294.

Green, L. (1995). Cleaning up drug hot spots in Oakland, California: The displacement and diffusion effects. *Justice Quarterly* *12*(4), 737–754.

Guerette, R. T., & Bowers, K. (forthcoming). Assessing the extent of crime displacement and diffusion of benefits: A systematic review of situational crime prevention evaluations.

Harrell, A. (2006). Towards systematic knowledge building: An anti-crime research and development continuum. *Journal of Experimental Criminology*, *2*(3), 339–344.

Hesseling, R. (1994). Displacement: A review of the empirical literature. In R. V. Clarke (Ed.), *Crime prevention studies* (Vol. 3, pp. 197–230). Monsey, NY: Criminal Justice Press.

Knaap, L. M., Leeuw, F., Bogaerts, S., & Nijssen, L. (2008). Combining Campbell standards and the realist evaluation approach: The best of two worlds? *American Journal of Evaluation*, *29*(1), 48–57.

Maxfield, M. G., & Babbie, E. (2008). *Research methods for criminal justice and criminology* (5th ed). Belmont, CA: Wadsworth.

Mazerolle, L., Kadleck, C., & Roehl, J. (1998). Controlling drug and disorder problems: The role of place managers. *Criminology* *36*(2), 371–404.

Miethe, T. D. (1991). Citizen-based crime control activity and victimization risks: An examination of displacement and free rider effects. *Criminology*, *29*, 419–39.

National Institute of Justice. (2008). *Solicitation: Crime and justice research.* Office of Justice Programs, U.S. Department of Justice, Grants.gov Funding Opportunity No. 2008–NIJ–1730, SL# 000820.

Nicholson, L. (1995). *What works in situational crime prevention? A literature review.* Edinburgh, Scotland: Scottish Office Central Research Unit.

Nieto, M. (1997). *Public video surveillance: Is it an effective crime prevention tool?* Sacramento, CA: California Research Bureau, California State Library.

Pawson, R., & Tilley, N. (1997). *Realistic evaluation.* London: Sage.

Poyner, B. (1993). What works in crime prevention: An overview of evaluations. In R. V. Clarke (Ed.), Crime prevention studies (Vol. 1, pp. 7–34). Monsey, NY: Criminal Justice Press.

Reppetto, T. (1976). Crime prevention and the displacement phenomenon. *Crime and Delinquency* 22(2), 166–177.

Sherman, L. W. (2000). Reducing incarceration rates: The promise of experimental criminology. *Crime and Delinquency, 46*(3), 299–314.

Smith, M., Clarke, R., & Pease, K. (2002). Anticipatory benefits in crime prevention. In N. Tilley (Ed.), *Crime prevention studies* (Vol. 13, pp. 71–88). Monsey, NY and Cullompton, Devon, UK: Criminal Justice Press and Willan Publishing.

Tilley, N. (2002). Introduction: Evaluation for crime prevention. In N. Tilley (Ed.), Crime prevention studies (Vol. 14, pp. 1–10). Monsey, NY and Cullompton, Devon, UK: Criminal Justice Press and Willan Publishing.

Welsh, B., & Farrington, D. (1999). Value for money? A review of the costs and benefits of situational crime prevention. *British Journal of Criminology, 39*(3), 345–368.

Welsh, B., & Farrington, D. (2002). *Crime prevention effects of closed circuit television: a systematic review.* Home Office Study 252, London: Home Office Research, Development and Statistics Directorate.

Welsh, B., & Farrington, D. (2003). Effects of closed-circuit television on crime. *Annals of the American Academy of Political and Social Science, 587*, 110–135.

Welsh, B., & Farrington, D. (2004). Surveillance for crime prevention in public space: Results and policy choices in Britain and America. *Criminology & Public Policy, 3*(3), 497–526.

Weisburd, D. (2003). Ethical practice and evaluation of interventions in crime and justice: The moral imperative for randomized trials. *Evaluation Review, 27*(3), 336–354.

Weisburd, D., Wyckoff, L., Ready, J., Eck, J., Hinkle, J., & Gajewski, F. (2006). Does crime just move around the corner? A controlled study of spatial displacement and diffusion of crime control benefits. *Criminology, 44*(3), 549–591.

Weisburd, D., & Green, L. (1995). Policing drug hot spots: The Jersey City drug market analysis experiment. *Justice Quarterly 12*(4), 711–735.

Weisburd, D., Lum, C., & Petrosino, A. (2001). Does research design affect study outcomes in criminal justice? In D. P. Farrington & B.C. Welsh (Eds.), *Annals of the American Academy of Political and Social Science, 578* , 50–70.

Weisburd, D., & Taxman, F. (2000). Developing a multicenter randomized trial in criminology: The case of HIDTA. *Journal of Quantitative Criminology, 16*(3), 315–340.

Whitcomb, D. (1979). *Focus on robbery: The hidden cameras project, Seattle, Washington.* Report prepared for the National Institute of Law Enforcement and Criminal Justice, Law Enforcement Assistance Administration, U.S. Department of Justice, Washington, DC.

Appendix: Overview of Randomized SCP Evaluations

Author	Date	Location	Environment	SCP Technique(s)	Follow-up Period	Cost/loss Data	Displacement	Diffusion	Anticipatory Benefits	Conclusion
Braga et al.	1999	Jersey City, NJ, US	Residential	Strengthen formal surveillance; disrupt markets; assist natural surveillance; use place managers	6 months	No	Examined	Examined	Not examined	Effective
Eck	1998	San Diego, CA, US	Residential	Use place managers	30 months	No	Not examined	Not examined	Not examined	Effective
Farrington, et al.	1993	United Kingdom	Retail	Screen exits; assist natural surveillance; strengthen formal surveillance	6 weeks	Computed	Not examined	Not examined	Not examined	Effective

(continued)

Appendix (continued)

Author	Date	Location	Environment	SCP Technique(s)	Follow-up Period	Cost/loss Data	Displacement	Diffusion	Anticipatory Benefits	Conclusion
Mazerolle et al.	1998	Oakland, CA, USA	Residential; retail	Utilize place managers; disrupt markets	5 months	No	Not examined	Not examined	Not examined	Effective
Weisburd & Green	1995	Jersey City, NJ, US	Public ways	Strengthen formal surveillance; extend guardianship	7 months post	No	Examined	Examined	Not examined	Effective
Whitcomb	1979	Seattle, WA, US	Retail	Strengthen formal surveillance	11 months	Allows for	Not examined	Not examined	Not examined	Effective

USING SIGNATURES OF OPPORTUNITY STRUCTURES TO EXAMINE MECHANISMS IN CRIME PREVENTION EVALUATIONS

by

John E. Eck
University of Cincinnati

Tamara Madensen
University of Nevada, Las Vegas

Abstract: *Interventions that block crime opportunity structures change crime signatures. Signatures are data patterns that describe how crime is associated with various features of the opportunity structure. The analysis of crime signature change, as part of crime prevention evaluations, can improve the internal validity of evaluation findings. This paper describes the logic of this argument, provides examples of how it works, and develops a four step procedure – SCEMA – for implementing this approach.*

INTRODUCTION

Evaluations of situational crime prevention programs have been based on the evaluation framework established by Campbell and Stanley (1963).

Crime Prevention Studies, volume 24 (2009), pp. 59–84.

This framework lists a set of evaluation designs and describes how they fare at removing threats to internal validity. Though highly robust, and consistent with the larger scientific framework of eliminating alternative explanations, this framework has three limitations. First, it does not pay sufficient attention to *how* the effect was created. That is, it does not address an intervention's mechanism (Pawson and Tilley, 2000). Mechanism is important because: a) it connects the intervention to the theory that sparked the intervention; b) it provides important guidance for generalizing the findings and creating replica interventions in other sites (Eck, 2006); and c) knowledge of the mechanism that is operating can help eliminate rival explanations.

The second deficiency – one more directly attributable to followers of the Campbell framework than the originators (Campbell and Stanley, 1963; Cook and Campbell, 1979; Shadish et al., 2002) – is that it does not address alternative methods for eliminating rival explanations. As Deborah Mayo (1996) has pointed out in her examination of scientific reasoning, scientists resort to a wide range of methods to show that experimental effects can be attributed to the intervention rather than some other factor. A focus on evaluations' designs to the exclusion of extra-design procedures to eliminate threats to internal validity, as can occur in systematic reviews, results in syntheses of studies that understate knowledge. Later, we will examine two examples of evaluations that have higher conclusion validity than one would estimate based on examining their designs alone. Their authors gained this higher conclusion validity by employing alternative methods.

The third deficiency, related to the previous two, is that the Campbell experimental framework, for all its merits, is too general. It is meant to be applicable in a wide variety of social interventions, from education to crime control, regardless of the setting and theoretical underpinnings of the intervention. Consequently it does not make use of domain-specific knowledge.

For these three reasons we suggest that crime prevention evaluations supplement the use of Campbell's design criteria with other procedures for eliminating rival explanations for the observed program effect. The approach we advocate can be considered a domain-specific version of what Shadish et al. (2002; pp. 105) call "coherent pattern matching." We start with the proposition that within the environmental criminology/crime science paradigm (Clarke, 2004) there are tools available to explicate mechanisms and eliminate rival explanations that are different from those available in other fields. The purpose of this paper is to begin a discussion of how domain-specific information from environmental criminology can be put to use in evaluations.

The thesis of this paper is as follows. Opportunity structures for crime create distinct patterns. We call these "signatures" (after Bowers and Johnson, 2004) to draw attention to the fact that patterns are not simply spatial distributions of crime (though the spatial distribution of crime is an important part of many crime signatures). Both academic research and crime analysis exploit signatures to understand how crime concentrations arise and to craft interventions that will reduce crime. Conversely, if opportunity structures did not give rise to distinct signatures, then it would make no sense to analyze crime or conduct other empirical research to determine how crime concentrations are created. To reduce crime we must disrupt, or change the opportunity structure (Clarke, 1995). This requires an intervention that alters the opportunity structure. Successful interventions change opportunity structures. That is, the intervention's mechanism operates on crime through the opportunity structure. Changes in opportunity structures change signatures. We can exploit these changes in signatures to determine if a crime prevention intervention's mechanism worked. Finally, information on the operation of the mechanism improves the internal validity of evaluations by eliminating rival hypotheses that evaluation designs may not be able to eliminate on their own. We develop a procedure called SCEMA: Signature Characterization, Expectation, Measurement, and Analysis that makes use of this argument. SCEMA is not a substitute for standard evaluation designs, but a supplement to them.

The outline of our paper is as follows. After this introduction we discuss ten propositions regarding opportunity structures, signatures, and signature change. In the process we define key concepts. The third section provides two examples of how changes in signatures can be used to help determine if a situational crime prevention intervention is effective. In the fourth section we describe the SCEMA procedure for operationalizing the approach described in the second and third sections. The fifth section examines several critical issues raised by the use of signatures crime prevention evaluations.

FROM OPPORTUNITY STRUCTURE TO EVALUATION DESIGN

Here we organize our argument in the form of ten propositions, some with subpropositions, and brief explanations. This set of propositions begins with basic theories of crime and crime concentration and ends with implications for conducting evaluations. It shows how crime prevention interventions are linked to knowledge about these crime concentrations. And it describes how understanding both theories of crime and the mechanism underlying the interventions can be used to design stronger evaluations of such interventions.

1. **Opportunity structures make crime possible.** This is the basic idea behind environmental criminological theories. Routine activity theory describes how the routines of everyday life create opportunities for offenders to exploit. The original paper on the topic showed how the variations in these opportunities are associated with temporal variations in crime (Cohen and Felson, 1979). The theory has been extended to explain why some targets and places have more crime than others (Felson, 1995; Clarke, 1999). Crime pattern theory looks at the way offenders search for targets and how they find opportunities in their everyday travels and activities (Brantingham and Brantingham, 1993). The rational choice perspective describes how people make decisions about offending given the characteristics of situations (Cornish and Clarke, 1986). Situational crime prevention reverses this explanation to show how altering the characteristics of situations can dissuade people from committing crimes (Clarke, 1995).

   1.1 – Opportunity structures are combinations of physical and social conditions in micro settings that influence offenders' perceptions proximate to their decision to commit crimes. Some opportunity structures prevent crime, while others make crime likely. The later are called "facilitating conditions" (Clarke and Newman, 2006). The opposite of facilitating conditions are "impeding conditions," which are aspects of the opportunity structure that make it difficult for crimes to occur. From an environmental criminology perspective, the conditions that matter for crime are those that are most proximate to the place and time at which the potential offender is considering committing the crime: temporal and spatial influences decline with greater time and space. Facilitating conditions are not uniformly spread across time and space, but tend to cluster. An opportunity structure is an array of conditions – in space, time, or along any dimension – that facilitate and impede crime. A particular opportunity structure may contain both facilitating and impeding conditions (e.g., a store may sell expensive small electronic devices that could be easily resold on a black market – facilitating conditions; – and use electronic surveillance, locked display cases, and trained staff to prevent theft – impeding conditions).

1.2 – It is the perceptions of offenders that matter most. Facilitating conditions must be detected and recognized by offenders. If an offender does not know a desirable target is nearby, then she cannot intentionally take advantage of this situation. However, impeding conditions may or may not be perceived by offenders. An offender may not perceive the target, or know that she did not perceive the target. Such an offender would be impeded. Other impeding conditions need to be perceived by offenders. Guardians, for example, block crime opportunities when they are perceived by offenders. But if the offender does not know of their presence, the offender may commit the crime in front of them. Though this may help crime detection, it may not prevent crime.

1.3 – Offender perceptions of facilitating and impeding conditions will vary spatially, temporally, and along other dimensions (Clarke, 1995). We can envision a perceived opportunity structure much like a geographic topography depicted on a map. That is, if we had the ability to combine the perceptions of all the offenders of interest, we could devise a map of an environment and show peaks and plateaus for facilitating conditions and valleys and plains for impeding conditions. We will call this "opportunity topography." Opportunity topographies vary temporally as well as spatially: by time of day, day of week, and season. Temporally, spikes represent time-dependent facilitating conditions, where troughs suggest time-dependent impeding conditions. Temporal regularities correspond to routines, such as commuting times, school sessions, methadone distribution schedules, tourist seasons, and so forth (Felson, 1981). Opportunity topographies also vary along dimensions other than time and space. Target characteristics, for example, present offenders with facilitating and impeding conditions. Cohen and Felson's (1979) VIVA, Clarke's (1999) CRAVED, and Clarke and Newman's (2006) EVIL DONE are all lists of target characteristics whose presence facilitates direct-contact predatory crime (VIVA), theft (CRAVED) or terrorism (EVIL DONE).[1] The absences of these characteristics are impeding conditions. The principle variables in environmental criminological theories describe many of these types of conditions.

2. **Offenders exploit opportunity structures.** As suggested in the explanation of the first proposition, it is not the opportunity alone that creates crime. Opportunities create necessary conditions for crimes to be committed, but these conditions are not sufficient. Not only are

offenders necessary for a crime, but they must make choices to exploit opportunities they encounter.

3. **Strong facilitating conditions produce more crime.** The stronger the perceived facilitating conditions relative to perceived impeding conditions, the more likely offenders will exploit an opportunity for crime. The weaker the perceived facilitating conditions relative to perceived impeding conditions, the less likely the offender will exploit the situation. In these circumstances we often claim the opportunity is blocked.

   3.1 – Offenders' exploitation of opportunity regions with strong facilitating conditions create dense concentrations of crime. In the low flat terrain of impeding conditions, crime will be scarce and spread out. At the extreme, it would appear random. Another way to think about this is to note that crime density maps, times series plots, and other frequency distributions describe many of the features of opportunity topographies. These crime distribution graphics will have gaps where offenders do not venture, much like an explorers map would have information gaps where there have been few if any explorations (the dark side of the moon, for example). Offender exploitation can be viewed as a non-random sampling process that estimates the underlying opportunity structure.

   3.2 – Frequency distributions showing patterns of crime provide the best available method for describing the topography of the opportunity structure. Such patterns are the "signatures" of opportunity structures. A hot spot map is an example of a partial signature. So is a time series plot. The full signature captures the distribution of crime on all dimensions that characterize the opportunity structure in question. In practice, we have to work with partial signatures, though some partial signatures are more complete than others, and these are more useful to practitioners designing crime prevention interventions.

4. **Variability in the terrain of the opportunity topography influences the prominence of the crime signature.** This directly follows from the previous proposition. Not only is there more crime in rough opportunity topographies than in smooth topographies, but crime is also more concentrated.

   4.1 – Strong crime signatures occur when there is great variability across opportunity topography. If there is high contrast between circumstances with facilitating conditions and those with impeding conditions (i.e., the opportunity topography has a rough terrain like British Columbia or western Colorado), then crime will stack in the uplands and be scarce in the opportunity topography's lowlands. The signature will be prominent in these conditions.

4.2 – Weak crime signatures occur when there is little variation across the topography of an opportunity structure. This produces greater uniformity in the distribution of crime. If the opportunity topography is made up of low rolling hills, then the signature will be weak: the contrast between high crime circumstances and low crime circumstances will be minor. At the extreme, the topography will look like Kansas or southern Saskatchewan. In such a circumstance, crime will be scarce and random along all observed relevant dimensions.

4.3. – Prominent signatures are more easily detected in statistical analysis. High-contrast opportunity topographies yield prominent signatures and low-contrast opportunity topographies yield weak crime signatures. Prominent signatures occur when facilitating conditions are heavily concentrated and are surrounded by impeding conditions. The contrast makes the crime signature easier to detect. It will be difficult to determine which dimensions are importantly linked to crime when observing low-contrast (and low-crime) topographies.

5. **Opportunity structures are observed by examining signatures.** The detection and analysis of crime signatures yield important information about the characteristics of the opportunity structure that gave rise to the crime pattern. This is the fundamental assumption of all crime analysis based on environmental criminological theories (Clarke and Eck, 2005). Information describing the opportunity structure may be ambiguous and incomplete, but it is the best information available. In short, both crime analysis and crime research work backward from the signature to the opportunity topography (the opportunity structure perceived by offenders) to the opportunity structure itself. And it is from this information that situational crime prevention interventions are derived.
6. **Interventions focus on normal processes, activities, or offender exploitation.** There are three forms of interventions that are of interest. Though we have described them separately, in practice they can be implemented together. Further, these forms are ideal types: some forms of interventions have attributes of two or three forms.

6.1 – Interventions that target normal processes and activities that give rise to the opportunity structure. These interventions fall within the framework of situational crime prevention. The mechanisms used by these interventions reduce facilitating conditions or increase impeding conditions.

6.2 – Interventions that alter offender perceptions of opportunity structures. These interventions do not change the opportunity structure. Their mechanisms only alter the way offenders perceive the opportunity structure. In their ideal form, the opportunity structure remains unchanged, but offenders have different perceptions of the opportunity structure. Posting signs that warn of dire consequences for violating laws (when unaccompanied by changes in other forms of prevention or enforcement) are examples. In practice, however, they are often coupled with one or both of the other types of interventions.

6.3 – Interventions that target offenders who exploit the opportunity structure. These interventions operate by removing offenders. These include specific deterrent, incapacitation, general deterrence efforts, early intervention of at risk individuals, and rehabilitation programs. When generally applied – not focused on particular opportunity structures – they are not a form of situational prevention. Rehabilitating offenders and general deterrence are general mechanisms that do not influence opportunity structures, or perceptions of opportunity structures, but instead alter general proclivities to engage in misconduct. An enforcement crackdown on a specific high-crime location applies a mechanism that has a space- (and time-) specific deterrent effect (and possible incapacitation effect) that may temporarily alter the opportunity topography, but it leaves the underlying opportunity structure intact.

Figure 1 summarizes propositions one through six, showing the role crime signatures play in diagnosing crime problems and pointing to the interventions which could alter the opportunity structure or opportunity topography and thus change the signature. The remaining propositions build on this set of relationships.

7. **Changes in crime frequency show the impact of the intervention.** If, following an intervention, crime declines (relative to some suitable control condition) then we have evidence supporting the conclusion that the intervention had the desired effect. If the crime change (relative to the control) shows no decline, then the evaluation has provided evidence supporting the conclusion that the intervention failed. This is the basic idea behind quasi-experiments and randomized experiments. The principle limitation is the suitability of the control condition; the

Figure 1. Opportunity Structure, Signature, and Intervention.

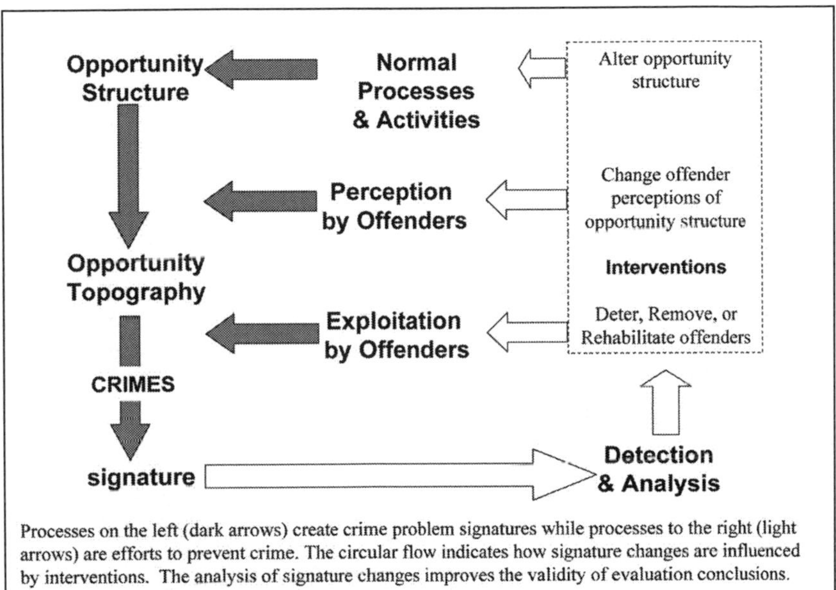

Processes on the left (dark arrows) create crime problem signatures while processes to the right (light arrows) are efforts to prevent crime. The circular flow indicates how signature changes are influenced by interventions. The analysis of signature changes improves the validity of evaluation conclusions.

less suitable it is, the less confidence we have that the change in crime is due to the intervention rather than some other explanation.

8. **Changes in the signature provide evidence that the intervention changed the opportunity topography or the opportunity structure.** If following an intervention the signature changed, this suggests that either the opportunity structure changed or offenders' perceptions of the structure (opportunity topography) changed. The original signature provided the information that described the original opportunity topography. If the intervention was crafted so as to alter the opportunity structure, then if the intervention worked, a change in the signature is the best evidence of a change in the opportunity structure or topography, or both.

   8.1 – Changes in the relationship between crime frequency and a specific dimension of the opportunity structure point to possible mechanisms by which the intervention influenced crime. For example, if there was a change in the types of targets attacked, this suggests that the intervention acted on target characteristics. If crimes decline at specific times, this implicates a mechanism that influences a temporal dimension. Or if former hot spot locations become cool spots, these signature changes suggest that the intervention operated through place characteristics or place management.

8.2 – Changes in the opportunity structure are more consistent with interventions stemming from situational crime prevention than other forms of interventions. Interventions that target offenders are less likely, in general, to alter opportunity structures. So these types of interventions are unlikely to reveal long term signature changes. However, in the short run, offender interventions may result in declines in crime concentrations where offenders are particularly active, particularly if the interventions successfully target most of the offenders involved (i.e., there is a decline in the sampling rate of the stable opportunity structure).

9. **Specific interventions use different mechanisms.** A cardinal rule of situational crime prevention (as well as the related approach, problem-oriented policing), is that interventions must be crime-problem-specific (Clarke, 1995).

9.1 – These mechanisms will influence different aspects of the opportunity structure or topography. Situational measures use any one or combination of 25 techniques to alter opportunity structures for crime (Cornish and Clarke, 2003). It follows that each technique uses a different mechanism (e.g., access control makes it more difficult for offenders to get to the target, while exit screening influences the chances of the offender being caught when leaving the crime. Though they are superficially similar, they are implemented in different ways and influence offender perceptions differently).

9.2 – Changes in different parts of the opportunity structure or topography will change signatures in different ways. Imagine two different interventions applied to very similar crime problems (i.e., they have the same opportunity structure and signatures). These interventions attack different parts of the opportunity structure or topography. After the interventions the two problems will have different opportunity structures. Thus, the two problems would have different signatures after the interventions even though they had similar signatures originally. This is what we mean when we say the signature has changed and that signature change is linked to changes in different parts of the original opportunity structure or topography.

9.3 – Signature change is diagnostic of the mechanism being used. This is the reverse of 9.2. If you were told that there was an intervention that reduced crime, but were not given specifics about the intervention, analysis of the signature change would give you important clues as to form of the intervention and the mechanism that was applied.

10. **Signature change complements standard quasi-experimental design conclusions.** Signature changes provide additional information regarding program effects that can assist in interpreting whether a relative decline in crime frequency was due to the intervention being evaluated. A signature change associated with a relative decline in crime suggests that the only viable explanations for the decline must be able to alter the opportunity structure or topography in a manner that could produce such a change.

    10.1 – Signature changes consistent with expected intervention mechanisms eliminate rival explanations. Any alternative explanation for the decline in crime that is inconsistent with evidence about the mechanism used is less plausible than the main hypothesis. This eliminates rival explanations that cannot alter opportunity structures or topographies.

    10.2 – Signature changes inconsistent with the expected intervention mechanism undermine the validity of the conclusion that the intervention produced the crime change. If an intervention was designed to apply a specific mechanism against a particular part of the opportunity structure or topography, then this should show up as a particular change in the crime signature. Failure to find this new signature implies that the intervention was not responsible for any measured decline in crime: something other than the intervention should get the credit.

    10.3 – The more specific and prominent the change in signatures, the fewer viable candidate explanations there can be. A dramatic decline in the association of crime and a particular dimension of the opportunity structure is highly definitive of the mechanism at work. This is because only a few rival explanations could produce a prominent signature change.

    10.4 – Evaluators should state expected changes in signatures if the intervention worked. This should be done while designing evaluations. Comparisons of expected signature changes to actual signature changes would serve as tests of the hypothesis that the intervention reduced crime.

These propositions lay out the argument for examining signatures as part of any evaluation of a situational crime prevention intervention, including those implemented as part of problem-oriented policing projects. Our argument is that standard evaluation designs are often insufficient to determine if the intervention actually worked, and by exploiting theories from environmental criminology we can produce evaluation conclusions with higher internal validity. In the next section we apply the theory to two evaluations to see how it might work. In the penultimate section we describe a general protocol for applying this approach.

EXAMPLES OF EXAMINING SIGNATURE CHANGE

In 1994, Barry Poyner published an article examining the effects on crime of the demolition of walkways connecting buildings in a large London housing project, Lisson Green. (Unless otherwise noted, Poyner [1994] is the source for the descriptions in this section, so we will not cite it further.) Lisson Green was complex of 23 six-story buildings containing 1,500 apartments connected by seven skywalks. Poyner's article contains a good example of the procedures we have been discussing (though he did not explain his procedures using the logic we have outlined). His evaluation was a very simple pre-post design without a control group. Poyner expanded this design by using monthly crime counts to create a short-time series design to show how various interventions were (or were not) associated with crime changes. This sort of design is common to situational prevention evaluations. The analyst is often stuck between two undesirable alternatives: conduct a weak evaluation and gain some knowledge, but with limitations to the validity of the conclusions, or conduct no evaluation and leave conclusions to speculations uninformed by any systematic treatment of data (Eck, 2006). The procedures we are advocating are designed to make such a tradeoff less onerous by improving the internal validity of evaluation designs.

Poyner begins his paper by noting that skywalks connecting residential apartment buildings (blocks) had been a popular design, but had fallen into disfavor because it was thought that the elevated connectors contributed to a number of maladies, including crime and particularly burglary. The original evaluation of the removal of the Lisson Green skywalks had claimed a large reduction in crime, including burglary, robbery, and thefts from and of vehicles. Poyner broke down the crime figures into three categories: burglary of apartments; muggings in the halls and on the skywalks; and thefts of and from vehicles in the adjacent parking areas. He noted that each type of crime had its own opportunity structure and that the removal of the skywalks was unlikely to have the same effect on all three crimes. Poyner showed that the number of burglaries was relatively stable over time and their numbers were too few to claim that the skywalk removal had an effect on them. He also noted that there was no plausible mechanism by which the skywalks could influence vehicle crimes at Lisson Green, as the parking areas were not connected to the buildings by these passages. However, the skywalk removal process provided a plausible mechanism: demolition activity required enforced restrictions on parking and this may have disrupted the vehicle crime opportunity structure. There were changes also in the parking area security guards after the skywalk demolition, and this too may have contributed to the vehicle crime drop.

For our purposes, however, the most interesting crime is robbery (muggings). The walkways gave uninterrupted access to all the buildings in the complex, so it is plausible that removing of the skywalks could alter the opportunity structure for robbery and thus reduce these events. However, the timing was wrong. The robberies dropped considerably before the skywalk removal. What could have caused this? Poyner interviewed the housing staff and found that entry phones had been installed in some buildings (blocks) prior to the removal of the skywalks.

> It was discovered from staff at the local estate office that four blocks near the main entry to the walkway system . . . were the first to be protected by entry phones. The main pedestrian access to the walkway system is via a ramp from the main street neighboring the estate at (this) point . . . Since the main line of the walkway system passed through the central corridors of two of these blocks, it seemed very likely that this would have closed direct access to the walkway system from this main street entrance. (page 139)[2]

So Poyner had a possible cause of the premature robbery reduction that had a mechanism that could disrupt the opportunity structure for robberies by curtailing unlimited access to the housing complex at the main entry point. But was the opportunity structure disrupted? Poyner plotted the spatial signature of robberies for three time intervals.

> Robberies and snatches that had occurred on the walkways were plotted onto the walkway diagram for three periods of six months: before the entry phones were installed . . . ; after installation of the entry phones but before walkway demolition . . . ; and after demolition . . . The results were very clear. . . . (N)early all the attacks . . . occurred before the first entry phones were fitted. A few (three) occurred in the next six months, and, by the time the seven walkway bridges were down, no more attacks were reported on the walkway system. (page 139)

Further, the majority of robbery locations before the entry phone installations were along corridors close to where the entry phones were placed, and these were the hot spots of robberies that virtually disappeared once the phones were operational. The remaining few robberies were much farther away from entry phone locations; a fact consistent with the hypothesis that other entrances (unprotected by phones) were more important for the other robberies.

By this analysis, Poyner was able to show not only that the intervention being evaluated (skywalk removal) probably had little effect or no impact on robbery (or burglary and vehicle crimes), but also that a previously undocumented change (entry phone installation) was probably responsible for most of the robbery reduction. The plausibility of the entry phones as the primary cause for robbery reduction stems not only from its timing (prior to the biggest drop in this crime) but also because its mechanism could cause the desired change in the opportunity structure, and because the crime signature change fits this mechanism.

How does examining the signature change improve the validity of evaluation conclusions? Take, for example, "history," one of the threats to the validity of Poyner's conclusion: something changed about the time the entry phones were installed and this caused the decline in robberies. This is the type of threat that defeated the hypothesis that the skywalk removal caused vehicle crimes to decline. In the case of the entry phones, the only viable history threats are those that occurred about the time the phones were installed and that were capable of causing the reduction in robberies closest to the phones, while having little impact on robberies elsewhere in Lisson Green. So, for example, stepped up police action in the neighborhood surrounding Lisson Green can be eliminated because it would not have created the spatial change in the robbery signature that Poyner observed. Although not all history threats could be eliminated, many could; and the few remaining must have characteristics in common with the entry phone intervention.

So, despite a weak evaluation design created to test a different intervention, Poyner was able to give reasonably strong evidence that the entry phones were probably effective (and that the Skywalk removal probably was not). The strength of his conclusion is in large part due to the fact that there were few if any rival explanations to the entry phone hypothesis that could explain the timing of the robbery drop and the change in the spatial signature. Further, the entry phone hypothesis had a highly plausible mechanism that was consistent with the signature change observed. Absent the examination of the robbery signatures, Poyner would only have been able to suggest that the entry phones were a credible rival explanation to skywalk removal.

Seven years before Poyner's article Paul Ekblom (1987) published a paper evaluating the impact of protective barricades at sub-post offices in London to prevent armed robbery. Like Poyner, he used a short time series, but with a control for background robbery trends. And like Poyner, Ekblom examined signatures to eliminate alternative explanations, particularly the pattern of successful and unsuccessful robbery attempts, the means of attack (sledge hammers, firearms, etc.), and other post office related robberies that the intervention could not prevent (attacks on post office delivery vehicles). However, where Poyner found that the intervention being tested had limited or no effect, Ekblom was able to establish that the barricades probably were a major contributor to the decline in sub-post office robberies. Careful examination of the opportunity structure and mechanism narrowed the rival explanations to those that could explain the drop in sub-post office robberies at the time of the intervention and were consistent with changes in robbery attack methods and success rates. While there may be a small probability of some viable alternatives, their numbers must be small.

In addition to providing illustrations of how examining signatures can strengthen evaluations, these two examples show that the basic idea we are advocating is not new. In fact, Campbell and Stanley (1963) are explicit in stating supplementary data analysis can strengthen evaluation designs (see also, Shadish et al., 2002). So the foundation of our argument has deep roots and we make no claim to originality in that respect. Our main objective is modest; to incorporate environmental criminology theory in evaluations of crime prevention interventions and to use these theories to systematize supplementary data analysis in these evaluations. We began by drawing a tight theoretical linkage between environmental criminological theories and evaluation procedures to not only justify the approach, but to give some guidance as to what forms of supplementary analysis can provide a foundation for what is often an ad hoc procedure. In the process we have linked opportunity structures and topographies with interventions and mechanisms, and introduced the idea of a crime signature. In the section that follows we will further systematize this approach by providing a four step procedure for applying these ideas.

SCEMA: A PROCEDURE FOR USING CRIME SIGNATURE CHANGE IN EVALUATIONS

This section outlines a procedure for using signatures to explore mechanisms in crime prevention programs. It is designed for use in evaluations of situational crime prevention. Consequently, we make no claims for its applicability to other forms of prevention. We call the procedure SCEMA, for Signature Characterization, Expectation, Measurement, and Analysis. Having defined signature earlier, we will describe the other four parts of the name. To illustrate the procedure, we will use a hypothetical example of a case study evaluation.

The hypothetical example involves a violent bar or pub. It is known to the police as a rowdy establishment, scene of many reports of fighting and assaults. We will give some important details about these assaults shortly, but for now we will jump ahead in the story and describe the standard evaluation design that will be used to evaluate the police intervention. We will assume that the evaluators will apply a non-equivalent control group design (Campbell and Stanley, 1963) wherein assaults are measured before and after the intervention for the treatment bar and before and after for a control bar with similar, but not identical characteristics. With non-random assignment and two cases, the principle threats to internal validity in this design involve treatment selection interacting with other threats. Selection-history interaction is the most likely. That is, there is some outside influence on the treatment bar around the time of the intervention that does not influence the control bar (or vice versa), and that this outside influence created the changes in crime found by the evaluation (rather than the intervention being tested). Nevertheless, this evaluation design is capable of eliminating a number of important threats to internal validity, even if it cannot eliminate all. The objective of applying SCEMA will be to narrow the class of viable rivals still further by applying theories from environmental criminology and the concept of mechanism.

Signature Characterization (Sc)

This is the first step in the SCEMA procedure. Here the evaluator describes the processes that create the signature. This is an explication of the opportunity structure and topography existing prior to the implementation of an intervention. This should be done while analyzing the crime problem, and as part of a search for an appropriate intervention. This is done by studying the association of crime with various hypothesized aspects of the opportunity structure. This is standard "problem analysis" (Clarke and Eck, 2006). In short, the evaluator is working backward from the signature to the opportunity structure to reveal (some of) the causes of the crime problem. We assume that if nothing is done, or if something is done but is ineffective, then the signature the evaluator observes at this time will be observed at later times. We will call this signature Sc.

Before the police agree on an intervention they conduct an analysis of this problem. They determine that the weekly distribution of assaults is bimodal; concentrated on Tuesday and Thursday nights. These are evenings when, to draw more customers to the bar, the owner advertises "lady's night" and offers half-priced drinks to women. On other days and evenings the treatment bar is indistinguishable from other bars. Close examination of the assaults on Tuesdays and Thursdays show that most occur in the parking area in front of the bar. Interviews and observations reveal that bouncers eject unruly patrons from the front door onto the parking area. The parking area is also a gathering place for male patrons, and some of the men bring their own alcohol and never enter the bar. It appears that the bar is simply moving fights from inside the bar to the parking area, where there is a ready audience to egg on the participants. In summary, we can summarize Sc with the statement that assaults are associated with Tuesday and Thursday evenings, bouncer actions, and with the parking area. It is assumed that if nothing is done, this signature will continue.

Signature Expectation (Se)

The second step in the SCEMA procedure begins once an intervention has been selected, and preferably before it has been implemented. Knowing what facets of the opportunity structure or topography the intervention is supposed to attack, as well as other features of the mechanism, the analyst creates an expected signature should the intervention be successful. This we will call Se. The evaluation should be designed so that it has sufficient power to detect meaningful crime reductions and so that it has sufficient power to detect meaningful departures of the measured signature from both Sc and Se.

The intervention planned by the police (working with the bar owners) is to eliminate "ladies night" and substitute karaoke night without reduced priced drinks. The owners also agree to have staff cut off drinks for inebriated patrons earlier, to ask patrons to leave before fights start, and to eject rowdy patrons through the side door where there is little room for people to congregate. The owners also agree to have their staff check the parking area to make sure there is no extra-curricular drinking. In return, the police agree that for the first month of the intervention officers will crack down on drinking in the parking area to reinforce the efforts of the bar staff. In short, the intervention addresses the salient features of the opportunity structure. The expected signature of this intervention (Se) is that that assaults will not be associated with Tuesday and Thursday nights. Assaults will not be associated with the parking area. And there will be no drinking associated with the parking area.

Signature Measurement (Sm)

During the evaluation of the intervention, while data are being collected in both treatment and control situations, data measuring the new signature should also be collected. We will call the new signature Sm.

In our running example, police crime analysts determine Sm by examining the time and location of assaults, documenting drinking citations in the parking area, interviewing bar staff and patrons, and making observations in the area around bar.

Signature Analysis

Finally, the evaluator compares Sm to both Sc and Se. If Sm is closer to Sc than Se, then the intervention's mechanism had little if any impact on either the opportunity structure or topography. If Sm is closer to Se than Sc, then the intervention triggered the mechanism. This comparison is illustrated in Figure 2. The signature is measured imperfectly, so there will be a distribution of possible signatures around this estimate. Consequently, significance tests could be used to determine if Sc or Se are within two or more standard deviations of the mean of Sm. The distribution of Sm_1 significantly overlaps Se, suggesting that the intervention's mechanism operated as desired and giving credence to the hypothesis that the intervention worked. The distribution of Sm_2 significantly overlaps Sc. This suggests that the intervention's mechanism failed to change the opportunity structure or topography and consequently the intervention probably did not cause assaults to decline. The distribution of Sm_0 has no overlap with either Sc or Se and consequently the results favor neither the main hypothesis nor its null.

Figure 2. Did the Signature Change? In the first scenario, the measured signature (Sm_1) is closer to the expected signature (Se) than the characterized signature (Sc). This suggests the mechanism operated as expected. In the second scenario, the measured signataure (Sm_2) is closer to Sc than Se, suggesting that the mechanism did not fire. If the measured signature is midway between Sc and Se (Sm_0), then the results are ambiguous. In each case, Sm_1) is measured with error so it has a distribution of possible values around the estimated value (the vertical lines).

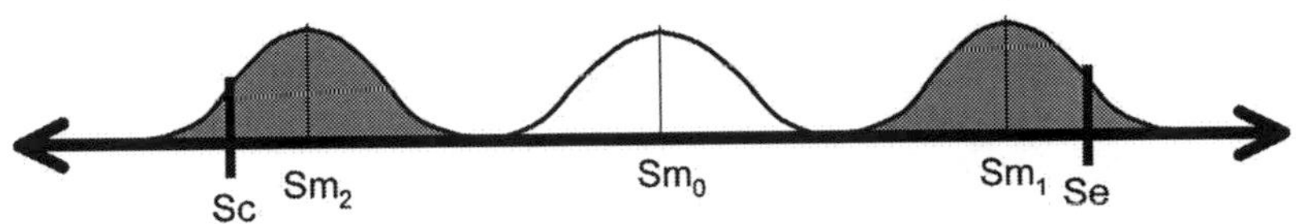

Figure 2 shows a highly simplified one-dimensional signature; i.e., the signature can be captured with a single variable. This is unlikely. In most situations the signature will be captured by multiple variables. If on all measured dimensions Sm is closer to Se than Sc, then the analyst has solid evidence to believe the intervention operated as desired. Similarly, if Sm is closer to Sc than Se on all dimensions, then there is solid evidence the intervention's mechanism failed to fire as expected. When some dimensions of Sm are close to Sc and others close to Se, the analyst will have to make a reasoned judgment about how and how much the intervention operated.

Continuing with our running example, the results of the post intervention analysis of the bar problem reveals a new signature. Assaults are no longer associated with Tuesdays and Thursdays and show a weekly pattern similar to other bars in the area. Assaults are no longer associated with the parking area. An initial spike in citations for illicit drinking in the bar's parking area declined precipitously (though this maybe due to changes in police activities). Interviews with staff and observations suggest that fewer people congregate in the parking area and there is little or no observed drinking there. They also suggest that bouncers and bar staff are complying with the agreement: drinks are being cut off earlier, staff are intervening in disputes prior to fights, and when someone needs to be forcibly removed from the bar, they are sent out the side door.

Once it has been determined that the intervention's mechanism operated as theorized (or failed to), the analyst compares the SCEMA results

Table 1: Scema and Impact Evaluation Interpretation Results of Impact Evaluation

Scema Results	Crime Down	Crime Constant	Crime Up
Mechanism Triggered	Intervention worked as desired and rival explanations inconsistent with SCEMA results are eliminated.	Intervention failed: it operated as expected but this was insufficient to reduce crime.	Intervention made things worse: it operated as expected yet crime increased.
Unclear if Mechanism Triggered	Little or no added information useful for eliminating rival explanations. Interpretation of results depends on whether SCEMA had sufficient power to detect changes in signature.		
Mechanism Failed to Trigger	Rival explanations are more likely than intervention hypothesis.	Theory failure: intervention does not operate as expected so it has no impact on crime.	Intervention did not make things worse, but was of little or no help either

to the results from a standard impact evaluation – generally a form of quasi-experiment. As shown in Table 1, if the quasi-experiment suggests the intervention may have been effective (first column) but cannot eliminate all threats to validity – i.e., there are rival explanations for the change in crime that cannot be rejected – and the SCEMA results show the mechanism operated as expected (top row), then the SCEMA results reinforce the quasi-experiment's conclusions. It does this by eliminating any still existing rival explanations that are inconsistent with the signature change shown by the SCEMA results. If the SCEMA results indicate that the mechanism did not operate (third row), the SCEMA results strengthen the case for some rival explanation being the cause of the results from the quasi-experiment. That is because SCEMA indicates that the intervention did not trigger its mechanism, and therefore may be incapable of creating the observed changes in crime. Finally, if the SCEMA procedure provides ambiguous evidence about signature changes, it adds little to the quasi-experimental conclusions. In such circumstances, we cannot eliminate any remaining threats to internal validity left over from the quasi-experiment.

Let's return to our example one last time. The quasi-experiment described earlier shows that the treatment bar had a larger decline in assaults than the control bar. This puts the results in the upper left cell of Table 1. The only rival explanations that are still in contention are processes that could reduce Tuesday and Thursday assaults, reduce crowds and drinking in the parking area, and at the same time reduce assaults more in the treatment bar than the control bar. All other possible rivals are eliminated. Absent specific knowledge of such an explanation unrelated to the police intervention, it is highly unlikely that a rival explanation exists that could have produced this specific combination of results. On the other hand, by focusing the search for rival hypotheses it is possible to find a specific plausible alternative explanation, just as Poyner (1994) was able to find a rival to the skywalk demolition explanation.

IMPLICATIONS AND CONCLUSIONS

In the preceding sections we have made an argument based on environmental criminology theories that signature change is important for evaluating opportunity blocking interventions. Simply put, opportunity blocking is designed to alter the opportunity structure and typical quasi-experimental methods do not take these changes into account. Information about opportunity structure changes can help evaluators determine if an intervention worked, and how it accomplished its objectives. If the intervention does not change the opportunity structure in the desired manner, then we cannot make a strong case for the intervention working.

We then gave examples from the literature to illustrate a) how the logic we outlined can be applied, and b) that the basic ideas we are advocating have been used, albeit less formally. The example from Poyner (1994) was also instructive in that it showed that signature change can help refute the viability of a proposed intervention, or support the hypothesis that it worked. In the previous section, we outlined a four step procedure, SCEMA, to augment standard evaluation designs. SCEMA is a general process. In this section we examine several critical considerations for evaluators applying this process.

Data Must Describe a Specific Crime

If the data describe multiple crimes, each with its own opportunity structure, then changes in crime patterns can come from any one, or combination, of several opportunity structures. This point is readily apparent from considering Poyner's (1994) work. When he began his investigation a previous report had claimed a 50% reduction in crime. By breaking the total crimes into three relatively homogeneous categories and explicitly addressing the opportunity structure for each, Poyner showed that burglary, vehicle crimes, and robbery had distinctive spatio-temporal signatures. By taking these into account, he was able to come to a much more plausible conclusion than had earlier accounts. Similarly, Ekblom (1987) separated robberies of sub-post offices from robberies of postal delivery vehicles on the grounds that they were different crimes that rely on different opportunity structures. Evaluators need to be concerned about the opportunity structures that a proposed intervention could address, even if its proponents claim that the intervention is a general palliative for crime.

The Signature Must Be Relevant to the Intervention

Imagine an intervention designed to reduce shoplifting of specific types of merchandise. The quasi-experiment would look at the relative decline in thefts of the relevant items in question in the stores, with the intervention compared to stores without the intervention. The signature we would be interested in is the distribution of thefts over all store items. If the intervention is successful we would expect to see a drop in thefts of the target items in the experimental store relative to the control store, and a signature change showing that total thefts declined coupled with a decline in the theft of the target item relative to other items. This is the same logic we would follow if the intervention focused on a crime hot spot: not only should the crime decline in the area relative to some control, but the hotspot should cool. If the intervention focuses on a temporal spike – a surge of aggravated assaults at bar closing times on Friday and Saturday nights – then the quasi-experiment should show the decline in these crimes over time. The signature would show the decline relative to other days of the week. The signature of robberies in Poyner's (1994) study changed in a way that was consistent with entry phones trigging the crime prevention mechanism, but not in a way that would be consistent with the walkway demolition.

By way of contrast, in the shoplifting example a change in the spatial signature of crime around the intervention store would not be informative. The patterns selected for examination should be linked directly to the expected opportunity structure. The fact that the Lisson Green vehicle crimes had a signature that was inconsistent with the opportunity structure created by the skywalks was in part responsible for Poyner (1994) rejecting the skywalk removal as a plausible cause of vehicle crime reduction. His additional investigations revealed other environmental changes that could interrupt the opportunity structure in the vehicle parking areas.

In some cases there are two or more competing possible opportunity structures (perhaps there is a debate among program personnel, or the theoretical literature is ambiguous or contradictory). In such circumstances, comparing signatures connected to one opportunity structure to signatures connected to another hypothesized opportunity structure can help tease out information about which opportunity structure, if any, was altered.

The Signature Must be Measured with Sufficient Precision that Change Can be Detected

If the signature measures are insensitive to changes in the opportunity structure then it will be difficult to determine if the opportunity structure was affected by the intervention. When crime is infrequent, signatures are hard to detect and changes in signatures can be easily confused with random variation. The less frequent the crime, the more time needs to elapse to allow the accumulation of crime to form a measurable signature. Victimization surveys may have to interview very large numbers of respondents to detect signature changes. On the other hand, high volume crimes and official police statistics make it easier to detect signatures and changes.

Because the intervention is supposed to suppress crime, it will be easier to detect signatures before a successful intervention than afterwards. Therefore, it might be necessary to extend the time period for data collection after the intervention to determine if the signature changed. Using the time period for data collection before as a benchmark, we might ask, "How long does it takes after the intervention to detect the same signature as we saw before?" The signature may reemerge long after the intervention if the program had a temporary impact on the opportunity structure. If it reemerges in the same time interval used to measure the signature prior to the intervention, then the program had a limited effect at best. Using the pre-intervention data collection period as the benchmark is rather arbitrary. It would be far better to determine the smallest time interval of data collection needed to detect a clear signature before the intervention, and then use this as the benchmark.

Much work needs to be done to quantify signature change. Some signature changes have established quantitative methods, while others are not well developed or widely used. There is considerable work to be done in the measurement of geographic patterns, for example. More rigorous methods need to be developed and employed. Though there has been considerable progress in applying spatial analysis tools to crime problems (Chaney and Ratcliff, 2005) there does not seem to be a set of standards for reliably detecting crime patterns or measuring their change.

A Caution Regarding Systematic Reviews

The procedures followed here have implications for the systematic reviews of crime prevention evaluations. It is standard practice to categorize evaluations by the rigor of the evaluation design (roughly based on the number of rival explanations that can be eliminated). The evaluations with the weakest designs (pre-post comparisons without controls, for example) are often dropped from the study on the grounds that their conclusions are too unreliable. If there are sufficient evaluations left with sufficient rigor, the researcher might compare results among the studies and control for design or measurement features (e.g., results from time series designs compared to results from randomized experiments, or results when using reported police data compared to results from using victimization surveys). However, systematic reviews do not control for efforts to strengthen the conclusions using supplementary data, probably because these efforts are highly idiosyncratic; they are highly dependent on the specifics of the study setting, intervention procedures, and other case specific factors. To the extent that systematic reviews ignore these extra-design efforts to strengthen the conclusion validity of evaluations, systematic reviews underestimate the knowledge of crime prevention programs. If the SCEMA process, or anything like it, becomes widely used then systematic reviews will become more biased toward understating what is known about crime prevention. Consequently, to avoid this bias, it is important to develop methods for accounting for signature change analysis in systematic reviews.

Final Remarks

This paper began with some basic concepts from environmental criminology, particularly situational crime prevention, and showed how these ideas suggest improvements in the evaluation of crime opportunity blocking interventions. We illustrated these ideas with two examples from the literature and developed a four step protocol, SCEMA. In the previous section we elaborated on this protocol by examining some basic concerns that evaluators using this approach will need to take into account. Our last point, about systematic reviews, suggests that the ideas we have developed here have broad implications and there is much work that needs to be done to elaborate, strengthen, and systematize the general approach we are advocating.

Acknowledgments: We thank the editors, Johannes Knutsson and Nick Tilley, as well as all the participants at the Stavern meeting, for their outstanding comments, criticisms and suggestions. Their assistance greatly improved this paper and we are extremely grateful to them for saving us from embarrassment. As much as we would like to lay off blame for any unfortunate statements that may remain in this paper, we are solely responsible.

Address correspondence to: John E. Eck, University of Cincinnati, Division of Criminal Justice, PO Box 210389, Cincinnati, Ohio 45226; e-mail: john.eck@uc.edu, or Tamara Madensen, University of Nevada, Las Vegas, Department of Criminal Justice, Box 455009, 4505 Maryland Parkway, Las Vegas, Nevada 89154-5009; e-mail: tamara.madensen@unlv.edu

NOTES

1. VIVA stands for Value, Inertia, Visibility, and Access (Felson, 2000). CRAVED is an acronym composed of Concealable, Removable, Available, Valuable, Enjoyable, and Disposable (Clarke, 1999). EVIL DONE comes from Exposed, Vital, Iconic, Legitimate, Destructible, Occupied, Near, and Easy (Clarke and Newman, 2006).
2. The omitted words in this and subsequent quotes from Poyner (1994) contained references to figures in Poyner's paper. As we did not include the figures in our paper we deleted the references to them.

REFERENCES

Bowers, K. J., & Johnson, S. D. (2004). Who commits near repeats? A test of the boost explanation. *Western Journal of Criminology*, 5, 12–24.

Brantingham, P. L., & Brantingham, P. J. (1993). Environment, routine, and situation: Toward a pattern theory of crime. In R. V. Clarke & M. Felson (Eds.), *Routine activity, and rational choice* (pp. 259–294). New Brunswick, NJ: Transaction Press.

Campbell, D. T., & Stanley, J. C. (1963). *Experimental and quasi-experimental designs for research*. Chicago: Rand McNally.

Chainey, S., & Ratcliffe, J. (2005). *GIS and crime mapping*. London: Wiley.

Clarke, R. V. (1995). Situational crime prevention. In M. Tonry & D. Farrington (Eds.), *Building a safer society: Strategic approaches to crime prevention. Crime and justice* (Vol. 19, pp. 91–150). Chicago: University of Chicago Press.

Clarke, R. V. (1999). *Hot products: Understanding, anticipating and reducing the demand for stolen goods*. Police research paper 112. London: Home Office, Research Development and Statistics Directorate.

Clarke, R. V. (2004). Technology, criminology and crime science. *European Journal on Criminal Policy and Research, 10*, 55–63.

Clarke, R. V., & Eck, J. E. (2005). *Crime analysis for problem solvers: In 60 small steps*. Washington, DC: U. S. Department of Justice, Office of Community Oriented Policing.

Clarke, R. V., & Newman, G. R. (2006). *Outsmarting the terrorists*. Westport, CT: Praeger Security International.

Cohen, L. E., & Felson, M. (1979). Social change and crime rate trends: A routine activity approach. *American sociological review, 44*, 588–605.

Cook, T. D. & Campbell, D. T. (1979). *Quasi-experimentation: Design and analysis issues for field settings*. New York: Houghton Mifflin.

Cornish, D. & Clarke, R. V. (Eds.). (1986). *The reasoning criminal: Rational choice perspectives on offending*. New York: Springer-Verlag.

Cornish, D., & Clarke, R. V. (2003). Opportunities, precipitators and criminal decisions: A reply to Wortley's critique of situation crime prevention. In M. J. Smith & D. B. Cornish (Eds.), *Theory for practice in situational crime prevention*. Crime prevention studies(Vol. 16, pp. 41–96). Monsey, NY and Cullompton, Devon, UK: Criminal Justice Press and Willan Publishing.

Eck, J. E. (2006). When is a bologna sandwich better than sex? A defense of small-N case study evaluations. *Journal of experimental criminology, 2*, 345–362.

Ekblom, P. (1987). *Preventing robberies at sub-post offices: An evaluation of a security initiative*. Crime Prevention Unit Paper 9. London: Home Office

Felson, M. (1981). Social accounts based on map, clock, and calendar. In F. T. Juster & K. C. Land (Eds.), *Social accounting systems: Essays on the state of the art* pp. 219–239. New York: Academic Press.

Felson, M. (1995). Those who discourage crime. In J. E. Eck & D. Weisburd (Eds.), *Crime and place*. Crime prevention studies (Vol. 4, pp. 53–66). Monsey, NY and Cullompton, Devon, UK: Criminal Justice Press and Willan Publishing.

Felson, M. (2000). The routine activity approach as a general theory of crime. In S. Simpson (Ed.), *On crime and criminality* (pp. 205–216). Thousand Oaks. CA: Pine Forge Press.

Mayo, D. (1996). *Error and the growth of experimental knowledge*. Chicago: University of Chicago Press.

Pawson, R., & Tilley, N. (2000). *Realistic evaluation*. New York: Sage.

Poyner, B. (1994). Lessons from Lisson Green: An evaluation of walkway demolition on a British housing estate. In R. V. Clarke (Ed.), *Crime prevention studies* (Vol. 3, pp. 127–150). Monsey, NY: Criminal Justice Press.

Shadish, W. R., Cook, T. D., & Campbell, D. T. (2002). *Experimentation and quasi-experimental designs for general causal inference*. New York: Houghton Mifflin.

COMMUNITY PERCEPTIONS OF POLICE CRIME PREVENTION EFFORTS: USING INTERVIEWS IN SMALL AREAS TO EVALUATE CRIME REDUCTION STRATEGIES

by

Anthony A. Braga
Harvard University
University of California, Berkeley

Brenda J. Bond
Suffolk University

Abstract: *Problem-oriented policing initiatives seem well positioned to generate positive community reactions to police intervention because this approach focuses on dealing with specific crime and disorder problems that cause ongoing concern to affected community members. This paper examines the use of interviews with community members in small areas to assess the effects of police crime reduction strategies on citizen perceptions of disorder problems, police behaviors, and fear of crime. Our study uses citizen interview data collected as part of a randomized controlled experiment in Lowell, Massachusetts to evalu-*

Crime Prevention Studies, volume 24 (2009), pp. 87–119.

ate the effects of problem-oriented policing strategies on crime and disorder hot spots. Our interviews with key community members revealed that selected place users noticed an increased police presence and that disorder problems were positively impacted in the treatment hot spots as compared to the control hot spots. However, the respondents did not detect any significant changes in police strategy, the willingness of the police to work with residents, or the demeanor of the police toward citizens. Our research suggests that small area interviews add considerable value to the evaluation of crime reduction strategies, but great care needs to be taken in analyzing and interpreting these data.

INTRODUCTION

Since the early 1990s, the police have become much more interested in a broader idea of crime prevention and the use of a wide range of crime prevention tactics (Roth et al., 2000). The search for more effective crime prevention alternatives to the traditional tactics used by most police departments led to the development of problem-oriented policing (Eck & Spelman, 1987; Goldstein, 1979). Problem-oriented policing challenges officers to analyze recurring crime and disorder problems and to implement appropriate preventive responses using a wide variety of innovative approaches. Sherman's (1997) review of problem-oriented policing evaluation findings and methods suggested that this strategy is "promising" in preventing crime. The U.S. National Research Council's Committee to Review Research on Police Policy and Practices also concluded that problem-oriented policing has promise in preventing crime because it uses a diverse range of approaches tailored to very specific crime problems (Skogan & Frydl, 2004; Weisburd & Eck, 2004).

In addition to doubts over the crime control effectiveness of the standard model of policing, police innovation in the 1980s and 1990s was also driven by high levels of community dissatisfaction with police services and a growing recognition that citizens had other concerns that required police action, such as fear of crime. Evaluations of community policing initiatives have generally found positive improvements in citizen perceptions of their neighborhoods and relationships with the police (Skogan, 2006). While some of these community policing programs engaged problem-oriented policing tactics, most evaluations of specific problem-oriented policing interventions focus on whether these strategies reduce crime and disorder problems rather on than determining whether these initiatives increase citizen satisfaction with police services, improve community members' perceptions of places, and decrease citizen fear of crime. Problem-oriented policing scholars, such as Ronald V. Clarke and John Eck (2005), recommend using qualitative community data to analyze the nature of crime and disorder problems and assess the effects of implemented responses on targeted problems. At face value, problem-oriented policing initiatives seem well positioned to generate positive community reactions to police intervention as the approach focuses on dealing with specific crime and disorder problems that cause ongoing concern to affected community members.

This paper examines the use of interviews with community members in small areas to assess the effects of police crime reduction strategies on citizen perceptions of disorder problems, police behaviors, and fear of crime. Our study uses citizen interview data collected as part of a randomized controlled experiment in Lowell, Massachusetts to evaluate the effects of problem-oriented policing strategies on crime and disorder hot spots. A previously published impact evaluation found that the intervention was associated with significant reductions in citizen calls for service to the police and systematic researcher observations of social and physical disorder in the treatment hot spots relative to control hot spots (Braga & Bond, 2008). In this paper, our analyses found that key community members, who worked and/or resided in the study hot spots area, noted significant reductions in physical and social disorder and significant increases in police presence in treatment places as compared to control places. Unfortunately, our analyses also found that there were no significant changes in citizen perceptions of police behaviors or fear of crime in the treatment hot spots relative to control hot spots. The appropriate use of small area interviews as outcome measures and the implications of these findings for problem-oriented policing practice are discussed.

COMMUNITY REACTIONS TO POLICE EFFORTS TO CONTROL CRIME AND DISORDER AT PROBLEM PLACES

The terms "community policing" and "problem-oriented policing" are sometimes referred to as essentially the same strategy (Walker, 1992; Kennedy & Moore, 1995), however others maintain a distinct separation between the two concepts (Goldstein, 1990; Eck & Spelman, 1987). Problem-oriented policing is typically defined as focusing police attention on the underlying causes of problems behind a string of crime incidents, while community policing emphasizes the development of strong police-community partnerships in a joint effort to reduce crime and enhance security (Moore, 1992). Indeed, community-oriented police officers use problem solving as a tool and problem-oriented departments often form partnerships with the community. In general, broad-based community policing initiatives have been found to reduce fear of crime and improve the relationships between the police and the communities they serve (Skogan & Frydl, 2004; Weisburd & Eck, 2004). Community policing strategies that entail direct involvement of citizens and police – such as police community stations, citizen contract patrol, and coordinated community policing – have been found to reduce fear of crime among individuals and decrease individual concern about crime in neighborhoods (Brown & Wycoff, 1987; Pate & Skogan, 1985; Wycoff & Skogan, 1986).

Community policing also has the potential to enhance police legitimacy. Citizen support and cooperation is closely linked to judgments about the legitimacy of the police (Tyler, 2004). When citizens view the police as legitimate legal authorities, they are more likely to cooperate and obey the law (Tyler, 1990). Public judgments about the legitimacy of the police are influenced by the citizens' assessments of the manner in which the police exercise their authority (Tyler, 1990, 2004). The available evidence suggests that the police generally obey the laws that limit their power (Skogan & Meares, 2004). However, minorities consistently express significantly lower confidence in the police when compared to whites (Tyler, 2004). Community policing has been a strategic innovation that has helped bridge the police "confidence gap" in minority communities. The available research evidence suggests that the approach improves citizens' judgments of police actions (Skogan, 2006). For example, over an eight-year period of community policing, Chicago residents' views of their police improved on measures of their effectiveness, responsiveness and demeanor (Skogan & Steiner, 2004). Importantly, these improvements were shared among Latinos, African-Americans and whites (Skogan & Steiner, 2004).

While there is a growing body of systematic research on the effects of community policing on citizen satisfaction with the police, there is a noteworthy lack of research assessing the effects of other police innovations on police-community relations. This gap in knowledge is noteworthy as many observers suggest a tension between the crime prevention effectiveness of focused police efforts and their potentially harmful effects on police-community relations (Meares, 2006; Rosenbaum, 2006; Taylor, 2006;

Weisburd & Braga, 2006). Certainly, legitimacy is linked to the ability of the police to prevent crime and keep neighborhoods safe. However, the police also need public support and cooperation to be effective in preventing crime. While residents in neighborhoods suffering from high levels of crime often demand higher levels of enforcement, they still want the police to be respectful and lawful in their crime control efforts (Skogan & Meares, 2004; Tyler, 2004). Residents don't want family members, friends, and neighbors to be targeted unfairly by enforcement efforts or treated poorly by overaggressive police officers. If the public's trust and confidence in the police is undermined, the ability of the police to prevent crime will be weakened by lawsuits, declining willingness to obey the law, and withdrawal from existing partnerships (Tyler, 1990, 2004). The political fallout from illegitimate police actions can seriously impede the ability of police departments to engage innovative crime control tactics.

In recent years, crime scholars and practitioners have pointed to the potential benefits of focusing crime prevention efforts on crime "hot spots" that generate a disproportionate share of criminal events (Pierce et al., 1988; Sherman et al., 1989; Weisburd et al., 1992). The appeal of focusing limited resources on a small number of high-activity crime places is straightforward. If we can prevent crime at these hot spots, then we might be able to reduce total crime. Police efforts to control hot spots can range from traditional approaches, such as directed patrols and crackdowns, to innovative "situational" problem-oriented policing strategies, where the police seek to understand underlying conditions, implement alternative responses, and collaborate with others (Braga, 2008; Eck, 1993). Regardless of the approach employed, "hot spots policing" efforts have been found to generate crime prevention gains (Braga, 2001, 2005).

Unfortunately, too little attention has been paid to the potential harmful effects of focused police action in hot spot areas. In general, police effectiveness studies have traditionally overlooked the effects of policing practices upon citizen perceptions of police legitimacy (Tyler, 2001, 2004). The concentration of police enforcement in specific hot spots could lead citizens to question the fairness of police practices. There is some evidence that residents of areas that are subject to focused police attention welcome the concentration of police efforts in problem places (McGarrell et al., 2001; Shaw, 1995). Nonetheless, focused and aggressive police enforcement strategies have been criticized as resulting in increased citizen complaints about police misconduct and abuse of force in New York City (Greene, 1999). Order maintenance and "quality of life" policing strategies that seek to prevent more serious crimes by arresting offenders for minor crimes, such as public drinking and smoking marijuana in plain view, have been criticized as exacerbating already poor relationships between the police and minority communities (Golub et al., 2007; Harcourt & Ludwig, 2007).

As in the case of understanding the effectiveness of police strategies, the potential impact of police crime prevention efforts in problem places on citizen perceptions of legitimacy may depend in good part on the types of strategies used and the context of the hot spots affected. Unfocused and indiscriminate enforcement actions seem likely to produce poor relationships between the police and community members residing in hot spot areas. Situational problem-oriented policing actions that engage community members and alleviate disorderly conditions may generate positive citizen perceptions of the police. But whatever the impact, policy makers and police executives need to know more about the effects of police crime prevention efforts on the communities that the police serve. We believe that the use of small area interviews to evaluate the effects of police crime prevention efforts in problem places can yield important insights into the micro-level context of community experiences with specific police actions. In this study, we examine the use of small area interviews with key community members to evaluate the impact of problem-oriented policing interventions implemented to control crime and disorder hot spots in Lowell, Massachusetts (a city of 105,000 residents located about 30 miles northeast of Boston). We examine whether the implemented police interventions impacted community perceptions of physical and social disorder problems, police behaviors, and fear of crime in the hot spot areas.

THE LOWELL POLICING CRIME AND DISORDER HOT SPOTS EXPERIMENT

Program Design

The program and evaluation design borrows from the Braga et al. (1999) study that generally followed the well-known steps of the SARA model used in many problem-oriented policing projects (Scanning, Analysis, Response, Assessment; see Eck & Spelman, 1987). During the scanning phase, computerized mapping and database technologies were used to geocode all 2004 crime and disorder emergency citizen calls for service and to identify the densest clusters of these calls in Lowell. Simple temporal analyses and ranking procedures were used to identify preliminary hot spot areas that had consistently high levels of citizen crime and disorder calls for service over time. Qualitative data on place characteristics, local dynamics, and LPD patrol officer perceptions of crime problems were used to determine hot spot area boundaries. This process left 34 discrete crime and disorder hot spot areas in Lowell for inclusion in the experiment. The hot spots accounted for 2.7% of Lowell's 14.5 square miles. In 2004, these places generated 5,125 citizen calls for service (23.5% of 21,810 total crime and disorder calls to the LPD). After the 34 violent crime places were identified, they were matched into 17 pairs for evaluation purposes (i.e., to be allocated to control and treatment groups). During the crime and disorder hot spots identification process, the Harvard research team trained police officers from each of Lowell's three police sectors in problem-oriented policing methods.

The analysis phase of the problem-oriented policing program started with the random allocation of the initial places for treatment. The 17 pairs of places were presented to LPD Superintendent Edward F. Davis III and a coin was flipped by the research team to determine randomly which of the places within the pair would receive the problem-oriented policing treatment. The locations that were not selected from each of the pairs were control places. The control hot spot areas were not identified to the captains, lieutenants, sergeants, and patrol officers in the sectors. Over the course of the experiment, they had no knowledge of control area locations. As such, these places experienced the routine amount of police strategies that such areas in Lowell would experience without focused intervention – arbitrary patrol interventions, routine follow-up investigations by detectives, and ad-hoc community problem-solving attention.

On September 1, 2005, Superintendent Davis assigned ultimate responsibility for the implementation of the problem-oriented policing intervention at the treatment places to the captains who managed Lowell's three police sectors. After receiving their assigned treatment hot spots, the captains were required to submit a report for each place that identified specific problems that generated repeat citizen calls for service, detailed the results of their problem analyses, and listed situational and enforcement responses that were logically linked to the underlying conditions that gave rise to these problems. Within each sector, lieutenants and sergeants spent time analyzing official data sources and discussing problems with community members. The intervention period lasted for one year, officially ending on August 31, 2006.

The captains were held accountable for the implementation of the problem-oriented policing interventions through Compstat-like monthly meetings with the command staff. At each monthly meeting, the LPD Crime Analysis Unit presented simple trend analyses of citizen calls for service in each of the treatment hot spots to determine whether identified crime and disorder problems were being positively impacted. If the data revealed that calls for service were decreasing in their hot spots, Superintendent Davis praised the captains and their officers for their hard work and asked them to explain why they believed their actions were producing the desired effects, how their strategies were affecting the identified problems at their places, and what else could be done to keep calls for service decreasing. If the analysis revealed that the number of citizen calls for service had remained the same or increased, Superintendent Davis peppered the captains with questions about their plans for dealing with recurring problems in the hot spot areas (e.g., whether or not they were making use of particular activities such as increased order maintenance approaches and alleviating identified physical disorder problems). The meetings also served as a venue for the command staff, captains, and other officers to explore and share ideas on plausibly effective prevention strategies for persistent problems in the treatment places. Careful notes were maintained by the research team on the implemented interventions discussed in these meetings and observed at treatment locations during weekly researcher ride alongs.

While the performance measurement accountability principles were borrowed from the well-known Compstat management process (Moore & Braga, 2003; Silverman, 1999), the activities at the monthly meetings represented an ongoing scanning, analysis, response, and assessment process. The routine measurement and review of strategies in the treatment places served as an important mechanism to ensure that there was a strong treatment dosage for the experiment. Police officers are generally known to be resistant to operational and strategic changes (Guyot, 1979), and often oppose restrictions imposed on them when participating in field experiments.[1] The monthly meetings were designed to ensure that the captains and their officers were implementing the problem-oriented policing program and adhering to the requirements of the experimental research design. While some observers suggest that standard department-wide Compstat systems may stifle the creativity of the problem-oriented policing process (Weisburd et al., 2003), the LPD monthly meetings were explicitly focused on implementing the approach by addressing local community concerns as measured by trends in citizen calls for service in the treatment hot spot areas, holding police managers accountable for dealing with identified problems, and serving as a venue to enhance the creativity of implemented responses through open discussion and idea sharing.

The Nature of LPD Problem-Oriented Policing Interventions

Prior to our review of impact evaluation findings and our examination of the value of small area interviews with community members in assessing crime reduction initiatives, it is important for police executives, policy makers, and academics to understand the nature of the LPD problem-oriented policing strategy as implemented. Throughout the program, ongoing contact and collaboration with community members in the treatment places were considered essential activities. However, community members were only used as an information source rather than viewed or recruited as "partners" or "co-producers" of public safety. Conversations between the officers and community members revolved around the nature of problems, the possible effectiveness of proposed responses, and the assessment of implemented responses. This observation is consistent with other studies examining citizen roles in problem-oriented policing programs (see, e.g. Capowich & Roehl, 1994). As Buerger (1994) suggests: " . . . the police establishment assigns a role that simply enhances the police response to crime and disorder" (p. 271).

As described earlier, the captains and officers were required to identify and analyze specific local problems in the 17 treatment hot spot areas that generated high volumes of citizen calls for service. The number of identified problems per place ranged from 3 to 7, with a mean of 4.3 specific crime and disorder problems per place. Unfortunately, like many problem-oriented policing projects, the problem analysis engaged by the LPD was generally weak, with many initiatives accepting the definition of a problem at face value, using only short-term data to unravel the nature of the problem, and failing to adequately examine the genesis of the crime problems (Clarke, 1998; Read & Tilley, 2000; Scott, 2000). Eck and Spelman (1987) suggest two classifications for the depth of problem analysis: limited analysis and extended analysis. Eck and Spelman (1987) grouped problem-solving efforts by the Newport News (VA) Police Department by determining whether there were obvious information sources that were not used, given the nature of the problem; if there were not any obvious unused sources, the effort was classified as extended. Using these definitions, slightly more than one-third (35.6%; 26 of 73) of the identified problems in this study received what could be described as an extended analysis.

As result, the interventions implemented by the LPD officers were much less nuanced than the carefully-designed responses advocated by scholars such as Ronald V. Clarke (1997) and Herman Goldstein (1990). Situational interventions broadly designed to modify underlying criminogenic conditions at a place were implemented at all 17 treatment places. On average, 4.4 situational strategies were implemented per place (range = 2 to 8 strategies per place). The strategies varied according to the nuances of the problems at places (e.g., cleaning and securing vacant lots, razing abandoned buildings, improving street lighting, adding video surveillance, and conducting code inspections of disorderly taverns; see Table 1). The LPD officers also implemented "social service" strategies at 12 treatment places, such as connecting problem tenants suffering from mental health problems to social workers, working with local shelters to provide housing for homeless individuals, and increasing youth recreational opportunities in local parks. On average, one social service strategy was implemented per place (range = 0 to 2 strategies per place). All treatment locations also experienced a number of aggressive order maintenance interventions to control the social disorder of the place. These tactics included repeat foot and radio car patrols, dispersing groups of loiterers, making arrests for public drinking, arresting drug sellers, and "stop and frisks" of suspicious persons. The weekly mean number of misdemeanor arrests in the treatment places increased significantly by 17.7%, from a pre-intervention mean of 12.9 arrests per week to a mean of 15.2 arrests per week during the intervention period (t (76)= 2.356, p = .021).

The experiences of the LPD officers closely reflect the nature of problem solving and problem-oriented policing as it is currently practiced in the field. Several academics have considered the gap between the rhetoric and reality of problem-oriented policing, and observed that many projects generate interventions that could be called "shallow" problem solving responses (Braga & Weisburd, 2006; Cordner & Biebel, 2005; Eck, 2006). In our formal impact evaluation, we described the resulting LPD treatment as a collection of specific problem-oriented tactics that could be broadly categorized as a "policing disorder" strategy (Braga & Bond, 2008).

Impact on Crime and Disorder

A randomized complete block design was used to assess the main effects of the intervention on citizen calls for service (Braga & Bond, 2008).

Table 1: "Situational" Problem-Oriented Policing Strategies at Treatment Places

Responses	Number of Places
Building and housing code enforcement	14
Video surveillance	8
Public works removed trash on street	8
Hung signs explaining rules (e.g., No Drinking, No Trespassing)	6
Removed graffiti from buildings and other physical structures	5
Evicted troublesome tenants	4
Cleared overgrown vegetation	4
Secured / razed abandoned and dilapidated physical structures	3
Vacant lots cleaned and fenced	3
Added / upgraded trash receptacles	3
Code enforcement and investigation of taverns and bars	3
Engaged private business to clean residential properties	3
Cleaned debris from city parking lots and garage	3
Required store owners to clean store fronts	2
Improved lighting in area	2
Towed abandoned cars	2
Required store to change merchandise displays to prevent theft	1
Relocation of bus stop	1

Randomized experimental designs allow researchers to assume that the only systematic difference between the control and treatment groups is the presence of the intervention; this permits a clear assessment of causes and effects (Campbell & Stanley, 1966; Cook & Campbell, 1979). In order to assess the effects of the intervention on the treatment places relative to the controls, citizen calls for service were compared for six month pre-intervention and post-intervention periods. The impact evaluation revealed that total citizen calls for service were reduced by a statistically significant 19.8% in treatment hot spot areas relative to control hot spot areas

(Braga & Bond, 2008). The analysis found statistically significant reductions in robbery, assault, and burglary calls, and non-statistically significant reductions in larceny and disorder calls, in treatment places relative to control places. The LPD intervention also did not result in significant immediate spatial displacement of crime into the two-block catchment areas surrounding the treatment hot spots relative to the control hot spots.

To unravel specific crime prevention pathways at work in the LPD strategy, mediation analysis was used to examine three isolated and exhaustive crime prevention mechanisms – misdemeanor arrests, situational prevention strategies, and social service strategies – in treatment and control places (Braga & Bond, 2008). Situational interventions broadly designed to modify criminogenic conditions at a place generated the strongest prevention effects, while increasing misdemeanor arrests at a place were associated with less powerful crime prevention benefits. Social service strategies, however, did not generate statistically significant short-term crime prevention benefits.

Like many evaluations of crime prevention initiatives implemented at specific crime hot spot areas (e.g., Braga et al., 1999; Sherman & Weisburd, 1995), the Lowell experiment used alternative performance measures to detect potential changes in social and physical disorder at treatment places relative to control places. *Physical observation data* were collected at both treatment and control places to detect changes in physical incivilities at places such as vacant lots, trash, and graffiti.[2] *Social observation data* were collected at both control and treatment places to examine variations in social incivilities such as drinking in public and loitering.[3] Subsequent analyses revealed that the LPD intervention resulted in significant reductions in physical and social incivilities at the treatment places in comparison to the control places (Braga & Bond, 2008). While these observational data documented that disorder problems in the treatment places had been reduced, it is also important to note that disorder was not completely eliminated at the treatment places. The LPD officers responsible for preventing crime at the treatment locations managed ongoing disorder problems in a more focused and diligent manner as compared to disorder problems in the control places.

SMALL AREA INTERVIEW METHODOLOGY

Our small area interview methodology was derived from a developing literature that suggests places have standing patterns of behavior or rhythms of recurring behavior and activity that are somewhat predictable and routine (see Felson, 2006; Taylor, 1997). Green Mazerolle, Kadleck, and Roehl (1998) suggest that the reliability and validity of on-site observations increase as the unit of analysis decreases. Their research proposes that street blocks and other small units of analysis have fewer and less complex patterns of street activity than neighborhoods, communities, or other larger units of analysis that have more complex and varied patterns of social behavior. This body of research suggests that individuals who reside and work at particular places may provide keen observations of the social dynamics and physical environment of small areas.

In our research, "key community members" in the hot spot areas were subjectively identified and interviewed to gain greater insight into the effects of the intervention in the treatment places relative to the control places. Rather than surveying a random sample of residents at each place, a systematic method was developed to identify a small number of specific place users. This decision was based on resource concerns (i.e., the cost of administering a large survey) and to explore the value of small area interview methods to study high-activity crime places. While interview methods to study places have been largely ignored by most researchers, Rosenbaum and Lavrakas (1995) have described the value of small area interviews and surveys in assessing community policing and problem-solving initiatives:

> . . . (small area) surveys are especially useful for estimating the effects of community mobilization programs or police interventions. Whether community mobilization can stimulate citizen participation, strengthen neighborhood self-regulation and improve perceptions of the area is most efficiently answered through self-reports. Constructs of interest might include: levels of social interaction among target area users; usage or avoidance of specific areas; territoriality and surveillance behaviors; perceived efficacy and control over activities in the area; crime prevention awareness and participation; perceived levels of crime and disorder; fear of crime; and overall assessments of the quality of life in the area. (Rosenbaum & Lavrakas, 1995, p. 294)

In this study, the "key community member" concept was operationalized as a person or group of people who, at some time during a normal day, makes a noteworthy contribution to the way a place is used. At the outset of the project, we designed our interview methodology to identify "place managers." A place manager is often defined as a person who has some responsibility for controlling behavior in the specific location, such as a bus conductor or teacher in school (see, e.g., Clarke & Eck, 2005). We felt that this definition was too restrictive to be applied across all 34 hot spot locations. For instance, in one hot spot location, many of the more serious crime problems were emanating from illicit drug selling and public drinking in a park located in a residential area. While we interviewed a community member in the hot spot area who had a vested interest in cleaning up the park, she did not have any direct responsibility for controlling the disorderly behavior in that location.

The following process was used to identify and interview key community members in the 17 pairs of hot spot locations included in the experiment.

1. **All available data on each of the hot spots were collected.** Information on each place was gathered from the following data sources during the pre-test period: interviews with police officers in the sector, interviews with the LPD community liaison representative, official data (calls for service, arrest, and incident data), maps, and direct researcher observations.
2. **These data were used to identify the problems of the hot spot and the specific locations within a hot spot these problems occur.** The problems of a hot spot and their specific locations were listed based on the available data. Some places had two or more discrete problem locations within their boundaries that contributed to the criminal activity. For example, there may have been assault and robbery problems emanating from a rowdy bar and an abandoned building within the same crime place. Information was reviewed on the links between the different problems of a place and how they were related.
3. **Based on the problem(s) of a place and their locations, individuals that have a stake in the problem(s) were listed.** Once the problems were identified and located within a place, people were listed who were affected by the discrete problems of a place. Different potential key community members were identified based on their stake in the distinct problems of a location. The location or physical layout of the place was also considered when choosing a key community member. It was possible for an individual to have valuable insight into one problem, but not have a direct stake in all the problems of the place.
4. **From this list of possible key community members, the minimum number of individuals who collectively provided insight**

into all the problems of a place was selected. These individuals were logically linked to the problem(s). The person who was reasonably able to provide the best overall picture of the problem was selected. For example, if there was a robbery problem in an apartment building, it made sense to talk to the resident manager of the building who was familiar with all of the incidents rather than to several of the residents who may have been familiar with their own experiences and not the experience of others in the building. Further, it did not seem reasonable to expect this resident manager to have valuable insight into the (hypothetical) loitering problem in front of a liquor store. The store owner or manager may be the correct person to interview for insight into this problem. Therefore, the number and types of person were driven by nuances of the problems of a place. However, in order to keep the same number of key community members interviewed, we required that the final number of key community members within a pair had to be the same. In other words, Place A and Place B within Pair 1 both had to have X key community members interviewed.

In order not to bias the data, the subject was interviewed by Harvard researchers without a direct police presence. In most areas, researcher safety was not a concern and interviews took place without any police presence. In those areas that were potentially dangerous, the interviewer was accompanied by a police officer. However, the police officer remained in the car and maintained surveillance on the researcher to ensure safety. To the extent possible, all business owners, managers, and professionals across the population of places were contacted via a phone call prior to the interview. A mutually convenient time and place was scheduled to conduct the interview with the subject. This step helped to avoid complications such as conducting an interview during busy hours, non-response due to fear of reprisal from hoodlums watching the business owner talk to an outsider (police informant), or other potential problems. All subjects were shown a map of the crime place to ensure that the respondent was describing problems and concerns within the boundaries of the hot spot. The instrument was tailored to residents and business owners / managers, but had the same basic structure and questions for all interviews.

After this process was completed, there were 52 key community members identified and interviewed during the pre-test and post-test time periods (26 each at the treatment and control places). Nine pairs of places (52.9% of 17 pairs) required two key community members to be interviewed to provide a complete assessment of the problems of a place between the pre-test and post-test observation periods. At these nine pairs of places, our review of the place-level data suggested that an additional key community member was necessary based on the geographic layout of the hot spot area and the place dynamics that influenced the number and types of problems. For example, at a hot spot that covered a four block geographic expanse in a busy downtown neighborhood, we interviewed the owner of a local variety store and the resident manager of an apartment building to capture their experiences and insights on the various problems of the place. The store owner was able to provide insights on the late night disorder and alcohol-related assault problems emanating from the surrounding bars. On the opposite side of the hot spot area (and out of direct view of the store owner), the resident manager provided insights on street-level drug sales occurring in a nearby alley and disorder problems generated by high school students and homeless vagrants congregating at a local bus stop in front of the apartment building. Without including both community members, we would have had an incomplete picture of important place dynamics.

During the pre-test interviews, the subjects were slightly more likely to be local business representatives (28 of 52, 53.8%) when compared to local residents (24 of 52, 46.2%). The key community members were 55.8% female (29 of 52), and 87.5% (49 of 52) were ages 30 and older. The respondents were 61.5% Caucasian (32 of 52), 25% Hispanic (13 of 52), and 13.5% Asian (7 of 52). A majority of the subjects had lived and/or worked in the hot spot area for five or more years (69.2%, 36 of 52). Only three respondents had lived and/or worked in the hot spot area for less than one year at the time of the pre-test interview (5.7%). Since the intervention period lasted only one year and most of the respondents were long-time fixtures at the places, attrition of key community members across observation periods was not a substantive problem. Only three of the 52 respondents (5.8%) from the first wave could not be located for an interview during the second wave. These three respondents were replaced by very similar key community members in all instances. For instance, if a business owner was not available for a second wave interview, he/she was replaced by a worker who had been working at the place prior to the start of the policing intervention.

The problem of statistical power is an important analytic issue in the use of a small number of carefully selected individuals to evaluate interventions at places. The small number of cases in this study undermined our ability to detect a treatment effect (if a treatment effect in fact existed) using standard statistical hypothesis tests. Indeed, statistical power is a very complex problem, especially in experimental research.[4] Researchers and analysts interested in using the small area interview approach need to consider research design sensitivity questions, such as the plausible intervention effect size and the number of cases, in planning evaluations based on this methodology. However, traditional survey methods with larger sample sizes do not guarantee powerful statistical tests. Indeed, the "total survey error" of large surveys can be greater than the total survey error in carefully selected small samples of informants (Groves, 1989). As Rosenbaum and Lavrakas (1995) describe, total survey error includes conventional sampling error (which is a function of the heterogeneity of what is being measured, the size of the sample, and the size of the population), coverage error (whether everyone in a population has an equal chance of selection), and measurement error (inaccuracies associated with the instrument and the mode in which the data are collected). Survey costs and the limits of available funding also impact the ability of the researcher to reduce and/or measure the potential effects of survey error in large survey samples.

Reliability and Validity of Key Community Member Data

It is important to note that these 52 key community members represent a non-probability purposive sample that was selected based on who we thought would be very knowledgeable about changes in the treatment and control hot spots over the course of the experiment. As Babbic (2003) notes, purposive sampling techniques are used primarily when there are a limited number of people who have expertise in the area being researched. Since community members were not directly involved in the LPD problem-oriented policing strategies, we were not overly concerned that the perceptions of the selected key community members would be skewed over the course of the evaluation by being party to the preventive actions introduced in the treatment hot spots areas. While research suggests that carefully selected community members can provide reliable and valid insights on place dynamics and problems (Green Mazerolle et al., 1998; Rosenbaum & Lavrakas, 1995), we investigated whether the key community member perceptions in this study were representative of the experiences of the larger community in the hot spot areas by examining the relationship between the number of pre-test disorder problems identified by the key community members and the total number of citizen calls to the police to report disorder concerns at the place during the six months prior to the intervention period.

Table 2 presents a summary of the general physical and social disorder problems identified by 52 key community members during the pre-test period at the 34 treatment and control locations. These identified problems were aggregated into an overall scale measuring the extensiveness of disorder problems at the hot spots according to the perceptions of key community members.[5] According to the Cronbach's Alpha coefficient (.71), the items that comprised the scale were well correlated and the scale was internally consistent in its reliability as a measure.

Citizen calls for service data are suggested to be more reliable and valid measures of crime and crime-related activity than incident data or arrest data (Pierce et al., 1988; Sherman et al., 1989). Most notably, citizen calls for service are affected less heavily by police discretion than other official data sources, and they represent the experiences and concerns of community members in specific places over time (Warner & Pierce, 1993). Therefore, call data are regarded as "the widest ongoing data collection net for criminal events in the city" (Sherman, et al., 1989: 35; but, see Klinger & Bridges, 1997). During the pre-test period, the correlation between the number of disorder problems identified by the 52 key commu-

Table 2: Physical and Social Disorder Problems Identified by Key Community Members

Type of Disorder	Number	Percent
Trash on street	41	78.8
Loitering	35	67.3
Public intoxication	32	61.5
Drug dealing	27	51.9
Graffiti	23	44.2
Abandoned buildings / damaged structures / vacant lots	19	36.5

N = 52
Cronbach's Alpha = 0.71
Note: These data represent the physical and social disorder problems identified by the 52 key community members in treatment and control hot spot locations during the pre-test observation period.

nity members and the number of disorder calls in the hot spot areas was large, positive, and statistically significant ($r = +0.64$, $p<.05$). The strong correlation suggested that key community members' views on one important issue in the hot spot area, the extensiveness of disorder problems, were representative of the experiences of the broader community as measured by the number of calls placed to the police to report disorder concerns at the place. Additional research on the reliability and validity of key community member perception data for other indicators, such as fear of crime and police-community relations, is clearly necessary. Nonetheless, we believe that this simple assessment provides some support for the position that carefully selected individuals can provide reliable and valid insights on broader community perceptions of the effects of crime reduction strategies implemented at specific places.

ANALYSIS AND RESULTS

Physical and Social Disorder Problems in the Hot Spot Areas

During the pre-test and post-test observation periods, key community members were asked whether specific types of physical and social disorder were problems in their hot spot areas over the previous twelve months. Respondents were specifically asked to rate whether a certain type of disorder, such as trash on the street, was "not a problem," "somewhat of a problem," or "a serious problem" in the hot spot area. For each respondent, their pre-test and post-test responses were examined to determine whether there was an improvement in their rating of specific disorder problems. If a respondent noted that "a serious problem" existed in the pre-test time period and that disorder was "somewhat of a problem" in the post-test, the respondent was recorded as noticing an improvement in that problem over the course of the intervention period. An improvement was recorded if the respondent rated a specific disorder issue as "not a problem" in the post-test period after rating the issue as "somewhat of a problem" or "a serious problem" in the pre-test period. If problems were rated worse or stayed the same across observation periods, no improvement was noted. Simple differences-in-group-proportions hypothesis tests were used to explore whether there were any statistically significant differences in the proportions of respondents noting improvements in disorder problems in the treatment and control hot spot areas during the pre-test and post-test observation periods.

Table 3 presents the results of the analysis of key community members' perceptions of improvements in physical and social disorder problems at the treatment hot spots relative to the control hot spots. Key community members in the treatment places noted non-significant improvements in trash and graffiti problems and statistically significant ($p<.05$) improvements in problems involving abandoned buildings, vacant lots, and damaged structures (such as broken fences) relative to key community members in the control areas. Over all, key community members in the treatment

Table 3: Pre-test v. Post-test Perceptions of Improvements in Physical and Social Disorder Problems at Treatment and Control Places

Problem	Treatment Improvement		Control Improvement				
	%	(X of 26)	%	(X of 26)	% Diff.	Z	P
Physical disorder	**42.3**	**(11)**	**15.4**	**(4)**	**+26.9**	**2.14**	**.032**
Trash	23.1	(6)	7.7	(2)	+15.4	1.54	.124
Graffiti	15.4	(4)	3.8	(1)	+11.6	1.42	.156
Abandoned buildings / damaged structures / vacant lots	30.8	(8)	7.7	(2)	+23.1	2.11	.035
Social disorder	**46.2**	**(12)**	**19.2**	**(5)**	**+27.0**	**2.08**	**.038**
Public intoxication	34.6	(9)	0.0	(0)	+34.6	3.29	.001
Drug dealing	26.9	(7)	7.7	(2)	+19.2	1.83	.067
Loitering	30.8	(8)	15.4	(4)	+15.4	1.32	.188
Any disorder	**61.5**	**(16)**	**26.9**	**(7)**	**+34.6**	**2.51**	**.012**

N = 52

Note: There were 26 individuals interviewed during the pre-test and post-test periods in the treatment group and 26 individuals interviewed during the pre-test and post-test periods in the control group.

hot spots noted statistically significant improvements ($p<.05$) in aggregate physical disorder problems as compared to their counterparts in the control hot spots. Key community members in the treatment places also noted statistically significant improvements in public intoxication ($p<.01$) and drug selling ($p<.10$) problems, and non-significant reductions in loitering problems relative to their control place counterparts. Taken as a whole, key community members in the treatment hot spots reported statistically significant improvements ($p<.05$) in social disorder problems as compared to key community members in the control hot spots. For example, as one elderly female resident noted after the LPD had several problematic tenants evicted from a public housing development, "I notice far less trash and fewer drunk people wandering around" (the housing complex). The key community member perceptions data supported the conclusion of the impact evaluation that found significant reductions in social and physical disorder associated with the policing intervention at the treatment places relative to control places.

Perceptions of Police Behaviors

During the pre-test and post-test observation periods, key community members were asked whether they noted any changes in police behavior in the hot spot areas over the previous twelve months. Respondents were specifically asked to report whether they experienced an increased number of contacts with police officers in the hot spot area, whether the demeanor of police officers towards citizens was respectful and courteous, whether the police had improved their crime control strategies, and whether police officers showed a willingness to work with citizens on crime and disorder problems. Respondents were asked whether they had any contact with a police officer, the number of contacts, and the circumstances of these contacts (reporting a crime, community meeting, interaction on the street, etc.) during the 12 months preceding the interview. For questions involving officers' demeanor and willingness to partner with community members, respondents were read statements about their experiences with the police in the hot spot area over the prior twelve months and then asked whether they strongly agree, agree, disagree, or strongly disagree with the statement. Open-ended questions were used to determine whether the respondent noticed any changes in police activities, such as policing strategies and/or styles, in the hot spot area over the previous twelve months.

Like the social and physical disorder analysis, for each respondent, their pre-test and post-test responses were examined to determine whether there was an improvement in their rating of police behavior in the hot spot area. Simple differences-in-group-proportions hypothesis tests were used to explore whether there were any statistically significant differences in the proportions of respondents noting improvements in police behavior in the treatment and control hot spot areas during the pre-test and post-test observation periods.

Table 4 presents the results of the analyses of changes in key community member perceptions of police behaviors in the treatment and control hot spot areas over the course of the experiment. Key community members in the treatment hot spots reported a large statistically significant improvement ($p<.01$) in the number of contacts between the police and themselves as compared to key community members in the control places. The interviews with key community members suggested a noteworthy increase in police presence in the treatment hot spots relative to the control hot spots. However, the key community members did not report statistically

Table 4: Pre-test v. Post-test Perceptions of Improvements in Police Behaviors at Treatment and Control Places

Police Behavior	Treatment Improvement		Control Improvement				
	%	(X of 26)	%	(X of 26)	% Diff.	Z	P
Number of contacts with police	73.1	(19)	15.4	(4)	+57.7	4.19	.000
Change in policing strategies / styles	34.6	(9)	19.2	(5)	+15.4	1.25	.211
Demeanor of police	19.2	(5)	11.5	(3)	+7.7	0.77	.441
Willingness to work with citizens	30.8	(8)	15.4	(4)	+15.4	1.30	.193

N = 52

Note: There were 26 individuals interviewed during the pre-test and post-test periods in the treatment group and 26 individuals interviewed during the pre-test and post-test periods in the control group.

significant differences in policing strategies or styles in the treatment places relative to control places. As a small business owner in a treatment place noted in the post-test time period, "I've noticed a lot of undercover surveillance by unmarked police cars and strong police visibility in uniform. Many officers stop at the store in their uniforms." Unfortunately, the same business owner did not report that he noticed any changes in their policing strategies or styles over the course of the experiment.

The respondents also did not note any significant improvements in the demeanor of the police towards citizens or the willingness of the police to work with community members on crime and disorder problems in the treatment hot spots relative to the control hot spots. It is important to note that, in contrast to concerns regarding potentially harmful effects of the focused police actions in specific areas, the policing disorder strategy did not generate negative appraisals of the LPD. In general, all 56 key community members, regardless of whether they were in treatment or control places, had generally favorable opinions of the LPD and the officers who worked in their areas.

In U.S. Department of Justice publications (e.g., Roth et al., 2000) and academic papers (e.g., Braga et al., 2006; Hartmann, 2002), the LPD has been described as thoughtful and diligent in its transition from traditional policing methods to community policing. Since the key community members were selected because of their prominent positions in the hot spot areas, they most likely have been exposed to, and perhaps involved in, the LPD's general community policing strategy and ad-hoc problem-solving projects. As such, it may not be very surprising to find that key community members noticed an increased amount of activity in treatment areas relative to control areas, but not any changes in policing styles, demeanor, or willingness to work with citizens. Since the LPD already had a tradition of community policing, it seems likely that they would have had to engage in community activities that went far beyond their routine efforts to make a significant impact on the perceptions of key community members.

Fear of Crime in the Hot Spot Areas

Key community members were also asked how afraid they were of being a victim of different types of crimes within the hot spot areas. Respondents were asked to appraise their fear of being the victim of a wide variety of illicit behaviors, ranging from being approached by panhandlers to being robbed on the street to being murdered. For each crime type, key community members were asked to rate their fear on a scale of one to ten, where one meant the respondent was not afraid at all and ten meant that they were very afraid. Simple differences-in-group-means tests did not reveal any statistically significant differences between the treatment and control groups in their ratings of fear for the various crimes. Respondents' fear was generally low for violent crimes and moderate for property crimes. When the respondents from both groups were pooled, the aggregate pre-test means were 2.2 for being approached by a panhandler, 2.3 for being raped or sexually assaulted, 2.5 for being murdered, 3.1 for being robbed or mugged on the street, 3.2 for being attacked on the street by a stranger, 3.7 for having their car stolen, 4.6 for having a break-in at their home or business, and 4.8 for having their property / vehicle damaged by vandals.

These fear of crime data were analyzed using ordinary least squares regression to compute a difference-in-differences estimator to determine whether there were any statistically significant changes in the mean fear ratings for specific crimes by key community members in treatment and control hot spots over the pre-test and post-test time periods.[6] Table 5 presents the results of the regression analyses of key community member perceptions of fear of crime in the control and treatment hot spot areas across the pre-test and post-test observation periods. In general, the analyses did not note any statistically significant changes in the community perceptions of fear across the various types of victimizations associated with the problem-oriented policing treatment. While there were consistent reductions in fear of victimization across the various violent crime categories, these positive changes in the perceptions of key community members were not large enough to generate a statistically significant reduction in fear of violent crime in treatment hot spots relative to control hot spots.

The available research literature suggests a strong link between fear of crime and disorderly conditions (see, e.g., Skogan, 1990). Unfortunately, in this study, decreased disorder and fewer calls for service to the police did not translate into significantly reduced fear of crime for the key community members. There are several other plausible explanations for this discrepancy. First, as discussed earlier, the small number of cases in our analyses may have undermined our ability to detect small, but substantive, treatment effects. The baseline level of fear in the treatment and control places was relatively low at the start of the intervention. To detect an effect, fear of crime would have to be nearly eliminated in the treatment places (or greatly increased in the control places). Given that the respondents worked

Table 5: Differences-in-Differences Estimators for Treatment Effects on Fear of Crime Measures for Specific Types of Victimizations in Treatment and Control Hot Spot Areas

How afraid are you of:	Coeff.	Std. error	t	P
Being approached on the streetby a beggar or panhandler	–.304	.793	–.384	.702
Having your property / vehicle damaged by vandals	.087	1.193	.073	.942
Having someone break into your home / business	–.174	1.327	–.131	.896
Having your car stolen	.967	1.126	.858	.393
Being attacked on the street by a stranger	–.110	1.115	–.099	.921
Being robbed or mugged on the street	–.695	1.112	–.625	.534
Being raped or sexually assaulted	–1.11	.979	–1.14	.259
Being murdered	–.808	1.029	–.786	.434

N = 52

Note: Respondents were asked how afraid they were in everyday life of being a victim of the different crimes listed above. All interviewers showed the respondent a map of the hot spot area and asked them to rate their fear of these crimes happening to them in the specific area. Respondents rated their fear on a scale of 1 to 10, where 1 meant they were not afraid at all and 10 meant they were very afraid. There were 26 individuals interviewed during the pre-test and post-test periods in the treatment group and 26 individuals interviewed during the pre-test and post-test periods in the control group.

and lived in an urban environment, it would be very difficult to drive fear levels in the treatment areas to near zero.

Second, crime and disorder problems were alleviated not eliminated. Although disorderly persons and drug sellers were not as deeply entrenched at the places as they once were, smaller numbers of these bothersome individuals were still present and could still frighten and threaten community members. As one resident commented, "there aren't as many kids drinking in the park at night. However, when the police move on from the area, some of the kids return to the park and drink near the basketball courts." Further, although the treatment places improved, the surrounding neighborhoods were not addressed. Crime hot spots exist in a larger neighborhood context (Bursik & Grasmick, 1993). Disorder and crime problems in the larger community, and the associated fear and perceptions of risk, may have influenced citizen appraisals of the place in a negative way. As a pizza parlor owner commented, "there is more police presence in the area, and officers are sitting and watching the corner. But, we have concerns for our delivery people who have been robbed elsewhere in city."

Third, a "key community member," by definition, knows more than the average citizen about the dynamics of a place and the surrounding neighborhood. These people are likely to be more deeply embedded within local social networks, and, therefore, receive more information about positive and negative events in the area. The enhanced flow of information can have negative and positive effects on their evaluative capacity. The key community member receives better coverage of events and this could either overestimate or underestimate the effectiveness of the intervention or the seriousness of crime and disorder problems in ways a general sample of people representing the spectrum of social embeddedness at the place would not.

CONCLUSION

Small area interviews with key community members added an important dimension to a multi-measure evaluation framework for crime reduction strategies implemented in specific crime places. In this study, the key advantage of the approach was the low-cost acquisition of important community insights from very knowledgeable individuals on the influence of police crime prevention strategies at specific places. Perceptions of disorder problems, satisfaction with police services, and fear of crime are distinct concepts that are related in complex ways and influenced by geography, socio-economic status, culture, and local crime levels, and other factors. Certainly, researchers and analysts using these data to evaluate interventions need to place insights from key community members in the context of their positions within neighborhoods, existing relationships with the police department, historical police activities in the area, the nature of the interventions being implemented, and other relevant social dynamics in the specific area and larger neighborhood and city environments. Through careful analysis, however, small area interview data make strong contributions to the development and evaluation of new crime reduction policies and programs directed in specific places.

In this study, the convergence and divergence of data on key community member perceptions, systematic researcher observations, and citizen calls for service shed some policy-relevant insights on how the community experiences police crime control efforts. While the main impact evaluation found that the LPD problem-oriented policing intervention significantly reduced citizen calls for service and indicators of social disorder, our analysis of key community member data suggested that these crime reduction strategies did not have the desired effects on police-community relationships. Community members noticed improvements in the level of disorder and increased police presence in the hot spot areas. Unfortunately, the informants did not experience significant changes in the style of policing, the willingness of the police to work with citizens on problems, and the demeanor of the police. These findings suggest that the problem of improving police-community relations may need to be addressed through an additional set of actions and programs beyond the strategies implemented to control crime and disorder at the targeted places. Indeed, consistent with the problem-oriented policing approach, the problem of improving police-community relations at specific places needs to be carefully analyzed and a portfolio of appropriate strategies that are logically linked to the underlying conditions and dynamics needs to be developed and implemented.

Address correspondence to: Anthony Braga, Program in Criminal Justice Policy and Management, John F. Kennedy School of Government, Harvard University, 79 John F. Kennedy Street, Cambridge, MA 02138; e-mail: Anthony_Braga@harvard.edu

Acknowledgments: This research was supported under award 2004-DB-BX-0014 from the Bureau of Justice Assistance, Office of Justice Programs, U.S. Department of Justice through the Programs Division of the Massachusetts Executive Office of Public Safety. The authors would like to thank former Superintendent Edward Davis, Superintendent Kenneth Lavallee, Captain Thomas Kennedy, Captain John Flaherty, Captain Jack Webb, Lieutenant Barry Golner, Lieutenant Paul Laferriere, Lieutenant Kevin Sullivan, Lieutenant Kelly Richardson, Lieutenant Frank Rouine, Lieutenant Mark Buckley, Sergeant Steve O'Neil, Officer Mark Trudel, Meghan Moffett, John Reynolds, Sara Khun, and other officers and staff of the Lowell Police Department for their valuable assistance in the completion of this research. Jesse Jannetta, Russell Wolff, Carl Walter, and Deborah Braga deserve much credit for their assistance with data collection and analysis. Finally, we would like to thank Sarah Lawrence for her support and patience in the successful completion of this research project and Johannes Knutsson, Nick Tilley, Ron Clarke, and Ross Homel for their helpful comments on earlier drafts of this manuscript. Points of view in this document are those of the authors and do not necessarily represent the official position of the U.S. Department of Justice, Massachusetts Executive Office of Public Safety, or Lowell Police Department.

NOTES

1. The landmark Kansas City Preventive Patrol Experiment had to be stopped and restarted three times before it was implemented properly; the patrol officers did not respect the boundaries of the treatment and control areas (Kelling et al., 1974). Likewise, the design of the Minneapolis Spouse Abuse Experiment was modified to a quasi-experiment when randomization could not be achieved because officers chose to arrest certain offenders on a non-random basis (Berk et al., 1988).
2. During the pretest and posttest periods, maps of each control and treatment hot spot area were created and every block face that comprised each individual hot spot was photographed. For example, if the hot spot consisted of a street intersection area with four adjoining street segments, the researcher took a photograph of each of the four blocks that comprised the area. To ensure consistency in data collection, the pictures were always taken at the midpoint of the block from the opposite side of the street. The resulting pictures were viewed and the physical characteristics of the places were reproduced onto maps. All physical disorder at the place were recorded, this included: abandoned buildings, vacant lots, trash, graffiti, abandoned cars, and other physical incivilities. These maps were coded and entered into a database for analysis.
3. Systematic social observations have long been used in criminological research to understand and measure deviant behavior (see, e.g. Sampson & Raudenbush, 1999; Reiss, 1971; Weisburd et al., 2006). The objective of the social observations was to get a measure of the amount and types of social activity occurring in the places during times they were known to be criminally active. These data were collected at both control and treatment places during the pretest and posttest periods by

making three separate visits to each place. Citizen calls for service data at each place were analyzed for temporal variations in criminal activity. All places were visited for five minutes at the time of day (morning, afternoon, or night) and day of the week that the location was most active. Drawing upon the methods used by Sherman and Weisburd (1995), a researcher, driven by a plainclothes police officer in an unmarked car, parked in an unobtrusive area that had a clear view of the place's "epicenter" of activity (636). After parking, the researcher then counted the number of people engaged in disorderly activities, such as loitering and drinking in public, over the next five minutes. These data were then coded and entered into a database for analysis.

4. Power estimates are often based simply on the number of cases in the study. By this measure, our estimate for power is relatively low. In our impact evaluation, using a standard sign test with 34 places (alpha=.05, two tails), our statistical power to detect a small effect size was about .24, a medium effect size was about .56, and large effect size was about .99 (Lipsey, 1990). However, as Weisburd (1993) points out, the number of cases is often a misleading measure. He finds that the smaller the experiment, the better control of variability in treatment and design. Statistical power may, in fact, be larger than expected.
5. The scale was created by aggregating specific disorder response categories "not a problem," "somewhat of a problem," and "serious problem" into a binary indicator that a particular issue, such as loitering, was a problem or not (0 = "not a problem" and 1 = "somewhat or a serious problem") in the place. The scale was derived by summing the six items described in Table 2 and dividing by six. The scale ranges from 0 to 1, where high values indicate more extensive disorder problems at the place and lower values represent less extensive problems at the place.
6. The basic regression equation was: fear rating = intercept + b_1(group) + b_2(period) + b_3(group*period) + error. Group was a dummy variable indicating whether a respondent was in the control (0) or treatment (1) hot spot area. Period was a dummy variable indicating whether the rating occurred during the pre-test (0) or post-test (1) time period. The b_3 coefficient was the difference-in-differences estimator which captured the effect of being in the treatment group relative to the control group over the two observation time periods (group*period).

REFERENCES

Babbie, E. (2003). *The practice of social research* (10th ed.). Belmont, CA: Wadsworth Publishing Company.

Berk, R., Smyth, G., & Sherman, L. (1988). When random assignment fails: Some lessons from the Minneapolis spouse abuse experiment. *Journal of Quantitative Criminology, 4*, 209–223.

Braga, A. (2001). The effects of hot spots policing on crime. *Annals of the American Academy of Political and Social Science, 578*, 104–125.

Braga, A. (2005). Hot spots policing and crime prevention: A systematic review of randomized controlled trials. *Journal of Experimental Criminology, 1*, 317–342.

Braga, A. (2008). *Problem-oriented policing and crime prevention* (2nd ed.). Monsey, NY: Criminal Justice Press.

Braga, A., & Bond, B. (2008). Policing crime and disorder hot spots: A randomized controlled trial. *Criminology, 46*, 701–731.

Braga, A., McDevitt, J. & Pierce, G. (2006). Understanding and preventing gang violence: Problem analysis and response development in Lowell, Massachusetts. *Police Quarterly, 9*, 20–46.

Braga, A., & Weisburd, D. (2006). Problem-oriented policing: The disconnect between principles and practice. In D. Weisburd & A. Braga (Eds.), *Police innovation: Contrasting perspectives.* New York: Cambridge University Press.

Braga, A., Weisburd, D., Waring, E., Green Mazerolle, L., Spelman, W. & Gajewski, F. (1999). Problem-oriented policing in violent crime places: A randomized controlled experiment. *Criminology, 37*, 541–580.

Brown, L., & Wycoff, M. (1987). Policing Houston: Reducing fear and improving service. *Crime & Delinquency, 33*, 71–89.

Buerger, M. (1994). The problems of problem-solving: Resistance, interdependencies, and conflicting interests. *American Journal of Police, 13*, 1–36.

Bursik, R., & Grasmick, H. (1993). *Neighborhoods and crime: The dimensions of effective community control.* Lexington, MA: Lexington Books.

Campbell, D., & Stanley, J. (1966). *Experimental and quasi-experimental designs for research.* Chicago: Rand McNally.

Capowich, G., & Roehl, J. (1994). Problem-oriented policing: Actions and effectiveness in San Diego. In D. Rosenbaum (Ed.), *The challenge of community policing: Testing the promises.* Thousand Oaks, CA: Sage.

Clarke, R. V. (Ed.). (1997). *Situational crime prevention: Successful case studies* (2nd ed.). Monsey, NY: Criminal Justice Press.

Clarke, R. V. (1998). Defining police strategies: Problem solving, problem-oriented policing, and community-oriented policing. In T. O'Connor Shelly & A. Grant (Eds.), *Problem-oriented policing: Crime-specific problems, critical issues, and making POP work.* Washington, DC: Police Executive Research Forum.

Clarke, R. V., & Eck, J. E. (2005). *Crime analysis for problem solvers in 60 small steps.* Washington, DC: U.S. Department of Justice, Office of Community Oriented Policing Services.

Cook, T., & Campbell, D. (1979).*Quasi-experimentation: Design and analysis issues for field settings.* Boston: Houghton Mifflin Company.

Cordner, G., & Perkins Biebel, E. (2005). Problem-oriented policing in practice. *Criminology & Public Policy*, *4*, 155–180.

Eck, J. E. (1993). Alternative futures for policing. In D. Weisburd & C. Uchida (Eds.), *Police innovation and control of the police*. New York: Springer-Verlag.

Eck, J. E. (2006). Science, values, and problem-oriented policing: Why problem-oriented policing? In D. Weisburd & A. Braga (Eds.), *Police innovation: Contrasting perspectives*. New York: Cambridge University Press.

Eck, J. E., & Spelman, W. (1987). *Problem-solving: Problem-oriented policing in Newport News*. Washington, DC: National Institute of Justice.

Felson, M. (2006). *Crime and nature*. Thousand Oaks, CA: Sage.

Goldstein, H. (1979). Improving policing: A problem-oriented approach. *Crime & Delinquency*, *25*, 236–258.

Goldstein, H. (1990). *Problem-oriented policing*. Philadelphia: Temple University Press.

Golub, A., Johnson, B. D., & Dunlap, E. (2007). The race/ethnicity disparity in misdemeanor marijuana arrests in New York City. *Criminology & Public Policy*, *6*, 131–164.

Green Mazerolle, L., Kadleck, C., & Roehl, J. (1998). Controlling drug and disorder problems: The role of place managers. *Criminology*, *36*, 371–404.

Greene, J. A. (1999). Zero tolerance: A case study of police practices and policies in New York City. *Crime & Delinquency*, *45*, 171–181.

Groves, R. M. (1989). *Survey errors and survey costs*. New York: John Wiley.

Guyot, D. (1979). Bending granite: Attempts to change the rank structure of American police departments. *Journal of Police Science and Administration*, 7, 253–284.

Harcourt, B., & Ludwig, J. (2007). Reefer madness: Broken windows policing and misdemeanor marijuana arrests in New York City, 1989–2000. *Criminology & Public Policy*, *6*, 165–182.

Hartmann, F. (2002). Safety first: Partnership, the powerful neutral convener, and problem solving. In G. Katzmann (Ed.), *Securing our children's future: New approaches to juvenile justice and youth violence*. Washington, DC: Brookings Institution Press.

Kelling, G., Pate, T., Dieckman, D., & Brown, C. (1974). *The Kansas City Preventive Patrol Experiment: A technical report*. Washington, DC: Police Foundation.

Kennedy, D., & Moore, M. H. (1995). Underwriting the risky investment in community policing: What social science should be doing to evaluate community policing. *Justice System Journal*, *17*, 271–290.

Klinger, D., & Bridges, G. (1997). Measurement error in calls-for-service as an indicator of crime. *Criminology*, *35*, 705–726.

Lipsey, M. (1990). *Design sensitivity: Statistical power for experimental research*. Thousand Oaks, CA: Sage.

McGarrell, E., Chermak, S., Weiss, A., & Wilson, J. (2001). Reducing firearms violence through directed patrol. *Criminology & Public Policy*, *1*, 119–148.

Meares, T. (2006). Third-party policing: A critical view. In D. Weisburd & A. Braga (Eds.), *Police innovation: Contrasting perspectives*. New York: Cambridge University Press.

Moore, M. H. (1992). Problem-solving and community policing. In M. Tonry & N. Morris (Eds.), *Modern policing*. Chicago: University of Chicago Press.

Moore, M. H., & Braga, A. (2003). Measuring and improving police performance: The lessons of Compstat and its progeny. *Policing: An International Journal of Police Strategies and Management*, *26*, 439–453.

Pate, T., & Skogan, W. (1985). *Coordinated community policing: The Newark experience*. Technical Report. Washington, DC: Police Foundation.

Pierce, G., Spaar, S., & Briggs, L. (1988). *The character of police work: Strategic and tactical implications*. Boston: Northeastern University, Center for Applied Social Research.

Read, T., & Tilley, N. (2000). *Not rocket science? Problem-solving and crime reduction*. Crime reduction research series paper 6. London, UK: Home Office.

Reiss, A. (1971). *The police and the public*. New Haven, CT: Yale University Press.

Rosenbaum, D. (2006). The limits of hot spots policing. In D. Weisburd & A. Braga (Eds.), *Police innovation: Contrasting perspectives*. New York: Cambridge University Press.

Rosenbaum, D., & Lavrakas, P. (1995). Self reports about place: The application of survey and interview methods to the study of small areas. In J. Eck & D. Weisburd (Eds.), *Crime and place*. Crime prevention studies, Vol. 4. Monsey, NY: Criminal Justice Press

Roth, J., Ryan, J., Gaffigan, S., Koper, C., Moore, M., Roehl, J., Johnson, C., Moore, G., White, R., Buerger, M., Langston, E. & Thacher, D. (2000). *National evaluation of the COPS program– Title I of the 1994 Crime Act*. Washington, DC: U.S. Department of Justice, National Institute of Justice.

Sampson, R., & Raudenbush, S. (1999). Systematic social observation of public spaces: A new look at disorder in urban neighborhoods. *American Journal of Sociology*, *105*, 603–651.

Scott, M. (2000). *Problem-oriented policing: Reflections on the first twenty years*. Washington, DC: U.S. Department of Justice, Office of Community Oriented Policing Services.

Shaw, J. (1995). Community policing against guns: Public opinion of the Kansas City gun experiment. *Justice Quarterly*, *12*, 695–710.

Sherman, L. (1997). Policing for crime prevention. In University of Maryland, Department of Criminology and Criminal Justice (Eds.), *Preventing crime: What works, what doesn't, what's promising*. Washington, DC: Office of Justice Programs, U.S. Department of Justice.

Sherman, L., & Weisburd, D. (1995). General deterrent effects of police patrol in crime hot spots: A randomized controlled trial. *Justice Quarterly*, *12*, 625–648.

Sherman, L., Gartin, P., & Buerger, M. (1989). Hot spots of predatory crime: Routine activities and the criminology of place. *Criminology*, *27*, 27–56.

Silverman, E. (1999). *NYPD battles crime: Innovative strategies in policing*. Boston: Northeastern University Press.

Skogan, W. (1990). *Disorder and decline: Crime and the spiral of decay in American neighborhoods*. New York: Free Press.

Skogan, W. (2006). The promise of community policing. In D. Weisburd & A. Braga (Eds.), *Police innovation: Contrasting perspectives.* New York: Cambridge University Press.

Skogan, W., & Frydl, K. (Eds.). (2004). *Fairness and effectiveness in policing: The evidence.* Committee to review police policy and practices. Washington, DC: The National Academies Press.

Skogan, W., & Meares, T. (2004). Lawful policing. *Annals of the American Academy of Political and Social Science, 593*, 66–83.

Skogan, W., & Steiner, L. (2004). *CAPS at ten: Community policing in Chicago.* Chicago: Illinois Criminal Justice Information Authority.

Taylor, R. (1997). Social order and disorder of street-blocks and neighborhoods: Ecology, micro-ecology, and the systematic model of social disorganization. *Journal of Research in Crime and Delinquency, 34*, 113–155.

Taylor, R. (2006). Incivilities reduction policing, zero tolerance, and the retreat from coproduction. In D. Weisburd & A. Braga (Eds.), *Police innovation: Contrasting perspectives.* New York: Cambridge University Press.

Tyler, T. (1990). *Why people obey the law: Procedural justice, legitimacy, and compliance.* New Haven, CT: Yale University Press.

Tyler, T. (2004). Enhancing police legitimacy. *Annals of the American Academy of Political and Social Science, 593*, 84–99.

Walker, S. (1992). *The police in America* (2nd ed.). New York: McGraw-Hill.

Warner, B., & Pierce, G. (1993). Reexamining social disorganization theory using calls to the police as a measure of crime. *Criminology, 31*, 493–518.

Weisburd, D. (1993). Design sensitivity in criminal justice experiments. In M. Tonry (Ed.), *Crime and justice: A review of research* (Vol. 17). Chicago: University of Chicago Press.

Weisburd, D., & Braga, A. (2006). Hot spots policing as a model for police innovation. In D. Weisburd & A. Braga (Eds.), *Police innovation: Contrasting perspectives.* New York: Cambridge University Press.

Weisburd, D., & Eck, J.E. (2004). What can police do to reduce crime, disorder, and fear? *Annals of the American Academy of Political and Social Science, 593*, 42–65.

Weisburd, D., Maher, L., & Sherman, L. (1992). Contrasting crime general and crime specific theory: The case of hot spots of crime. *Advances in Criminological Theory, 4*, 45–69.

Weisburd, D., Mastrofski, S., McNally, A., Greenspan, R., & Willis, J. (2003). Reforming to preserve: Compstat and strategic problem solving in American policing. *Criminology & Public Policy, 2*, 421–457.

Weisburd, D., Wyckoff, L., Ready, J., Eck, J.E., Hinkle, J., & Gajewski, F. (2006). Does crime just move around the corner? A controlled study of spatial displacement and diffusion of crime control benefits. *Criminology, 44*, 549–592.

Wycoff, M., & Skogan, W. (1986). Storefront police offices: The Houston field test. In D. Rosenbaum (Ed.), *Community crime prevention: Does it work?* Thousand Oaks, CA: Sage.

WHAT'S THE "WHAT" IN "WHAT WORKS?" HEALTH, POLICING AND CRIME PREVENTION

by

Nick Tilley
University College London

Abstract: *There are many meanings of "What" in "What Works?" Five are identified in this chapter. These relate to: particular interventions; classes of measure; mechanisms; strategies; and context-mechanism-outcome pattern configurations (CMOCs). Randomized Clinical/Controlled Trials (RCTs) are often treated as the gold standard for evaluation research in health. They have been used as the same standard in policing and crime prevention, though there are far fewer examples of them than there are in medicine. The "what" questions answered in RCTs relate to particular interventions or classes of measure. The adequacy of RCTs for evaluations in policing and situational crime prevention is considered herein through the detailed examination of an exemplary study. It is found to fail, in spite of its technical strengths. Its logic and assumptions are found to be seriously flawed. There are evaluation designs in health that do not involve RCTs. These also tend to answer different "what" questions from those asked in RCTs. Policing and situational crime prevention evaluations have more to learn from these than from RCTs.*

Crime Prevention Studies, volume 24 (2009), pp. 121–145.

INTRODUCTION

Health provides an attractive model for those attempting to improve crime prevention and policing through evidence-based policy and practice (Sherman, 1998; Shepherd, 2003). Crime science takes part of its inspiration from medical science (Laycock, 2003). Although there have been disappointments over the uptake of evidence in medical practice, there is a long history of basic research and of tests of treatments, the most influential of which have been clinical trials. Moreover, enormous efforts have been made to bring findings to the attention of practitioners. To support this, very substantial sums of money have been made available to pay for both fundamental research and tests of the efficacy and effectiveness of diverse treatments. Approval systems (such as those of the U.S. Food and Drug Administration) have been put in place in most countries before drugs can be used. Pharmaceutical companies are clearly motivated to provide funding where their profits turn on the development of new treatments and on the results of rigorous, well-designed trials that command credibility.

This chapter considers the evaluation questions asked in medicine – and the methods used to answer them – to see whether the equivalent questions and methods are applicable in policing and crime prevention. Is the medical model one we could or should mimic? Or, notwithstanding its appeal, are there key differences? In the end the argument will be a) that the received model of questions and methods in medicine is of rather limited relevance to policing and crime prevention, but b) that there are still important commonalities between questions and methods in the two domains, although not those that have been most emphasized in the past.

The key outcome-related issue addressed in evaluations, in the fields of health or crime prevention, is "what works?" Various meanings of "what," however, can distinguished. These are briefly laid out here, and their significance will become clearer as the chapter unfolds.

1. The "what" of "what works?" may refer to a *particular intervention*. In health this could refer, for example, to a particular drug to treat depression, say Prozac. In crime prevention it could refer to a particular type of property marking to reduce domestic burglary, say Smartwater.

2. The "what" of "what works?" may refer to a *class of measures*. In health this could refer, for example, to Selective Serotonin Reuptake Inhibitors (of which Prozac is one type) to treat depression. In crime prevention it could refer to property marking to reduce burglary, of which Smartwater is one type.

3. The "what" of "what works?" may refer to the *mechanism* through which an outcome is be produced (i.e., how the effect is brought about). In relation to Selective Serotonin Reuptake Inhibitors (SSRIs), the Mayo Clinic states on its website that, "It's not clear precisely how SSRIs affect depression. Certain brain chemicals called neurotransmitters are associated with depression, including the neurotransmitter serotonin. Some research suggests that abnormalities in neurotransmitter activity affect mood and behavior. SSRIs seem to relieve symptoms of depression by blocking the reabsorption (reuptake) of serotonin by certain nerve cells in the brain. This leaves more serotonin available in the brain. As a result, this enhances neurotransmission — the sending of nerve impulses — and improves mood. SSRIs are called selective because they seem to affect only serotonin, not other neurotransmitters" (http://www.mayoclinic.com/health/ssris/MH00066 – accessed March 13th 2008). By crime prevention standards this may seem to describe quite a precise mechanism, but evidently not by the standards of health research! In crime prevention, property marking might reduce burglary by increasing actual or perceived risk to offenders, respectively by either making it more likely that they will be caught or by making offenders think that they are more likely to be caught. It might also reduce burglary by making it less rewarding, either by making it harder for offenders to dispose of the marked goods or by making burglars think they will find it harder to dispose of them. Or there may be other mechanisms.

4. The "what" of "what works?" may refer to a more general *strategy* to address a problem. In health, this can go from broad approaches such as surgery or drugs or even evidence-based medicine, to national initiatives such as the British Health Action Zones, to local multi-strand efforts to deal with specific problem such as a Scottish Patient Pathway project to reduce coronary heart disease. In crime prevention, this can go from broad approaches such as situational crime prevention or problem-oriented policing or even evidence-based policing, to national initiatives such as the British Crime Reduction Programme, to local multi-strand efforts to deal with specific problems such as the Boston Gun Project.

5. The "what" of "what works?" may refer to context-mechanism-outcome pattern configurations, where positive, negative and nil-effect sub-group pathways are identified. In health, thalidomide appears (among other as yet not fully understood mechanisms) to inhibit angiogenesis, or the growth of new blood cells that feed tumor cells, as an effective treatment for myeloma, a cancer that develops from plasma cells in bone marrow (see

http://www.multiplemyeloma.org/treatments/3.04.php – acces sed August 2008), but thalidomide also crosses the placenta and the same angiogenesis seems to work its way through in pregnant women to teratogenic effects on their offspring, notably foreshortened limbs (see http://www.cancercare.on.ca/pdfdrugs/Thalidomide.pdf – accessed August 2008). In crime prevention naming and shaming (public disclosure) works for aspirant members of mainstream society (such as car manufacturers) who have a strong stake in being seen to be behaving as expected, but not for those rejecting or resisting or indifferent to being seen to be behaving as expected (such as terrorists or poll tax protesters) (see Pawson, 2003).

THE RECEIVED MEDICAL MODEL OF EVALUATION

The model of evaluation from the health field that those in policing and crime prevention have been invited to try to emulate is the RCT. The randomized clinical trial (RCT) in medicine is a thing of beauty. It takes a specific treatment and asks whether it works or not. It allocates potential recipients randomly to control and treatment conditions and measures the change in each before and after the treatment has been provided. The difference in differences provides a measure of effect size. If the effect size is positive, and large enough in relation to cost, then the treatment can be endorsed. If it is negative, or the effects too small in relation to costs, it can be discouraged or prohibited. RCTs sort the treatment wheat from the treatment chaff. In particular they help identify treatments that unintentionally cause harm, which can then be avoided. RCTs are concerned with answering the first two "what" questions in the list given immediately before this section of the paper.

The simple logic and powerful conclusions for practice and policy that emanate from RCTs in medicine have made them attractive in other areas of policy and practice, where RCT generally refers to Randomized *Controlled* rather than Randomized *Clinical* trial. The Cochrane Collaboration, which was developed to draw together trial findings in health, has been followed by the establishment of the Campbell Collaboration, which attempts the same for social policy, and which includes a group specifically concerned with Crime and Justice (Petrosino et al., 2001; Farrington and Petrosino, 2001). One of the big apparent advantages of the RCT is not only that the results of series of studies can be compared. They can also be aggregated in meta-analyses to provide larger samples from which conclusions can be drawn with greater statistical certainty.

The practice of RCTs in medicine can be complex, despite their straightforward underlying logic. Estimates of effect size can easily be biased. RCTs are used to try to make a "fair" measurement of outcomes by creating equivalent treatment and control groups, but even within them sources of bias can still rear their ugly heads. In particular, treatment recipient expectations, practitioner expectations and even scientists' hopes and expectations can all produce biases. To eliminate these sources of bias, complex efforts at blinding are ordinarily included in clinical trials. Double blinding[1] involves administering a placebo (and/or alternative treatment) to one randomly selected set of subjects. The other set is administered the treatment containing the active ingredient of interest. Members of neither set know whether they have received the placebo, substitute or trial treatment. In addition the person administering the treatment will not know which they have administered to any given subject. In "triple blinding" those collecting data on results and analysing those data will also not know either. This "triple blinding," the 24-carat-gold standard in medical trials, thus involves treatment subject, treatment administrator, results collector and data analyst all unable to tell whether they belong to, are administering to, or are conducting aggregate analysis in relation to members of a treatment or control group.[2]

Random allocation and triple blinding in clinical trials are intended to eliminate a series of biases that may otherwise arise:

- Statistical analysis effects: selective fishing for positive effects.
- Outcome measurement effects: clinician, researcher or treatment recipient skewed assessment of patient condition.
- Treatment/placebo/non treatment selection effects: prejudicial allocation of patients to one modality or another.
- Natural disease courses: changes that would occur even in the absence of intervention.
- Regression to the mean effects: allocation of treatments to extreme states that would naturally tend to revert towards the mean.
- Placebo effects: patient expectation effects on their condition.

Results of clever research designs suggest that all risks of bias are real (see Bratman, 2004). Bias can certainly operate insidiously. It does not require any intention of those involved to deceive. Randomization and blinding are used as much to guard against self-deception as to protect from fraud.

There have been Randomized Controlled Trials relevant to policing and crime prevention that attempt to match the exacting standards of the Randomized Clinical Trial. A strong example is a study by Alison Warburton and Jonathan Shepherd (2000). Jonathan Shepherd is a distinguished medical researcher, who brought extensive experience and technical expertise to the conduct of the research. He is also, of course, well-known in criminology and crime prevention as an enthusiastic advocate and user of experimental methods of the sort used in medicine. His standing in criminology is properly reflected in his award of the 2008 Stockholm Prize.

Warburton and Shepherd's study examined the effectiveness of introducing toughened "nonic" pint glasses in bars in Britain as a means of reducing injury. Nonic glasses are those without a handle, but with a bulge towards the top. The paper reporting their findings begins by noting that, "Bar glasswear is responsible for about 10% of assault injuries that present in U.K. emergency units and these usually lead to permanent, disfiguring facial scars" (Warburton and Shepherd 2000, p. 36), and adds that in three quarters of the incidents, "nonic" glasses are involved. It goes on to cite previous research by Shepherd et al. (1993), which had found that toughened glasses are more impact resistant than their annealed counterparts, especially when the glasswear is new, and that when toughened glasses do break they shatter into relatively harmless small cubes. Because toughened glasses seemed less likely to produce assault injury, many bars had switched to their use. However, to date the authors note that there had been no field trials to see whether in practice they prevent injury. This was the rationale for Warburton and Shepherd's study.

The trial was set up to produce a large enough sample for data over a six month period to yield statistically significant variations in numbers of injuries across the experimental (toughened glass) and control (annealed glass) conditions.

No records were kept of the precise number of bars approached to take part in the trial. It is said, though, that the number "exceeded 700" (p. 37), before the threshold number of staff required for the trial (at least 600) was met. Sixty bars were eventually available for randomization. They had to meet a variety of conditions, including reported injuries in the past year, willingness to cooperate with researchers and at least four participating bar staff. Three bars withdrew in the end. Those taking part had their entire stock of nonic glasses replaced by new ones to be used in the trial. New glasses were needed because wear and tear evidently makes older glasses less impact resistant. Twenty-three bars received control glasses (four didn't receive those allocated). Thirty bars received the toughened, intervention glasses. In the end 14 bars receiving the control glass completed the trial, with the return of 576 questionnaires, and 16 of the bars receiving the intervention glasses completed the trial, with the return of 653 questionnaires.

The bars were not told which type of glass they were being provided, though the packaging did show the identity of the glasses. Moreover, the researchers did not know which type of glasses was more impact resistant. There was, thus, a good effort at double blinding. An unknown number of questionnaires were distributed monthly to staff to record injuries. Because the number of questionnaires distributed, and of staff, were not known, response rates clearly could not be calculated. At the end of the trial a further general questionnaire was administered to all staff.

One incidental oddity of the study is that it turned out, when ten examples of each form of glasswear were tested for impact resistance, that the experimental *toughened* glasses were slightly less tough than the control *annealed* glasses, although the difference did not reach statistical significance ($p=0.35$). However, annealed glasses broke into sharp shards whilst toughened glasses disintegrated into small lumps. The staff reported that some toughened glasses spontaneously disintegrated, even when on the shelf!

In this study, the results of the trial were estimated using differences only in after rates, assuming they would otherwise have been the same. The toughened trial glasses underperformed in comparison with the control annealed glasses. The injury rate was reported to be 60% higher ($p<0.05$) in the intervention (toughened glass) group, with no difference in severity, although "Bearing in mind the sample size, the true 'statistical disadvantage' of toughened glass could be a few per cent more injuries, or could be a doubling or more" (p. 38). Across the whole sample only three of the 115 injury events were severe enough to require time off work, and only one resulted from an assault. Nearly all injuries sustained were, thus, minor accidents.

The authors conclude that new standards for toughened glass are required, since evidently not all toughened glasswear performs to the same level. They also quote one experienced publican saying that, "although the glasses (toughened) were stronger and easier to collect, the staff tended to treat them with less care and we tended to have more injuries" (pp. 39-40). In the light of this, Warburton and Shepherd comment that, "a proportion of the injuries in the intervention group may have been due to staff complacency or carelessness" (p. 40).

One objection to RCTs of the sort used in medicine, in the evaluation of much crime prevention and policing, is that RCTs are ill-equipped to deal with intentional behavior. Clinical trials are designed to rule out the intentions, understandings and expectations of the participants. Blinding and placebos aim to achieve just this, to allow the effects of the treatment and the treatment alone to be estimated. Placebo (expectation and perception-affected) effects are subtracted. Yet in situational crime prevention, expectations and perceptions comprise crucial mechanisms through which effects are brought about. "Anticipatory benefits," for example, occur in advance of the implementation of a crime prevention measure and one of the key mechanisms producing them relates to the (mis)perceptions of offenders (Smith et al., 2003). Except for the one injury caused by assault in Warburton and Shepherd's study, all were accidents. They did not involve intentional action aimed at causing injury. The injury was an unintentional side-effect which befell the victim. Thus, the encounter with the broken glass and the injury sustained happened inadvertently to the victim. It was not inflicted on them by another person's deliberate action. In this sense, perceptions of the glass (or the programme of glass replacement) by offenders is irrelevant. Moreover, the effects of any perception of the significance of particular glass types were discounted by the blinding of the bars to the types of glass with which they were being supplied.

Warburton and Shepherd's study neatly seems to side-step issues of intentionality by looking almost exclusively at accidents, where there is no intentional agent causing the injury. The downside is obvious. Whilst the issue with which the study begins is assault injuries, and assaults emphatically do involve intentionality on the part of the assailant, the substantive focus is on accidental injuries caused to bar workers as they go about their chores. Although the study might plausibly claim internal validity in relation to the effects of differing types of glasswear on accidental injury, it can tell us little or nothing of the effects of differing forms of glasswear on the injuries caused by the intentional action entailed in assaults. Of course it is perfectly plausible that an assailant's use of a glass that breaks into small cubes will cause less injury than a glass that breaks into sharp spikes, but that was realised before the research was undertaken. As a field trial to test whether that is indeed the case, the study fails. Indeed the study design risks misleading inferences. Any suggestion (which the authors certainly do not make, although it seems to be implicit in the study design), that a type of glass that produces fewer self-inflicted, unintended, minor hand injuries will also produce fewer major, intended, facial injuries inflicted by an assailant, would be absurd. In the case of the experimental and control glasses used in this study, common sense would suggest that there would be a trade-off between reducing minor and major injuries. The evidence collected suggests that the experimental, toughened glasses led to more of the self-inflicted, unintended, minor hand injuries than the control glasses. But the original proposition, that these glasses would produce fewer major, intended, facial injuries inflicted by an assailant than the control glasses continues to be highly plausible. Hence, minor hand injuries would be better prevented by using the control glasses and major injuries would be better prevented by using the experimental toughened ones.

There are other ways in which the study fails as an assessment of the effects of glass type on facial injuries caused by *intentional* assaults and we will come to them in due course. For the moment, let us pause to see whether the trial really does stand up as a study of the effects of changes in glasswear type on *accidental* injuries. Is intentionality entirely eliminated in the injurious accidents that befall bar workers as they go about their work? To grasp this, more would need to be known about how bar workers define their work and the glasses with which they deal. Warburton and Shepherd's quotation from the "experienced publican," cited above is, however, illuminating in this regard. The idea that levels of care by bar staff in collecting glasses are a function of their perceptions of the strength of the glasses and that this, in turn, affects the rates of breakage and injury, comprises an interesting and potentially illuminating hypothesis. It raises the possibility that a key mechanism in generating higher rates of accidental injury, when toughened glasses are used, has to do with perceptions of them and in this case the intentional action involved in the level of care taken when the glasses are handled by staff. The experienced publican's comments also raise some doubts about the level of blinding achieved in Warburton and Shepherd's study. It sounds as if at least some staff realised what sort of glasses they were handling. But, even if this were not the case, in understanding the effects of the changed form of glasses on actual levels of accidental injury, the notion that perceptions affect care and that this, in turn, influences injury level, suggests some of the complex processes of adjustment to the introduction of measures with which we are familiar when we look genuinely at offending behavior. Notions of displacement (Reppetto, 1976) , diffusion of benefits (Clarke and Weisburd, 1994) and longer term adaptation in crime prevention (Ekblom, 1997) are all concerned with the ways in which measures are interpreted by offenders and how this is then relevant to decisions about criminal behavior. The potential significance of perceptions and intentionality in relation to accidental injuries is not, of course, exhausted by the experienced publican's hypothesis. Warburton and Shepherd refer to the deterioration in impact resistance in glasses as they age. Publicans' decisions about replenishment rates will affect the pattern of glasswear held. The actual glasswear in stock, combined with staff members' perceptions of its robustness and the way in which they then handle it, may very well influence trends, longer-term levels and patterns of accidental injury.

The issues of intentionality and adaptation bring us to a further major failing in Warburton and Shepherd's methodology for examining the effects of toughened nonic glasses on levels injury produced by assaults in bars. Warburton and Shepherd concede that they have to depend on accidental injuries, given (mercifully) the relative rarity of those caused by assaults. The injuries covered in their study occurred mostly to the hands of bar workers (101 of the 115 injuries). Assaults presumably cause injury mainly to other parts of the body, at least so far as the victims are concerned. It is far from clear whether and how assailants may change what they do by way of assaults if the form of glasswear is changed. Most of us might guess that it would have no effect and that is presumably the working assumption of Warburton and Shepherd's study. But the question is an empirical one. The following hypotheses, though, might be true:

- If assailants believe they risk greater hand injury by using toughened nonic glass, they might select an alternative weapon, say a bottle or non-nonic glass.
- If assailants believe the toughened nonic glass will not produce significant injury, they may decide not to commit an assault at all.
- If bar staff (and/or others in the bar) believe that an assailant is about to use a relatively non-injurious toughened glass, they may make fewer efforts to prevent the assault from taking place.
- If, on the occasion of a heated argument, both parties believe that the risks to them from violence using non-toughened glasses are very high, they will be more likely to back down.

None of these hypotheses may be true, and there may be others also. They are listed here only as examples designed to show how understanding, intentionality and adaptation are crucial to the effects that glasswear types may have on the patterns of assaults and the injuries that follow.

These hypotheses relate to mechanisms through which changes in types of glasswear used in bars might alter the behavior either of the assailant or of those nearby in ways ultimately affecting the numbers of injuries produced.

For medical trials, the mechanisms may not matter much. What is important is the bottom line: in whatever way the intervention may have worked, did it produce the intended outcome and did it produce unintended harms that more than offset its benefits? These are the issues addressed in the first two "what" questions laid out towards the start of this paper. Questions about the mechanisms at work, of the sort mentioned in this paper in relation to the ways in which the introduction of toughened glass nonics might have an effect on accidental injuries or injuries from assaults in bars, are beside the point. They address the third of the "what" questions that were listed. They may be interesting but do not matter much. For crime prevention at least, however, the issue does matter. It does so for three reasons.

First, the conclusions of RCTs can only strictly be applied to the population from which the random allocation is made. If the findings are applied beyond that population it has to be assumed that the population from which the randomized allocation took place stands for a wider population. In the case of the Warburton and Shepherd study, remembering that the bars from which the randomised allocation was made were those that met the eligibility criteria, which amounted to 60 of an invited number which "exceeded 700," this will be what? All bars everywhere at all times? All bars included in the telephone directories of Cardiff, Gwent, Shropshire, Staffordshire, Stoke-on-Trent, West Midlands and Bristol, which were the source of the invitations to take part in the project? All bars that agreed to take part in the project? Or, are the conclusions valid only for the bars that had the required attributes to be eligible to take part in the project and who stayed the course (30 of the original 60 that were available for random allocation). In the case of medical trials, it is generally assumed that the population from which randomized allocation is made is representative of the total population with the condition of interest and that they remain relatively unchanging. This is not so clearly the case with units of interest in crime prevention, such as bars which may well vary and change in ways that are relevant to the efficacy of measures put in place. Replications are often advocated for trials to determine whether the findings of RCTs can be generalized. In practice, unless the conditions from which the populations in the differing trials can be taken to be representative of all populations from which randomized allocations take place, this does not take us very far.

Second, the population of potential recipients of interventions in crime prevention is heterogeneous and changing, and the mechanisms activated by crime prevention measures tend to vary by sub-population. If the findings are to be applied, an understanding of how they work through in differing sub-populations is needed. Warburton and Shepherd do not consider sub-populations of bars or bar workers and how the change in type of glass activates differing mechanisms amongst them. We do not know how the incidents are spread amongst the bars taking part in the trial. We do not know anything about the attributes of the staff receiving accidents as against those not experiencing them. We also do not know about customer experience of injuries. How might these be significant for the mechanisms through which the type of glass used might generate variations in level of injury? In relation to the experienced publican hypothesis (that perceptions of the attributes of glasses might influence their perceptions of risk of breakage and hence the care they take with the glasses), a range of hypotheses might be advanced.

Third, setting aside the first and second problems for a moment by assuming that those randomly allocated can be taken to be representative of a wider population, if each trial tells us only about the association between a particular treatment and changes in numbers of crimes or injuries, many large-scale and expensive trials will be needed. Take Warburton and Shepherd's concern: types of glasswear for pint-sized nonics and serious injuries caused by their use in fights in bars. It is clear from the foregoing arguments that non-accidental injuries to the hands of bar workers will not do as proxies. Only one facial injury was sustained within the 60 bars initially included in the Warburton and Shepherd trial, and more than 700 bars were needed for that trial to find the 60 that were suitable. The remaining 114 injuries came from other sources. The sample of bars to include in the trial would need to increase perhaps 100-fold to obtain a sample size big enough over six months to yield findings that were statistically significant. That would mean approaching 70,000 bars to find 6,000 for the trial, which would then need to have glasswear of the appropriate kind supplied. It was estimated that there were only 58,250 public houses in the U.K. in 2006 (http://www.caterersearch.com/Articles/2006/12/15/53051/industry-data-number-of-pubs-in-the-uk.html – accessed August 2008). Even then, however, it turned out that not all toughened glass is the same. Some types are tougher than others. The same might go for control glasswear. Assuming only two types of each, the sample size would need to be increased still further. Then, let us assume that replications are needed. Moreover, pint-sized nonics are not the only form of weapon available to potential assailants in bars: bottles, half-pint glasses, and tankards make up three further glass objects that might also be used. The numbers of trials and numbers of participants needed quickly become entirely unrealistic. The decisions by Warburton and Shepherd to take changes in any injury as a measure, and to accept the simple toughened/non toughened comparison are perfectly understandable, but the price paid in terms of the validity of findings for all toughened glass and for facial injuries cause by assaults is very high. If we refuse to pay that price the scale of what would be required becomes quite unrealistic.

Warburton and Shepherd's study, as a crime-related example of an RCT, is well-chosen in that the intervention is a very simple one – the use of one form of pint-sized nonic glasswear rather than another in bars. The problems in drawing any useful inferences from it for assault-related injuries should by now be clear. Some theory is needed about how and why it reduces crime-related harms (its mechanisms) and the conditions in which these mechanisms operate (its contexts). The evaluation needs to be designed to test or refine that theory. The tested theory can then be applied. The simple RCT that was undertaken, which looked for an association between all injuries (in practice mostly minor ones to the hand) across all bars, using only one type of glass (albeit the one most often used in assaults), leaves us little the wiser with its findings. This is not to say that we learn nothing from the study, nor is it to disparage a well-conducted piece of research. It is only to point out that what we learnt from it, alone, was rather limited.

Most other crime prevention interventions are much more diverse than the replacement of one type of pint glass with another in the expectation that when used as a weapon fewer disfiguring injuries will be produced. Take property marking, which as crime prevention interventions go, is still simple. The technologies are multifarious. They also change and hence what and how it can work will also change. There are and have been diverse marking methods and settings. Consider simple labels, Radio Frequency Identification (RFID) tags, dye tags, "Smartwater," "Alphadot," "Identi-dot," serial numbers, cattle branding, sheep ear-marking, etching, engraving, UV pens, stamps and car number plates as methods. Consider libraries, houses, shops, farms, and vehicles as immediate sites, and the nature of the wider localities in which these are found. This gives thirteen types of

Table 1: Property Marking Types and Settings

Method	Libraries	Houses	Shops	Farms	Vehicles
Labels	✓		✓		
RFID	✓		✓		
Dye-tags			✓		
Smartwater	✓	✓	✓		
Alphadot	✓	✓	✓	✓	✓
Identidot	✓	✓	✓	✓	✓
Serial numbers		✓	✓		✓
Cattle branding					✓
Ear marks					✓
Etching		✓	✓		✓
Engraving					✓
UV pens		✓			✓
Stamps	✓	✓			✓
Number plates					✓

property marking, and five types of site for it. Some types of property marking are site specific, such as ear-marking sheep on farms, but others can be used in different settings. Table 1 attempts to show what might be used in each setting. This suggests 33 possibilities. These sites could occur in different community settings. Suppose we restricted types of community setting to three: urban, sub-urban and rural, all of which are relevant to all types of marking and setting except for cattle-branding and sheep's ear-marks which we assume are restricted to rural areas. That gives up to 101 possibilities. Suppose we needed four trials for each. That would require 404 trials, in each of which multiple, independent non-communicating, long-term stable experimental and control sites would be needed (see Marchant, 2004). This, of course, underestimates the potential variability and hence volume of trials that would be required. Number plates, for example, are produced and applied in quite disparate conditions and have different designs, varying the ease with which they can be made, acquired, stolen or recognised (see http://www.designcouncil.org.uk/en/Case-Studies/All-Case-Studies/Anti-theft-number-plates/ – accessed August 2008).

Even if it were conceivable that this large number of trials were possible, how far would they take us in understanding property marking and deciding whether, where and how to use it? Unlike glasswear type replacement in bars, property marking, as with most other crime prevention interventions, aims mainly to alter the decisions made by offenders. This makes the processes involved in each application of property marking much more complex. A variety of mechanisms may be at work.

Property marking might increase the risk to offenders by making it more likely that they will be caught with stolen property, successfully prosecuted and punished. This in turn may mean:

1. More offenders are incapacitated (where offender decisions are not affected).
2. Some offenders are deterred from future crime.
3. And/or other prospective offenders are deterred as they come to appreciate what will happen to them if they try to commit the crime.

Alternatively (or in addition), the perceived increased risk of apprehension, regardless of the reality:

4. May lead (some) prospective offenders not to commit crime in the first place.

For property marking to "work" in relation to any individual offender in the first way,

a) Property that is liable to be stolen has to be marked;
b) Offenders have to fail to remove or disguise the marks;
c) Authorities have to check that property that might be stolen has property marks on it;
d) Police have to link the marked property back to those from whom it has been taken;
e) Those found with the stolen property have to be unable to cook up a plausible enough story about why they legitimately have it in their possession;
f) The prosecutor has to be persuaded that the case is worth taking to court;
g) The judge/jury have to be persuaded by the evidence;

h) A custodial sentence has to be passed; and

i) There have to be offences that the incarcerated person would otherwise be committing but for the fact that he or she is in prison.

For property marking to work in the second way, conditions “a” through “i” have to be in place, and,

j) The penalty has to be sufficiently salient that the offender makes decisions that do not lead to further offences or which lead to fewer offences.

For property marking to work in the third way, conditions “a” through “j” have to be in place, and,

k) Prospective offenders need to know, appreciate and sufficiently fear the penalties applied that they will make decisions not to commit offences that would otherwise commit.

For property marking to work in the fourth way, conditions “a” through “k” need not be in place, but,

l) Prospective offenders must know that property is (or may very likely) be marked;

m) Prospective offenders must be persuaded that the marking significantly increases their risks of being caught and penalised if they steal the marked goods; and

n) The expected penalties must be sufficient to lead them to decide not to commit the offences they would otherwise commit.

If a net fall in crime is to be produced by property marking, further conditions are needed:

o) The crimes prevented by any of the four means must not be substituted in terms of volume, value or severity, either by the same or substitute offenders; and/or

p) Offender uncertainty about the range of offences, goods and places where property marking has taken place leads them to avoid offences even where or in relation to goods not property marked.

Thus, what might work to bring about a crime drop through property marking depends on contextual contingencies. Though simple by the standards of most crime prevention measures, it would appear that property marking depends on complex processes if it is to produce preventive effects.

In what has become a classic study of property marking as a means of reducing domestic burglary, in practice Laycock (1985, 1992) found that although short-term falls were associated with its introduction in the three South Wales villages where her study was sited, these falls were not attributable to the property marking per se. There was no evidence of the expected means by which domestic burglary would be reduced, for instance, recovery of stolen property and convictions of those caught in its possession; losses of unmarkable goods (such as cash) fell as much as markable ones; and a second fall was found when publicity alone was given to the property marking when the results of the original study were published but no further measures had been put in place. Instead, Laycock argues that property marking activated preventive mechanisms (changed offender perceptions) in the specific implementation (high take-up and massive publicity) and place (relatively isolated communities with local offenders) contexts of the study, had generated a short-term fall in local levels of domestic burglary. So, for Laycock what had worked was not property marking as such but the preventive mechanisms it had managed to activate as it had been introduced in the (relatively isolated) circumstances of the South Wales villages.

Laycock cleverly works out what would be required for property marking to work in one way or another, and she traces the actual patterns to see whether they do or do not correspond to the theoretical requirements. This is very different from an RCT. Laycock's study addresses the fifth of the "what" questions shown at the start of this paper.

In practice, property marking is often introduced as one of a suite of measures within broader crime prevention initiatives. For instance it has been one of the components delivered in many versions of neighbourhood watch. Looking at complicated multi-component initiatives takes us to our fourth type of "what" question, that relating to strategy. Running trials for each type of property marking in each setting in each community type in each possible set of accompanying interventions would make the challenges of toughened and non-toughened glasswear in bars seem very simple indeed. Running trials of every permutation would clearly be impossible in practice even if it made sense methodologically.

General strategies, with complex causal and implementation chains, multiple components, and diverse sets of interests and interactions at work as the programme unfolds are not susceptible to RCTs. They are in need of theoretical reconstruction that can then be matched to practice, although the details of this lie beyond the scope of this paper (see Tilley, 2004). Much problem-oriented policing involves multi-component strategic work, albeit targeting a specific problem.

EMERGING MEDICAL MODELS OF EVALUATION

So far this paper has concentrated on the RCT as the received medical model for evaluation. The argument has been that it offers rather little. There are, however, developments challenging the dominance of the RCT, that may be rather more promising as models for evaluating policing and crime prevention, although researchers involved in assessing either type of program would freely admit that the use of RCT is often invaluable.

The first development relates to pharmacogenetics. The argument here is that RCTs have been helpful in estimating net effects where "block-buster" drugs are sought that will treat large numbers of patients with relatively common complaints. The RCT establishes whether net benefits across that population exceed the net costs of the treatment, even though some recipients of the treatment might not benefit. The field of pharmacogenetics focuses on individual differences. What leads one person to benefit but not another? The human genome promises something closer to boutique treatments attuned to the specific genetic constitution of differing sub-groups.

As Wolf et al. (2000, pp. 987-90) put it:

> Individual variation in response to drugs is a substantial clinical problem. Such variation ranges from failure to respond to a drug to adverse drug reactions and drug_drug interactions when several drugs are taken concomitantly. The clinical consequences range from patient discomfort through serious clinical illness to the occasional fatality. . . . (A) recent U.S. study estimated that 106,000 patients die and 2.2 million are injured each year by adverse reactions to prescribed drugs. . . .
>
> It is now clear that much individuality in drug response is inherited: this genetically determined variability in drug response defines the research area known as pharmacogenetics. . . .
>
> Our increasing knowledge of the mechanisms of drug action, the identification of new drug targets and the understanding of genetic factors that determine our response to drugs may allow us to design drugs that are specifically targeted towards particular populations or that avoid genetic variability in therapeutic response. The extent of genetic polymorphism in the human population indicates that pharmacogenetic variability will probably be an issue for most new drugs.

> The development of pharmacogenetics provides at least one mechanism for taking prescription away from its current empiricism and progressing towards more "individualised" drug treatment.

This comes close to the logic and methodology of problem-oriented policing and situational crime prevention. In both, the presenting setting for an identified problem is analyzed as a basis for working through promising solutions, which are rooted in theory about causal mechanisms and the conditions in which they are activated, to produce intended positive effects and avoid unintended negative ones. Outcomes feed back into improved theory. Evidence-based "individualized" treatments are provided. "Blockbuster" solutions are, of course, welcome if they can be devised. Immobilizers in cars comprise one recent example of what seems to have been a crime prevention blockbuster. Interestingly, though, even here a compelling evaluation by Brown (2004) worked out what pattern (or footprint) of changes in theft of vehicles would be required were the introduction of immobilizers to be having preventive effects and looked at the available data to check on this; he was unable to and did not need to conduct an RCT or anything like one.

The second development in health evaluation relates to complex changes in medical regime. The RCT had been especially well suited to seemingly simple, readily standardized treatments that were given to discrete individuals, such as the administration of a particular drug: the sort alluded to in the quotation just made from Wolf et al. Many health-related interventions are a good deal more complex. They may, for example, involve changing the patterns of care provided in the hospital or the community. Here, randomly allocated treatment and controlled units of analysis cannot be blinded to what is going on as easily as those taking part in drug trials, if they can be blinded at all. Non-treatment units may appropriate some or all of the intervention and thereby subvert the comparisons intended. Those who are skeptical within the treatment groups may not deliver it at all or deliver it in a half-hearted way. Determining what, for the purpose of the trial, shows adequate fidelity to the intended treatment may not be self-evident where treatment and non-treatment groups fall on a scale of compliance.

In the case of medical emergency teams for example, many of those complex processes involved in strategy development in crime prevention are at work compromising the possibility of RCTs and raising queries about their adequacy for producing valid evaluation findings (see Berwick, 2007).

In addition to these two relatively recent examples, it should be remembered that the history of health-related research evaluating practices and policies has not always involved RCTs. The evaluative research on the best ways of providing safe blood for transfusion purposes has used multiple methods. It began with Richard Titmuss's *The Gift Relationship* (Titmuss, 1970). This was a comparative study of the American and British ways of collecting blood in the late 1960s, that used a range of methods and data sources but no RCT. Titmuss drew on administrative data, reviews of existing research and he conducted a small scale "pilot" survey. His work was followed up by multiple studies using multiple methods in multiple disciplines, in the end suggesting quite significant modifications to Titmuss's original hypothesis that voluntarily given blood was consistently less contaminated than that which was paid for: mechanisms and contexts varied for the production of good and bad blood through payment and volunteering (Pawson and Tilley, 2001).

An even earlier example of significant non-RCT evaluation in health comes from one of the founding fathers of epidemiology: the Hungarian doctor, Ignaz Semmelweis. Semmelweis began with a natural experiment in his mid-nineteenth century evaluations of the significance of handwashing. A decree of 1839 had required that one maternity ward of the Vienna General Hospital be used for training midwives and the other for teaching medical students. Semmelweis noted the variations in levels of death from childbed fever in the two wards. The ward used for training midwives consistently had a substantially lower rate than the one used for medical students. Semmelweis assessed a range of hypotheses about the source of epidemics of childbed fever and in particular the variation in rates between the two wards at the hospital. Eventually, following the death of a colleague from symptoms akin to those caused by childbed fever after an autopsy where he had accidentally cut his finger, Semmelweis conjectured that it was the transmission of "cadaveric matter" from the autopsy to the women in the maternity ward that caused the childbed fever. This matter is evidently difficult to remove thoroughly and routine washing fails to do the trick, at least as measured by smell. Semmelweis instituted handwashing in a strong solution of chlorinated lime when doctors went from the mortuary to the maternity ward. The death rates in the two wards immediately equalised. Semmelweis went on to assemble large volumes of comparative epidemiological data that were consistent with his hypothesis. His colleagues did not believe his findings. He became extremely unpopular. He failed to secure a permanent position in Vienna and had to return to Hungary. He did not overturn the prevailing orthodoxy. This may in part have had to do with a very belligerent manner in which he did nothing to endear himself to those he was asking to follow him. It has been suggested, also, however, that he was not persuasive because he paid insufficient attention to the mechanisms through which "cadaveric matter" caused childbed fever (Nuland, 2003). He did not consider what it was about it that produced the symptoms and development of childbed fever. He did not therefore collect any evidence about this. It was not until Pasteur and Lister that germ theory developed, which specified more fully the mechanisms behind the patterns Semmelweis had identified and the effectiveness of the strong solution handwashing response he developed. Evidently had Semmelweis looked through a microscope all would have been revealed! So Semmelweis used a natural experiment and administrative data to test his initial hypothesis. This was later only found persuasive for practice when supplemented with tested theory specifying the mechanisms through which the disease developed. No RCTs were involved.

Looking at health for models that might usefully be drawn on in evaluations in situational crime prevention and problem-oriented policing is perfectly sensible. The RCT, however, is not the only show in town that is or has been worth watching and learning from.

CONCLUSION

Let us draw some threads together by returning to toughened and annealed glasswear in bars. What might comprise more useful evaluation research in relation to this than the RCT conducted by Warburton and Shepherd? I should stress that the issue is an enormously important one and Jonathan Shepherd, in particular, deserves great credit for his work in identifying the problem of facial injuries caused by the use of glasswear in assaults and in figuring out ways of reducing the harm. The critical sections in the early part of this paper are strictly of the methodology, not of the individuals. No lack of respect for them, the quality of their research, the problem identified or their contributions to applied research should be inferred. But it is clear that I do think that the RCT discussed earlier added very little to what had already been shown to be a powerful case for replacing those glasses that could be and evidently had been used in assaults to inflict serious facial injuries, with glasswear that is less liable to cause that injury.

This is no place to develop details of an alternative research design. However some general pointers are possible:

1. Qualitative research on bar life, in particular as it relates to injuries to bar workers and customers, would be a good starting point. This would involve participant and non-participant observations of what goes on in bars; informal interviews with customers, workers and managers; and discussions of the details of individual accidents and assaults. Such research could produce promising hypotheses about how and under what conditions incidents of the sort producing injuries of different types occur. The experienced publican's careless barworker hypothesis is a nice example from the Warburton and Shepherd study. Barry Poyner (1986) drew on partial descriptions of incidents to construct coherent "crime sets." Likewise assault and unintended injury-sets could be produced using partial descriptions, to develop models of the ways in which injuries are produced. Further qualitative research could also be conducted to refine the initial hypotheses. The most promising hypotheses might then be tested with any suitable quantitative data that are available.

2. A research review, to encompass not only formal evaluations but also other cognate qualitative and quantitative studies, for example of bar life, industrial accidents, and use of weapons in violent crime, could be undertaken. The purpose would be to distil from the literature promising hypotheses about how deliberate and accidental injuries are generated in different types of bar setting.

3. The very small-scale experiments to test the breaking point of glasses described in Warburton and Shepherd's paper seemed sensible. The field trial equivalent of this, drawing on the qualitative research, would be to simulate fights in bars to see what happens when glasses, or other objects such as bottles, are used as they generally are used in fights. Rather as in car crash tests, dummies might then be used to examine the extent of the injuries sustained by different types of weapon to hand in a bar, constructed using different materials.

4. Experiments simulating the behavior of bar workers as they handle glasses and are thought to incur hand injuries would be useful. Heat of water in washing up, use of mechanical devices to wash glasses, numbers of glasses carried, clearing up broken glasses, taking the glasses from their packaging, and lighting levels as glasses are picked up might all be examined using artificial limbs designed to show points of injury that would be sustained with glasses of differing kinds.

5. Warburton and Shepherd helpfully identify an expected prevalence rate for bar worker injury (in their case in estimating the required sample size to produce statistically significant variations in rates of injury from

different glass types). This might be used as a basis for a study examining variations in the ratio of actual to expected injury rates for bars having attributes that hypotheses suggest furnish more or less conducive conditions for generating intended and unintended harms from broken glass. Variations in glasswear in terms of type and age could be built into the equation.

6. Natural experiments might also be tried with newly established or refurbished bars, using variations in glass type, tracking forward rates of injury and contextual conditions and mechanisms that are expected to produce varying rates of injury depending on the type of glasswear used.

7. It might be possible to simulate expected variations in injury outcome of different kinds using glasswear of different kinds (in terms for example of numbers, times, trends, sites, and seriousness of incident) in computer models, manipulating what are conjectured through the findings of 1, 2 and 3 to be relevant contextual attributes of bars.

The purpose behind the research would be to devise and refine theories specifying what type of glass in what conditions generates what pattern of accidental and deliberately inflicted injuries to different parts of the body. For most practical purposes, enough could probably be learned through 1-4. What the reader should note is the wide range of qualitative, quantitative, social and physical science research techniques listed in 1-7. They can all help achieve the evaluation purpose.

Situational crime prevention and problem-oriented policing have indeed developed by using a wide range of research techniques to build a knowledge base for use in the specific circumstances of particular persistent problems as they are addressed or as new problems (for example suicide bombing or internet crime) emerge. Genuine RCTs, following the received medical model, have been rare. The diverse research methods used have served theory, policy and practice well. The use of varying forms of evaluation also accords with recent thinking in health evaluations as well as some influential evaluative work from the past.

There may sometimes be a role for RCTs in situational crime prevention and problem-oriented policing, but there is no reason to put them on a pedestal as the only or best method of obtaining evidence on what to do. They answer question types one and two of the list given at the start of this paper, but are not well-suited to the others, which are more important in informing practices within problem-oriented policing and situational crime prevention.

✦

Address correspondence to: Nick Tilley, Jill Dando Institute of Crime Science, University College London, Brook House, 2-16 Torrington Place, London WC1E 7HN; e-mail: NickJTilley@aol.com

Acknowledgments: This is a heavily revised version of a paper originally presented at the Stavern meeting where the papers collected in this volume were first discussed. I am grateful to those at the meeting for their comments and suggestions. I am also indebted to Johannes Knutsson and Gloria Laycock for reading through and correcting a later draft.

NOTES

1. The term "masking" is now sometimes used instead if "blinding."
2. This is much more demanding than Sherman's highest level of evaluation, which requires only "Random assignment and analysis of comparable units to program and comparison groups" (Sherman, 1997, pp. 2-10)

REFERENCES

Berwick, D. (2008). The science of improvement. *Journal of the American Medical Association*, *299*, 1182–1184.

Bratman, (2004). *Double-blind studies: A major scientific advance of the 20th century*. Retrieved March 13th 2008 from http://www.mendosa.com/bratman.htm

Brown, R. (2004). The effectiveness of electronic immobilisation: Changing patterns of temporary and permanent vehicle theft. In M. Maxfield & R. Clarke (Eds.), *Understanding and preventing car theft. Crime prevention studies*, Vol. 17. Monsey, NY: Criminal Justice Press.

Clarke, R., & Weisburd, D. (1994). Diffusion of crime control benefits: Observations on the reverse of displacement. In R. Clarke (Ed.), *Crime prevention studies*, Vol. 2. Monsey, NY: Criminal Justice Press.

Ekblom, P. (1997). Gearing up against crime: A dynamic framework to help designers keep up with the adaptive criminal in a changing world *International Journal of Risk, Security and Crime Prevention*, *2*, 249–265.

Farrington, D., & Petrosino, A. (2001). The Campbell Collaboration Crime and Justice Group. *Annals of the American Academy of Political and Social Science*, *578*, 35–49.

Laycock G. (1985). *Property marking: A deterrent to domestic burglary*? Crime Prevention Unit Paper 3. Home Office: London.

Laycock, G. (1992). Operation Identification or the power of publicity? In R. Clarke (Ed.), *Crime prevention: successful case studies*. Monsey, NY: Criminal Justice Press.

Laycock, G. (2003). *Launching crime science*. London: UCL Jill Dando Institute of Crime Science.

Marchant, P. (2004). A demonstration that the claim that brighter lighting reduces crime is unfounded *British Journal of Criminology, 44*, 441–444.

Nuland, S. (2003). *The doctors' plague: Germs, childbed fever and the strange story of Ignac Semmelweis*. New York: W.W. Norton.

Pawson, R. (2006). *Evidence-based policy*. London: Sage.

Pawson, R., & Tilley, N. (2001). Realist evaluation bloodlines. *American Journal of Evaluation, 21*, 317–324.

Petrosino, A., Boruch, R., Soydan, H., Duggan, L., & Sanchez-Meca, J. (2001). Ê Meeting the challenges of evidence-based policy: The Campbell Collaboration. *Annals of the American Academy of Political and Social Science, 578*, 14–34.

Poyner, B. (1986). A model for action. In K. Heal & G. Laycock (Eds.), *Situational crime prevention: From theory to practice*. London: HMSO.

Reppetto, T. (1976). Crime prevention and the displacement phenomenon. *Crime & Delinquency, 22*, 166–177.

Semmelweis, I. (1983). *Etiology, concept and prophylaxis of childbed fever*. Madison, WI: University of Wisconsin Press. (original work published 1861)

Shepherd, J. (2003). Explaining feast or famine in randomised field trials. *Evaluation Review, 27*, 290–315.

Shepherd, J., Huggett, R., & Kidner, G. (1993). Impact resistance of bar glasses. *Journal of Trauma, 35*, 936–938.

Sherman, L. (1997). Thinking about crime prevention. In L. Sherman, D. Gottfredson, D. MacKenzie, J. Eck, P. Reuter, & S. Bushway, *Preventing crime: What works, what doesn't, what's promising*. Washington, DC: U.S. Department of Justice, Office of Justice Programs.

Sherman, L. (1998). *Evidence-based policing*. Washington, DC: Police Foundation.

Smith, M., Clarke, R., & Pease, K. (2002). Anticipatory benefits in crime prevention. In N. Tilley (Ed.), *Analysis for crime prevention*. Crime prevention studies, Vol. 13. Monsey, NY and Cullompton, Devon, UK: Criminal Justice Press and Willan Publishing.

Tilley, N. (2004). Applying theory-driven evaluation to the British Crime Reduction Programme. *Criminal Justice, 4*, 255–276.

Titmuss, R. (1970). *The gift relationship*. London: Allen and Unwin.

Warburton, A., & Shepherd, J. (2000). Effectiveness of toughened glasswear in terms of reducing injury in bars: A randomised controlled trial. *Injury Prevention, 6*,, 36–40.

ESTIMATING AND EXTRAPOLATING CAUSAL EFFECTS FOR CRIME PREVENTION POLICY AND PROGRAM EVALUATION

by

Gary T. Henry
University of North Carolina, Chapel Hill

Abstract: *Central to achieving the potential of evaluation is the ability to estimate the impact of crime prevention policies and programs on crime and to extrapolate the findings to other settings. The potential outcomes framework presented in this paper is the most compelling theory of causality, but its implications for extrapolating results have not been fully considered. The paper demonstrates the importance of balancing treated and untreated study samples as well as the study population and the target population for accurately estimating effects, generalizing them to the study population, and extrapolating them to other target populations. Alternative methods for producing unbiased estimates of program effects and the implications for extrapolating the estimates to other target populations are discussed.*

INTRODUCTION

The full promise of evaluation is not in determining whether a social intervention is being carried out as it was intended, but in providing

Crime Prevention Studies, volume 24 (2009), pp. 147–173.

trustworthy evidence concerning whether socially desirable outcomes could be achieved through that intervention. At one level, the issue is to assess the effects of a social intervention in terms of socially desirable outcomes. This expectation for evaluation is no mean feat given the incredible complexity of assessing the outcomes of an intervention that is set in the midst of an ongoing set of deeply ingrained social interactions (Mark et al., 2000; Pawson and Tilley, 1997). Somewhat ironically, it is often asserted that the complexity of social settings requires an approach to assessing causes and effects, such as randomized control trials, that cuts through the complexity in an effort to confront confounds – which are factors other than the intervention that could affect the outcomes – even if the approach requires a degree of artificiality (Boruch et al., 2008).

But expectations for causal analysis in evaluation have been set higher still. Many, if not most, evaluators, evaluation sponsors and consumers of evaluation findings expect that evaluations should be capable of influencing subsequent actions, such as expanding an intervention in its original setting or adopting the intervention in another jurisdiction or setting. Some members of the evaluation and policymaking communities have acted as though strong causal inferences would ensure that replication of the intervention could be expected to produce similar outcomes. However, replication studies have shown that repeating interventions in other settings frequently does not produce similar results. For example, the replications of the Minneapolis Domestic Violence Experiment (Berk and Sherman, 1988) produced distinctly different patterns of results in other sites across the U.S. (Sherman et al., 1992; Berk et al., 1992; Pate and Hamilton, 1992). In this instance, extrapolating evaluation findings from Minneapolis into the future at the same or other sites would not have been a socially beneficial reaction. The original study found that arrest of the abusing spouse in a domestic violence situation was likely to reduce subsequent abuse, but the replication studies showed that immediate arrest either had no effect on subsequent abuse or increased subsequent abuse, particularly among unemployed abusers.

In short, for evaluation to reach its full potential we need causal methods that provide accurate assessments of cause-effect relationships and provide reliable expectations for the effects that can be expected in other settings where better outcomes are desired. For practicing evaluators, the ambitious objective to provide trustworthy and accurate evidence concerning causal effects of social interventions must be tempered with realistic ideas about what can be achieved in a single study or even in a carefully coordinated set of studies. Clearly, the decision to replicate the Minneapolis experiment in additional sites was a wise and cautious step in this process. But we must continually reexamine our methods and practices in an effort to draw nearer to realizing the full potential for evaluation in democratic societies.

Unfortunately, many practicing evaluators leap directly from the need to provide causal inferences to the exclusive use of evaluations that randomly assign units to treatment or control groups, which are referred to in a variety of ways, including randomized experiments or randomized control trials (RCT). It is true that RCTs are the preferred method for most evaluators conducting causal impact studies, but to understand their strengths it is important to understand the theory that supports their ability to produce unbiased estimates of the treatment effect(s). It is also important to understand the limitations of RCTs, which can be illustrated using the same theory. But perhaps more important is developing a comprehensive theory of causality and scientific inquiry. We need a theory that allows for a consideration of alternatives to RCTs, to be assessed alongside RCTs, in order to develop the strongest possible assortment of evaluation methods.

In this paper, I will attempt to describe the theory of causal analysis that has the broadest support within the community of social intervention evaluators interested in assessing causal claims. The theory can be made sufficiently general to cover both RCTs and alternative methods that may yield accurate evidence about the effects that can be expected from an intervention. My first objective is to lay out a theory of causality that has become the received standard against which causal claims are assessed. The theory is known as Rubin's causal model (RCM) because of the fundamental contributions that statistician Donald Rubin and several distinguished collaborators have made to its development (Rubin, 1974, 2005, 2006; Holland, 1986). It is extremely important to note at the outset that while Rubin's causal model provides a theoretical basis for the preference for random assignment studies and, therefore, the justification for random assignment studies, the model is more general and allows us to consider the issue of extrapolating findings in addition to estimating causal effects. In addition, it is being more widely recognized as a way to bridge the chasm between two alternative approaches to causal inference: random assignment studies (randomized control trials) and observational (non-experimental and quasi-experimental) studies.

In addition, as Rubin has shown (2005), the model provides: (1) a formal basis to make causal inferences from study designs other than random assignment studies; (2) guidance for addressing some of the common flaws that arise in many random assignment studies; (3) guidance about the reduction of bias in observational studies; (4) guidance for estimating causal effects for target populations that extend beyond the population from which the study samples were selected; and, (5) criteria against which evaluation findings can be assessed in an effort to be constantly self-critical in pursuit of accurate, trustworthy information for improving social conditions. But we should not get ahead of ourselves; first, we should better understand the central ideas that underlie Rubin's causal model.

THE RECEIVED THEORY OF CAUSALITY: RUBIN'S CAUSAL MODEL (RCM)

The theory of causality that dominates 21st century social science has been labeled by Holland (1986) as Rubin's causal model (Rubin, 1974, 2005, 2006). While substantial parts of the theory have been fairly well established for several years, it is often misunderstood and has been frequently updated and extended, as is the case with any theory that underlies a progressive research program (Lakatos, 1970), but its core remains intact.

We should at the outset take care to distinguish this approach to causality from: the Campbell and Stanley (1966) design-based approach to improving internal and external validity of social science research, the Cook and Campbell (1979) approach to ruling out plausible threats to validity, and the Shadish et al. (2001) approach to ruling out threats to generalizable causal inferences. The objectives of the approach of Campbell and his colleagues have been to: (1) establish that a causal relationship exists; (2) correctly label the cause and effect; and, (3) reduce the plausibility of reasons that the relationship should not be applied beyond the particular study or evaluation. The principal focus of the approaches is on the elements of design that can enhance or inhibit causal inferences. These approaches focus on the problems inherent in drawing causal inferences from specific designs. In the most recent development of the approach, Shadish et al. (2002) present an encyclopedic list of design problems for nearly every conceivable research design and provide guidance about the embellishments to commonly used designs that can strengthen the causal inferences drawn from each type of design. They often recommend design enhancements such as adding pre-test measures or cross-over designs (switching individuals from treatment to no treatment regimes during the course of a study) in an effort to eliminate alternative rival hypotheses such as pre-existing differences between individuals exposed to an intervention and those who were not. (For a more thorough critique of the approach of "ruling out threats to validity," see Reichardt, 2008). These approaches to causality have successfully guided design-based improvements in social science research and evaluation, but they are distinctly different from Rubin's causal model (RCM). The advice from the approaches developed by Campbell and his colleagues and RCM is similar on a majority of practical issues, such as the benefits of randomization. The approach taken by Campbell and his colleagues separates experiments, quasi-experiments, and non-experiments into distinct categories, while the formal grounding of RCM allows us to put randomized studies and observational studies into a common framework to assess their relative strengths and weaknesses.

RCM sets out a very specific objective: to assess the magnitude of the effect of an intervention, which is referred to as the treatment effect. This focus on the magnitude of an effect is especially appropriate for evaluation (Cook et al., 2008). Evaluation should inform subsequent decision making. Decisions about the adoption, expansion, continuation, or even identification of a promising intervention should be based on the amount of effect that can reasonably be expected in the future. It is the size of the effect that is of greatest importance in justifying the costs of expanding an existing policy or reforming it.

RCM has three key variables: (1) potential outcomes; (2) treatment or control condition; and (3) the switch or mechanism by which individuals are allocated to either treatment or control conditions. So we begin with the idea that each individual (or other unit) has the possibility of alternative outcomes (Y). Rubin (2005) and many others, including Fienburg (2007), have acknowledged the intellectual debt of this formulation to Neyman (1923), but have also shown that this perspective was not explicit in Fisher's formulation of the randomized experiment (1925).

The two potential outcomes of immediate interest for evaluation purposes are the outcome for an individual that could be observed after participation in an intervention (Y_T) and the outcome that could be observed for the same individual at the same time if no intervention or change in current practice had occurred (Y_C), which is referred to as the control condition.[1] This possibility of alternative outcomes is in fact intrinsic to the way we think about social interventions; that is, we believe that a successful intervention will result in better outcomes for participants and communities than would have occurred without their participation in the intervention.

For example, Petrosino et al. (2003) show that many persist in the belief that a juvenile awareness intervention that has been commonly labeled "Scared Straight" will reduce subsequent arrests among participating youth. These beliefs persist in spite of several studies that show that troubled adolescents will be more likely to commit a crime during the next year after participating in a "Scared Straight" intervention than the same adolescent would have if he had not been exposed to the intervention. The two potential outcomes in this case are arrest (Y=0) and no arrest (Y=1) for each troubled juvenile (*i*) in the target population during a period of time after the intervention has been conducted. We follow the convention where Y=1 indicates success and Y=0 indicates failure. We expect that a "Scared Straight" type intervention can affect the probability that juveniles are arrested after the intervention, although the expectations based on prior studies may differ from naïve beliefs. In this case, any individual in the target population has two potential outcomes, but only one of these potential outcomes can actually be observed for an individual youth during the same measurement period.

We will consider an evaluation such as one of "Scared Straight," in which we wish to contrast the difference in outcomes between being exposed to an intervention and exposure to an alternative state, which we will label "control" for convenience. The control condition could mean either experiencing the current social program or intervention, withholding any social services, or an alternative intervention to the one under consideration. In Figure 1, the four strata that define the four possible combinations of assignment to treatment/control and the two outcomes (arrest/no arrest) are presented as strata. For example, in strata one are those individuals who would succeed (no arrest) if exposed to treatment and would have failed after exposure to the control condition. These are the individuals for whom the intervention is successful and has benefited them. In Figure 1, we illustrate a target population in which 100 individuals experienced success or no arrest. For strata 2 and 3, the intervention has no effect. The individuals in strata 2 had the same potential outcome, success, whether they were exposed to the treatment or the control situation. Strata 3 contains individuals for whom both of their potential outcomes were arrest or failure, which also indicates that this group were unaffected by the intervention. Finally, in strata 4, we find the individuals for whom the treatment backfired. After exposure to treatment, they were arrested but after exposure to the control they succeeded in not being arrested. Strata 2, 3, and 4 have 50 members of the target population in each.

Figure 1. Potential Outcomes for the Four Groups in the Target Population.

	Strata	Target Population N	*Potential Outcomes (1=success; 0=failure or subsequent arrest)*		*Total Net Effects*
			Y_T	Y_C	
Target Population	1	100	1	0	100
	2	50	1	1	0
	3	50	0	0	0
	4	50	0	1	-50
	Totals	250	150	100	50

To formalize the example, we define an observation as the application of a measurement process to an individual (or unit) at a particular time. Our interest from an evaluation standpoint is in the measurement of an outcome (Y) on individual i after an intervention has occurred (Y_i). In this case, we use two outcomes, success and failure, but the situation could be expanded to include continuous outcomes as well. Rubin's causal model defines a treatment effect for an individual (ô*i*) as the difference between the value of an outcome after experiencing an intervention (Y_T) and the value of an outcome for the same individual i after not experiencing the intervention (Y_C):

(1) $$\tau = (Y_T - Y_C)$$

In Figure 1, we see that the treatment effect for each individual in strata 1 is 1, which is aggregated to 100 successes when all of the individuals in the strata are combined. Strata 2 and 3 do not contribute any net gains in successes. Strata 4 contribute 50 arrests or net failures (-50). After aggregating across strata, we see that 50 more successes occurred when exposed to the intervention than when exposed to the control. The mean difference in successes is .20 (150/250 –100/250). The ratio of success in treatment and control is 1.5 ((150/250)/(100/250)). In other terms, the odds ratio for success is 1.5 (.6/.4) for the potential outcomes after exposure to treatment and .667 (.4/.6) for the potential outcomes after exposure to the control condition. An alternative way to express the treatment effect is the ratio of these two numbers or 2.25.

This example makes explicit that this theory of causality rests on two fundamental premises. First, as we have stated above, each individual has two potential post-intervention values on the outcome variable (Y), one if the individual has experienced the intervention (Y_T) and one if the individual did not experience the intervention (Y_C). These may be the same or different. In other words, for some the treatment may not change their outcomes and for some the treatment may cause an undesirable outcome. To be specific, strata 1 and 4 are the strata of individuals for whom the treatment and control condition yield different outcomes, success and failure, respectively. As long as the percentage of the population in strata 1 is larger than the percentage of the population in strata 4, the treatment effect is a socially desirable outcome.

Second, while the theory rests on the possibility of two outcomes, only one outcome value could be actually observed in the same period after an intervention, either exposure to treatment or exposure to control. As Paul Holland states: "It is impossible to observe the value of [Y_T and Y_C] on the same unit [i], therefore it is impossible to observe the effect of [T on i]" (Holland, 1986, p. 947, with [ ] noting different symbols used for this presentation). For example, if we only observe the outcomes for individuals who are exposed to the treatment, individuals in strata 1 and strata 2 cannot be distinguished, and neither can the individuals in strata 3 and strata 4. The inability to directly observe causal forces is widely attributed to Hume's formulation of causality. Rubin's formulation provides a formal basis for specifying the assumptions needed to infer causality.

The term "potential outcomes" is a more precise alternative to the term "counterfactual" which has been used to describe the need to observe an outcome that is counter to fact in order to directly assess the effect of an intervention (Rubin, 2005). Counterfactual, while it could be regarded as a term of art, can have a meaning that is broader than the one required for the causal inference and can be nonsensical (e.g., the arrest of a seven-year-old adolescent). Therefore, we will use the "potential outcomes" language in place of the more commonly used term "counterfactual." In

Figure 1, the outcomes were recorded for purposes of clarifying the idea, but could not be observed in practice, of course.

The fundamental problem of observing the alternative potential outcomes for the same individual is overcome in Rubin's causal model by the notion of a switch (*S*) that determines whether a particular individual experiences the intervention or does not:

(2) For $S(i)=T$, then Y_T is observed

(3) For $S(i)=C$, then Y_C is observed.

A switch is the means by which individuals are allocated to either the treatment condition or the control condition. Common switches are self-selection into a program, administrative assignment to treatment, or randomization. The average treatment effect (ATE) can be converted from an impossible to calculate quantity in the first equation to a possible to estimate quantity:

(4)

$$\tau = E(Y_T - Y_C)$$

$$\tau = E(Y_T) - E(Y_C)$$

$$\tau = (Y_T) - (Y_C)$$

Where the ATE is represented by τ and the expected value of the difference between the potential outcomes summed across individuals in the study population is represented by $E(Y_T - Y_C)$ which is shown to be equivalent to the difference in means for the part of the study population exposed to the intervention and the unexposed but only if a specific assumption holds as we will explain now. The treatment effect ô in the last equation above is an unbiased estimate of the true treatment effect, if the switch (*S*) has assigned individuals to the intervention *T* or no intervention *C* independent of outcomes, that is:

(5) $$E(Y_i \mid S_i = 1) = E(Y_i \mid S_i = 0)$$

In more straightforward language, this means that the switch has operated such that the mean value of the outcome is expected to be the same for the group assigned to the intervention and the group that is not, in the absence of the intervention. A switch that achieves independence is random assignment or drawing two probability samples from the study population and assigning one sample to the intervention and one to the control status.

See Figure 2 for an illustration of the function of a switch which allows the assumption of independence. A virtue of random assignment is that it allows for estimates of the treatment effect with the fewest possible assumptions, although the following assumptions are required:

1) the treatment received by one subject does not affect the outcome of other subjects;
2) there are no hidden versions of treatment; and,
3) the same measurements would be observed whether or not the subjects know they are being studied (Rubin, 2005; Baker and Kramer, 2007).

With these assumptions accepted, random assignment studies can be said to yield unbiased estimates of the true treatment effect, asymptotically. Random assignment has converted the fundamental problem of causal inference to a problem of statistical inference by distributing the confounders or other factors that might affect outcomes equivalently across those assigned to treatment and those assigned to control. When the ideal conditions for implementation of the random assignment study can be assumed, the difference in outcomes between treatment and control are an unbiased estimate of the treatment effect.

In Figure 2, S represents the randomization switch, X the indicator variable for treatment (1) or control (0), and Y the outcome observed after the intervention has occurred. The solid lines indicate that the arrow

Figure 2. The Function of the Randomization Switch.

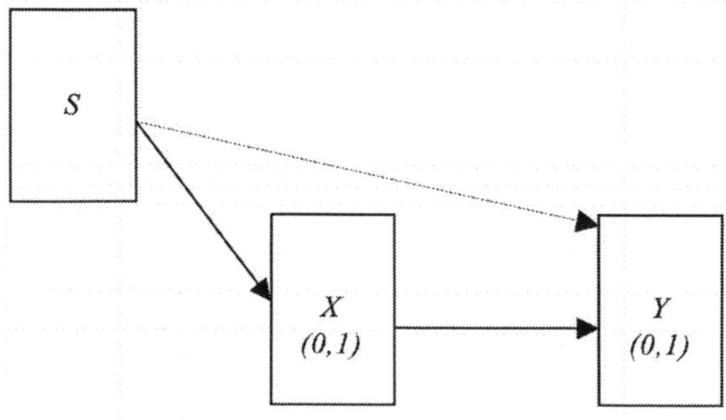

points in the direction of presumed effects. The dashed line between the switch and outcome indicates that there is no effect of the switch on the outcome, which is required to fulfill the assumption of independence.

In Figure 3, we depict the basic structure of the random assignment studies reviewed by Petrosino et al. (2003), in which random assignment is used as the switch for assigning juvenile offenders to either a Scared Straight intervention or control. The outcome of interest is either arrest or no arrest during the study period. In this case, the investigators randomly assigned juveniles to the intervention independently of outcomes. Independence is an assumption since it cannot be tested directly at the time of assignment. Quite often, independence is assumed to be a substitute for equivalence of the two groups, but even with randomization, chance variation occurs, which will make the two groups different. It is important to note that in the meta-analysis of "Scared Straight" type interventions, Petrosino et al. (2003) found that the failures (subsequently arrested juveniles) exceeded the successes, which in our illustrative Figure 1, would mean that strata 4 is larger than strata 1.

Figure 4 illustrates the importance of achieving balance between the treatment and control groups. For this example, the target population of 500 has been split evenly, with one-half in the treatment group and one-half in the control group. As the illustration makes clear, calculating the correct treatment effect depends on the correct balance of the strata in the treatment and control group. In this case, we define balance as having equal numbers in each stratum of the treatment and control groups. Variations in strata proportions, even chance variations, will bias the treatment effect.

Figure 3. Random Assignment to Scared Straight Intervention.

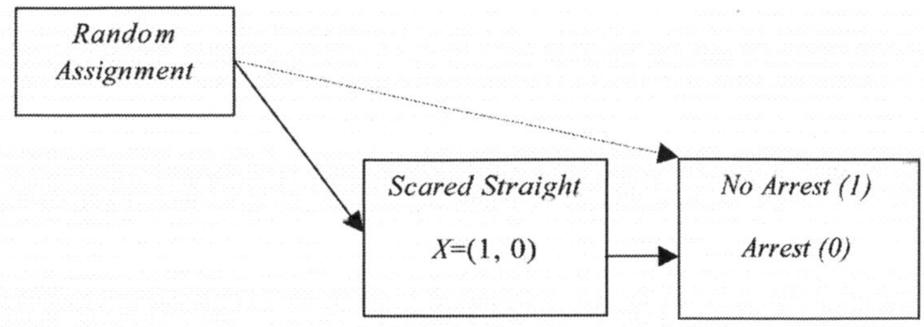

Figure 4. Equivalent Assignment of Four Strata of Target Population into Treatment and Control Groups.

	Strata	N	*Potential Outcomes*		*Observed outcomes*		
			Y_T	Y_C	X	Y_T	Y_C
Control Group	1	100	1	0	0	*	0
	2	50	1	1	0	*	1
	3	50	0	0	0	*	0
	4	50	0	1	0	*	1
Treatment Group	1	100	1	0	1	1	*
	2	50	1	1	1	1	*
	3	50	0	0	1	0	*
	4	50	0	1	1	0	*
	Observed Totals	500				150	100

We can see that the treatment group has 50 more successes than the control and the ratio of treatment successes to control successes in 1.5, as was the case with the previous illustrative example in Figure 1.

If the strata proportions are not balanced with respect to treatment and control, the treatment effect will not be accurate. Randomization will produce some chance deviations, which necessitates testing the hypothesis that any observed difference is due to chance. However, in practice the strata are unobserved. We can examine any difference in the means of treatment and control for variables that have been shown to relate to the outcome of interest as a test for observed equivalence in the two groups and use regression to adjust for any chance differences.[2] Independence does not assure equivalence of the intervention and control groups. Independence establishes that confounds are distributed across both groups or, said another way, departures from equivalence are a function of chance. As Rubin (1974) demonstrated, matching or balancing on observed covariates prior to randomization can improve equivalence in addition to achieving independence.

Thus, it is also difficult to imagine the justification for not using blocking in any random assignment study in which blocking is possible. However, it is not hard to imagine a randomized study in which blocking is not possible. For example, in the Minneapolis Domestic Violence Experiment (Berk and Sherman, 1988), officers responding to complaints about domestic violence randomized assignment to one of three alternative treatments, including: a) arrest of the abuser, b) requiring the abusing spouse to leave the premises, or c) providing advice or mediation. The investigators provided color-coded report notebooks to the officers in order to simplify the assignment to alternative treatments. It is difficult to imagine a scenario in which calls could have been placed into blocks prior to assignment to treatment that would have achieved substantial compliance.

The model used to estimate the treatment effect from an experiment provides a concrete indication about how the randomization switch functions. The treatment effect is estimated by subtracting the mean of the group exposed to the intervention from the mean of the group in the control and the confidence interval estimates the range of values in which the true mean is likely to fall for a specified degree of confidence, most commonly 95 out of 100 times. The analytical model that is used to estimate the effect of treatment is shown below, where X is the dichotomous indicator of assignment to the intervention ($XT = 1$; $XC = 0$).

(6) $$Y_i = \mu + \beta_i X_i + e_i$$

In this model, the switch (randomization) is assumed to be ignorable since independence assures that extraneous disturbing influences are distributed across both the treatment and the control based on chance alone and the effects of these influences reside in the error term, making $\beta 1$ an unbiased estimate of the unobservable treatment effect. However, as Rubin has counseled, when we know something about the causes of the outcome other than treatment, it is important to adjust for them (2005).

Up to this point we have concentrated on how a randomized controls trial can lead to unbiased estimates of the treatment effect. The reason that the theory is more important than this is that it provides a bridge to causal inferences from observational studies. In addition, we can use our elements of Rubin's theory of causality to set up the second important issue concerning evaluation: extrapolating from the past in a specific setting or settings to the future in the same setting with a target population that may differ or other settings.

Causal Effect Estimates from Observational Studies

In their review of matched sampling for observational studies, Cochran and Rubin (1973) list six justifications for conducting observational studies:

1) If random assignment cannot be conducted for political or ethical reasons.

2) If random assignment study is too expensive and/or results will not be available for years.

3) If units in observational study can be "more representative" of the target population because of the restricted environments in which random assignment studies can be conducted.

4) If ascertaining which treatments should be the focus of future randomized experiments.

5) Because many random assignment studies are more like observational studies where there are broken protocols (violation of assignment, attrition, missing data, etc.).

6) Because many important questions in random assignment studies are observational.

Fortunately, the theoretical framework that Rubin has established provides a basis for describing and assessing observational study methods such as regression discontinuity, matched sample designs, and instrumental variables.

The switch for regression discontinuity designs is a quantitative variable on which a cut-off value is established such that the individuals on one side of the cut-off are assigned to treatment and those on the other side are assigned to the control condition. The design is considered a sharp regression discontinuity design when no exceptions to the assignment rule are observed. While the switch clearly results in a treatment and control group, the switch is likely to be correlated with the outcome, which in most cases would produce biased estimates of the treatment effect. However, the assignment variable is perfectly correlated with the assignment to treatment. By including the assignment variable in a regression equation to estimate the treatment effect, the correlation of the error and the assignment variable eliminates the bias in the estimate of the treatment effect (coefficient of the treatment indicator variable) by eliminating the correlation of the treatment indicator with the error term. However, the correct specification of the functional form of the relationship between the assignment variable (switch) and the outcome is needed to ensure unbiased estimates (van der Klaauw, 2002, p. 1259). To achieve correct specification, the analytical model generally includes squared and cubic terms for the assignment variable (Trochim et al., 1991).

While criminologists such as Minor et al. (1990) have long been aware of the potential for applying regression discontinuity approaches to evaluation of criminal justice interventions, apparently the design has been rarely used. It seems that assignment to treatment on the basis of risk or need could be used in evaluations of crime prevention evaluation, perhaps more persuasively than random assignment, which raises questions about why the design has not been employed in such studies. In other fields such as education it has been used frequently. For example, in a study of supplemental funding for districts with high levels of educational disadvantage, Henry et al. (2008) used the sharp discontinuity created by the cut-off in funding on an index of educational disadvantage to estimate the effect of the intervention. They found that the test scores of high school students in the 16 districts that received the funding was 1.5 points higher than those of high school students in other districts when controlling for the assignment variable and its polynomial functions and other student characteristics and school compositional variables. This estimate of the effect is unbiased by selection into treatment.

Other designs, including matching using propensity scores (Rosenbaum and Rubin, 1983) and instrumental variables (Reiss, 2003), have been described and assessed using the framework established by RCM. A propensity score matching method balances the treated and control groups in observational studies by pair matching on the conditional probability of being selected into treatment and, in situations in which assignment to treatment is strongly ignorable, the estimates of treatment effects are unbiased (Rosenbaum and Rubin, 1983). Assignment to treatment is strongly ignorable when the observed covariates are sufficient to consider assignment to treatment independent given the covariates. When the covariates include the variables that define membership into the strata, that is the strata depicted in the illustrative example presented in Figure 1 and resulting in equivalent treatment and control groups as shown in Figure 2, the balancing from propensity score matching can produce unbiased estimates of the treatment effect. However, the possibility that other variables that relate to the strata are not included in the observed covariates leaves the possibility that bias distorts the estimates.

For instrumental variables, the identifying instrument is the switch which is used to "break up" the correlation between the treatment variable and the error term in the analytical model, thereby rendering the estimate of the treatment effect unbiased if the instruments perform well (Reiss, 2003). When the instrument performs well, the effects of assignment to treatment are completely mediated by the use of an instrument, but the performance of the instrument is largely untestable. Randomization has the fewest untestable assumptions of these different switches reducing the possibility of bias to chance. But since any particular evaluation is only likely to have one of the nearly infinite possible chance allocations to treatment and control conditions, the possibility of inaccurate treatment effect estimates remains. Further, if the necessity of volunteering for a randomized experiment and those who do not choose to volunteer creates an imbalance between the four exhaustive potential outcomes strata (Figure 1) in the study population and the target population, the treatment effects may not accurately be extrapolated to the population from which the volunteers were recruited.

In a very promising development in research synthesis, these alternative methods for estimating treatment effects are being systematically assessed. In the first generation of assessments, estimates of the differences in standardized treatment effect sizes were assessed for their relationship to study design (Lipsey and Wilson, 1992; Petrosino et al., 2003). Results were mixed, but the study populations in this first generation of studies were so limited that other sources of extraneous variation were not well controlled. In a second generation of these syntheses, Glazerman et al. (2003) compared matched pairs of estimates of treatment effects in which the estimate from a randomized experiment is subtracted from the estimate from an approach that simulates an observational study but uses the same treatment group as the RCT (also see Cook, Shadish, and Wong (2008). Their matched pairs design overcomes a limitation of earlier studies that compare estimates from unrelated RCT and observational studies. While an improvement, the authors' assumption that the experimental studies are unbiased seems to be a stretch given the messiness of real world conditions such as differential attrition between treatment and control groups. However, their approach is clearly a step in the right direction.

Glazerman et al. (2003) find that bias is significantly reduced when regression adjustments and matching are used to estimate treatment effects. Further they show that some regression adjustments (those that meet an equivalence specification test that the treatment effect estimate on pretest data is not statistically significant) and some matching techniques (such as one-to-one matching with an extensive set of covariates) are better at approximating results from a randomized experiment than others. This work goes further than hand wringing over the differences between experimental and observational studies to provide some concrete guidance for the refinement of these approaches which have promising theoretical properties but are known to be flawed in at least some specific applications. However, most of the debates on causal methods to date do not tackle the issue associated with extrapolation to the target population for subsequent policy decisions.

EXTRAPOLATING CAUSAL ESTIMATES

An evaluation task (or in some cases, a task for policy analysis) can include the extrapolation of the effects found in a study to the target population of interest. The target population may be those unaffected by the current intervention, including individuals in other settings, individuals who could receive the intervention in the future, or those who would be served as a result of program expansion. In reviewing Cochran's contributions to observation study methods, Rubin (1984) makes clear that evaluators should, at a minimum, consider adjusting the estimates of treatment effect to accurately assess the likely effects of an intervention on the target population.

To understand why this is important, the previous example has been extended further. First, we must add some additional notation to our perspective on potential outcomes: Y_{obs} includes the observed Y_{T} and Y_{C} for the treatment and control group respectively; and Y_{mis} includes three types of unobserved potential outcomes: unobserved outcome Y_{misC} that corresponds to the observed Y_{T} for the treatment group; Y_{misT} for control in which Y_{C} is the possible outcome that was actually observed; and $Y_{\text{mis*}}$ for members of the target population that were not observed at all. Again by recourse to the assumption of independence, we can understand that

$\beta 1$ in the analytical model for randomized experiments presented above is an unbiased estimate of the unobservable treatment effect for the target population, if:

$$(7) \qquad E(Y_i \mid Y_{misc^*}) = E(Y_i \mid Y_{obs}, S_i = 1) = E(Y_i \mid Y_{obs}, S_i = O)$$

This equation indicates that the expected value of the outcome of interest for the unobserved individuals in the study population is equal to the expected value of the outcome for the individuals whose outcomes are observed as a part of the study either as the treatment or control group. In other words, the means for these three groups should differ only by chancc. For illustrative purposes, in Figure 5 I provide a more extensive data matrix that represents the theoretical and observed situations in Figure 1 and 4. The matrix corresponds to the studies which are reviewed by Petrosino et al. (2003) or the domestic violence experiment in which a dichotomous variable, arrest, is the outcome of interest (no arrest = success). The matrix includes the same four strata, but expands from treatment and control to three groups: control, treatment, and the unobserved sample from which the two samples that characterize treatment and control have been drawn. Furthermore, I assume that the three groups constitute the target population and each group is a random sample of the population. It follows that equivalence between the three samples in terms of the proportionality of each of the four strata is only distorted by chance variation.

The change in the probability of success after exposure to the intervention is .20. We may be interested in the ratios of successful outcomes as well. Using the target population's potential outcomes, the ratio of arrest from the treatment compared to the control is 1.5 (60/40) which is equal to the ratio of arrest comparing the treatment sample arrests to the control sample arrests in the study (15/10).

This formulation allows us to consider the problem of extrapolation as a missing data problem. When data are missing completely at random, for example, when the treatment and control groups are random samples of the target population, the sample estimate of the treatment effect can be extrapolated to the target population. However, when the target population percentages of the strata deviate from the treatment and control sample percentages, the estimates will be biased. This simple example shows the sensitivity to the density function for the strata, in particular strata 1 and 4 in which the outcomes differ depending on the assignment to treatment

Figure 5. Equivalent Assignment of Four Strata Groups to Treatment and Control from Target Population.

	Strata	Target Population	*Potential Outcomes*		*Observed outcomes*		
			Y_T	Y_C	X	Y_T	Y_C
Control Group	1	10	1	0	0	*	0
	2	5	1	1	0	*	1
	3	5	0	0	0	*	0
	4	5	0	1	0	*	1
Treatment Group	1	10	1	0	1	1	*
	2	5	1	1	1	1	*
	3	5	0	0	1	0	*
	4	5	0	1	1	0	*
Unobserved Sample	1	20	1	0	*	*	*
	2	10	1	1	*	*	*
	3	10	0	0	*	*	*
	4	10	0	1	*	*	*

or control. The effect size estimates will be biased if the proportions of the treatment and control groups in strata 1 and 4 are not equivalent in these samples and are not correctly adjusted by imputation or covariate analysis. However, most evaluations that use randomized designs routinely violate this assumption, a near necessity given that in most situations participants must volunteer for the study with full knowledge that they may be assigned to either treatment or control. In addition, individual study site samples often depart from the target population percentages of the four strata.

The Minneapolis Domestic Violence Experiment (Berk and Sherman, 1988) and its replications in other sites across the U.S. (Sherman et al., 1992; Berk et al., 1992; Pate and Hamilton, 1992) may be used to illustrate the problems of extrapolation. In this case, the original randomized experiment, which was assiduously although imperfectly carried out, indicated that arrest reduced post-intervention offences relative to advice or temporary removal of the abusing spouse (the magnitude of the effect varies depending on the assumptions about assignment to treatment or receiving treatment as the appropriate way to estimate the treatment effects). In contrast to the original study in Minneapolis, which found a deterrent effect for arrest, the replication studies' findings were summed up by four of the investigators as follows:

> Replications in Omaha, Charlotte, and Milwaukee found no evidence for a long-term deterrent effect of arrest on recidivism. Instead, they found significant long-term *increases* in subsequent incidents (Dunford, Huizinga, and Elliott 1990; Dunford forthcoming; Hirschel et al. 1990; Sherman et al. 1992). However, the Colorado Springs and Dade County replications found evidence of long-term deterrent effects, . . . (Berk et al., 1992; Pate et al., 1991). (Sherman et al., 1992, p. 680)

In Sherman et al. (1992), the unemployed were twice as likely to commit a subsequent assault if arrested, and the employed were half as likely to commit a subsequent assault when arrested (p. 695), further muddying the picture and making the policy advice intractable. For example, it seems to violate the principle of fairness to arrest employed spouse abusers and let unemployed spouse abusers remain free.

While there is no certainty about why the results were mixed across these multiple randomized experiments, it is possible that the variations of percentages of the site study population comparable to strata 1 and 4 in Figure 5 caused the differences. That is, those whose potential outcomes were different if assigned to treatment or control were more common in some sites than others. However, since the strata membership cannot be recovered from the actual outcomes, although post hoc (and biased [Berk et al., 1992, p. 699]) analysis indicated that it was related to employment, we cannot be certain about the differences in the distributions of strata membership. It is clear that extrapolating the findings from the multiple studies without knowledge of the proportional distributions to the two critical strata in the treatment group, the control group and the target population is based on one of two questionable assumptions: (1) equivalence of the study population and the target population or (2) uniform effect for members of the study population and target population.

Of course, there are approximations that could yield more accurate extrapolations of treatment effects with assumptions that may be less questionable. One method Rubin (2006, p. 21) discusses is the Belden-Peters estimator, in which an outcome *Y* is regressed on covariates in the target population. Then the predicted value of *Y* is estimated for the individuals in the treatment group using the estimated coefficients from the regression. Finally, the treatment effect is estimated subtracting the value of the predicted value of the individuals in the treatment group from their actual scores. Adjustment methods may be developed that incorporate other approaches, for instance multiple imputation of missing data. It is important to incorporate adjustments using variables that have been shown to systematically relate to the outcome of interest even if the prior studies are not causal. This can improve the balance between the strata in the study groups and the target population when estimating and extrapolating treatment effects.

In addition, even a cursory analysis of Figure 5 raises another possibility. It may be the case that studies of a probability sample of the population that draw from the four strata with an equal probability may be less biased in terms of the extrapolated estimates for the target population of interest than a RCT which depends on a highly stylized sample, for example, volunteers for the study in organizations or jurisdictions that volunteer to be a site for the RCT. More empirical investigation will need to be done to assess the extent of bias. But the illustration should motivate more critical consideration of any attempt to directly apply the estimates from RCTs on an ill-defined population to a target population of interest. As Rubin previously demonstrated (1974), there are times when a matched sample study could be preferred to a RCT because the former would yield closer equivalence than might be produced when left to chance through random draws. I raise the possibility that bias may be reduced through careful observational studies to suggest that the rich and fertile development of causal evaluation is still in process and the research program can and should continue to progress.

CONCLUSIONS: A RATIONALE FOR COMBINING STATISTICAL AND SUBSTANTIVE KNOWLEDGE

Evaluation of the effectiveness of social interventions encounters two formidable expectations: estimating the effect of an intervention and extrapolating the effects to a target population for the intervention. In this paper, the basic elements of the theory of causality that prevails in the scientific evaluations of program effects have been presented and related to meeting both of these expectations. We have indicated that randomized experiments are particularly effective at minimizing the assumptions needed for causal inference because they distribute "extraneous" sources of variation in the outcome of interest across the treatment and control groups and reduce the effects of confounds to the error term.

A payoff from attending to this theory is that it helps to pinpoint the nature of problems that arise from violations of the assumptions in field settings, define problems that arise, guide evaluators to potential solutions, and suggest tests for the adequacy of the solutions that can be attempted. The implications of this theory have been used to energize a progressive research program in the methods for policy and program evaluation. The point of departure for this research lies in the fundamental problem for causal inference: the ideal comparison to determine the effects of an intervention is not possible. The oft-used description of "gold standard" notwithstanding, a random assignment study is not the "ideal," but it is the best available in terms of making the fewest assumptions. However, for the estimates of treatment effects to be directly extrapolated to a target population, evaluators must be reasonably able to assume that expectations for equivalence that are expected from the assumption of independence are actually obtained *and* that the proportion of individuals for which potential outcomes under assignment to treatment differ from those under assignment to control is the same in the treatment group, the control group, and the target population.

An extremely constructive outgrowth from this theory is research on alternative approaches for effect size estimation. Alternative switches have been proposed which, when combined with appropriate analytical models (and additional assumptions), can produce arguably unbiased treatment effects, at least from a theoretical standpoint. Regression discontinuity designs, in which assignment to treatment is strictly based on a continuous variable, can be used for unbiased estimates of effects. When proper specification of the assignment variable is included in the model, the presence of a sharp regression discontinuity along the assignment variable removes the correlation between the dichotomous assignment to treatment (*X*) and residual error, thereby neutralizing selection bias. Instrumental variable designs in which a variable (S) is correlated with the treatment variable but is not directly correlated to the outcome, except through variables that are measured and included in the analytical model, can yield unbiased estimates of the effect of the intervention (see Reiss, 2003). However, instrumental variable estimates have not fared well in terms of reducing bias in at least one empirical study in which they appear to increase bias (Glazerman et al., 2003). Propensity score matching is another promising approach to reducing the bias in treatment effect estimates. The large number of studies that use propensity score matching and attempt to assess the differences that arise from employing different approaches to matching is evidence of the productivity of this research program (Rubin, 2005). We are at the beginning of the empirical efforts to understand how propensity score matching should be carried out to minimize bias and how to comparatively assess estimation bias and extrapolation bias.

One such empirical study provokes us to think seriously about substantive knowledge in evaluation (Glazerman et al., 2003), which Rubin himself has persistently encouraged (1974, 2005). These authors find that an extensive set of covariates can reduce the bias that exists between propensity score matched estimates of treatment effects and estimates generated from large scale randomized experiments. In most of the research on evaluation methods, covariates are rather abstractly mentioned. Even in the Glazerman et al. study, the best that it was possible to do was to distinguish the quantity of covariates. However, their findings suggest that substantive knowledge of the extraneous sources of variation or confounds affecting the outcomes can improve our quest for more accurate information for policy decisions. This leads us to an irony noted by Reiss (2003) in the context of inferring cause from observational data:

> . . . the whole approach would be ineffective unless background assumptions (in addition to the general assumptions) are made. (p. 12)

He points out the one approach for estimating causal effects, instrumental variable analysis, requires the identification of a switch based on causal background knowledge. This implies that improving causal inference rests on evidence that would not necessarily meet the tests of causality that RCM specifies, in other words, systematic, carefully constructed correlational assessments of the variables influencing the outcomes. The same may be true in the selection of covariates for inclusion in propensity score matching procedures. Better covariates may lead to less bias. From this we can begin to see the importance of realist approaches to causality (Pawson and Tilley, 1997) and the development of substantive knowledge about the outcomes of interest. We can also see that gathering evidence linking changes in interventions to changes in outcomes in real time can inform more widespread adaptations of policies and procedures on an ongoing, routine and systematic basis (Sherman, 2003). This approach is illustrated in the applications of evidence-based approaches to crime reduction (Bullock et al., 2006). Rubin's causal model directs our attention to issues of bias in the study of the effects of specific causes (an intervention). The realist and pragmatic approaches incorporating evidence in day-to-day decision making about interventions can help to enumerate and gauge the potential causes of specific effects. The former starts with the cause and assesses the effect; the latter starts with an effect and assesses possible causes. It seems that progress in research on methods for estimating causal effects will depend, in part, on progress in the science pertaining to identification of factors that systematically affect the outcomes of interest as well as those that moderate the effects. If we can include these causal variables extraneous to the intervention being evaluated and the moderators of effects as covariates or blocking variables, we are likely to increase balance between the strata from our illustrations and thereby improve the estimates and extrapolations that are produced from evaluations.

Address correspondence to: Gary T. Henry, Carolina Institute of Public Policy, CB 3435, University of North Carolina at Chapel Hill, Chapel Hill, NC 27599-3435; e-mail: gthenry@unc.edu

NOTES

1. I will primarily use the term intervention to indicate the social policy, program, or treatment, but the words can be interchanged without significant harm to the argument. I choose the term intervention for this manuscript because a social program, whether operated by a government agency or non-governmental organization, intervenes in an ongo-

ing social situation with the publicly stated intent to make the existing conditions better.

2. Glazerman, Levy & Myers (2003) show that using a specification test to find a regression equation that produces statistically insignificant difference between treatment and control groups on pretest scores can significantly reduce bias in the estimate of the treatment effect.

REFERENCES

Baker S. G., & Kramer, B. S. (2007). Randomized trials for the real world: Making as few and as reasonable assumptions as possible. *Statistical Methods in Medical Research*, *1*, 1–10.

Berk, R. A., & Sherman, L. W. (1988). Police responses to family violence incidents: An analysis of an experimental design with incomplete randomization. *Journal of the American Statistical Association*, *83*(401), 70–76.

Berk, R. A., Campbell, A., Klap, R., & Western, B. (1992). The deterrent effect of arrest in incidents of domestic violence: A Bayesian analysis of four field experiments. *American Sociological Review*, *57*, 698–708.

Bullock, K., Erol, R., & Tilley, N. (2006). *Problem-oriented policing and partnerships*. Portland, OR: Willan Publishing.

Campbell, D. T., & Stanley, J. C. (1966). *Experimental and quasi-experimental designs for research*. Chicago: Rand McNally.

Cochran, W.G. & Rubin, D.B. (1973). Controlling bias in observational studies: A review. *Sankkya*, A, *35*, 417–466.

Cook, T. D., & Campbell, D. T. (1979). *Quasi-experimentation: Design and analysis issues for field studies*. Boston: Houghton Mifflin.

Cook, T. D., Shadish, W. S., & Wong, V. C. (2008). Three conditions under which experiments and observational studies often produce comparable causal estimates: New findings from within-study comparisons. *Journal of Policy Analysis and Management*, *27*, 724–750.

Dunford, F. W. (1992). "The Measurement of Recidivism in Cases of Spouse Assault." *Journal of Criminal Law and Criminology*, *83*(1), 120–136.

Dunford, F. W., Huizinga, D., & Elliott, D. S. (1990). The role of arrest in domestic assault: The Omaha experiment. *Criminology*, *28*, 183–206.

Fienburg, S. E. (2007). Comment: Complex causal questions require careful model formulation: Discussion of Rubin on experiments with "censoring" due to death. *Statistical Science*, *21*, 317–318.

Fisher, R. A. (1925). *Statistical methods for research workers*. Oliver & Boyd, London.

Glazerman, S., Levy, D. M., & Myers, D. (2003). Nonexperimental versus experimental estimates of earnings impacts. *Annals of the American Academy of Political and Social Science*, *589*, Misleading Evidence and Evidence-Led Policy: Making Social Science More Experimental, 63–93.

Henry, G. T., Thompson, C. L., Rickman, D. K., Fortner, C. K., et al. (2008). *Improving teacher quality in the DSSF pilot districts: A comparison of progress from*

2004-05 to 2005-06. Chapel Hill, NC: Carolina Institute for Public Policy, University of North Carolina at Chapel Hill.

Hirschel, J. D., Hutchison, I. W. III, Dean, C. W., Kelley, J. J., & Pesackis, C.E. (1990). *Charlotte Spouse Assault Replication Project: Final report*. Grant No. 87-IJ-CK-K004. Washington, DC: National Institute of Justice.

Holland, P. W. (1986). Statistics and causal inference, *Journal of the American Statistical Association, 81*, 945–970.

Lakatos, I., & Musgrave, A. (Eds.). (1970). *Criticism and the growth of knowledge*. Cambridge: Cambridge University Press.

Lipsey, M. W., & Wilson, D. B. (1998). Effective intervention for serious juvenile offenders: A synthesis of research. In R. Loeber & D. Farrington (Eds.), *Serious and violent juvenile offenders: Risk factors and successful interventions*. Thousand Oaks, CA: Sage.

Lipsey, M. W., & Wilson, D. B. (1993). The efficacy of psychological, educational, and behavioral treatment: Confirmation from meta-analysis. *American Psychologist, 48*, 1181–1209.

Mark, M. M., Henry, G. T., & Julnes, G. (2000). *Evaluation: An integrated framework for understanding, guiding, and improving policies and programs*. San Francisco, CA: Jossey-Bass.

Minor, K. I., Hartmann, D. J., & Davis, S. F. (1990). Preserving internal validity in correctional evaluation research: The biased assignment design as an alternative to randomized design. *Journal of Contemporary Criminal Justice, 6*, 216–225.

Neyman, J. (1923). Sur les applications de la théorie des probabilités aux experiences agricoles: Essai des principes. Roczniki Nauk Rolniczych 10 pp. 1–51, D. M. Dabrowska, & T. P. Speed (trans.). (1990). *Statistical Science, 5*, 465–480 (with discussion).

Pate, A., Hamilton, E. E., & Annan, S. (1991). *Metro-Dade Spouse Abuse Replication Project: Draft final report*. Washington, DC: National Institute of Justice. Unpublished manuscript.

Pawson, R., & Tilley, N. (1997). *Realistic evaluation*. Thousand Oaks, CA: Sage.

Petrosino, A., Turpin-Petrosino, C., & Buehler, J. (2003). Scared Straight and other juvenile awareness programs for preventing juvenile delinquency: A systematic review of the randomized experimental evidence. *Annals of the American Academy of Political and Social Science*, Misleading Evidence and Evidence-Led Policy: Making Social Science More Experimental, *589*, 41–62.

Pate, A. M., & Hamilton, E. E. (1992). Formal and informal deterrents to domestic violence: The Dade County spouse assault experiment. *American Sociological Review, 57*, 691–697.

Reiss, J. (2003, October). Practice ahead of theory: Instrumental variables, natural experiments and inductivism in econometrics. *Causality: Metaphysics and methods technical reports* CTR 12/03, CPNSS, LSE.

Reichardt, C. S. (2008, November). *A critique of the Campbellian conception of validity*. Presentation at the American Evaluation Association annual meeting, Denver, CO.

Rosenbaum, P. R., & Rubin, D. B. (1983). The central role of the propensity score in observational studies for causal effects. *Biometrica, 70*, 41–55.

Rubin, D. B. (1974). Estimating causal effects of treatments in randomized and nonrandomized studies. *Journal of Education Psychology*, *66*, 688–701.

Rubin, D. B. (1984). William G. Cochran's contributions to the design, analysis, and evaluation of observational studies. In W. G. Cochran, S. R. S. Rao Poduri & J. Sedransk (Eds.), *W. G. Cochran's impact on statistics*. New York: Wiley.

Rubin, D. B. (2005). Causal inference using potential outcomes: Design, modeling, decisions. *Journal of the American Statistical Association*, *100*, 322–331.

Rubin, D. B. (2006). *Matched sampling for causal effects*. Cambridge: Cambridge University Press.

Shadish, W. R., Cook, T. D., & Campbell, D. T. (2001). *Experimental and quasi-experimental designs for generalized causal inference*. Boston: Houghton-Mifflin.

Sherman, L. W. (2003). Experimental evidence and governmental administration. *Annals of the American Academy of Political and Social Science*, Misleading Evidence and Evidence-Led Policy: Making Social Science More Experimental, *589*, 226–233

Sherman, L. W., Smith, D. A., Schmidt, J. D., & Rogan, D. P. (1992). Crime, punishment, and stake in conformity: Legal and informal control of domestic violence. *American Sociological Review*, *57*, 680–690.

Trochim, W. M. K., Cappelleri, J. C., & Reichardt, C. S. (1991). Random measurement error does not bias the treatment effect estimate in the regression-discontinuity design II. When an interaction effect is present. *Evaluation Review*, *15*, 571–604.

van der Klaauw, W. (2002). Estimating the effect of financial aid offers on college enrollment: A regression–discontinuity approach. *International Economic Review*, *43*, 1249–1287.

POTENTIAL USES OF COMPUTATIONAL METHODS IN THE EVALUATION OF CRIME REDUCTION ACTIVITY

by

Shane D. Johnson
University College London

Abstract: *According to Moore's law, increases in computing power are roughly exponential over time. As a consequence, the application of computational methods to old and new problems becomes ever more possible, even with desktop computing. Such methods, and in particular computer simulation, have considerable potential in the study of crime but their application is relatively novel at this time. Consequently, the aim of this chapter is to consider the possibilities with a particular focus on how they might be used to inform the evaluation of crime reduction activity. A number of different types of computational methods will be discussed and examples of the types of policy-related questions for which they might be used considered. The strengths and weaknesses of the approaches described will also be discussed.*

INTRODUCTION

Computational methods, and in particular computer simulation (e.g., Liang et al., 2001; Groff, 2007a), have considerable potential in the study of

Crime Prevention Studies, volume 24 (2009), pp. 175–217.

crime. The aim of this chapter is to discuss some of the possibilities with a particular focus on the evaluation of crime reduction activity. In writing this chapter, two possibilities regarding the scope and direction of the material to be covered suggested themselves: 1) to focus on a particular type of simulation and provide a detailed exposition of that method; or, 2) to discuss a number of different types of computational method to provide the reader with a more general understanding of the possibilities. As the use of simulation for the evaluation of crime reduction activity is novel, I chose the latter. In addition to illustrating the benefits of the methods discussed, some of the issues that need to be addressed before their potential may be realised will also be considered.

The chapter is divided into four sections, each considering different research questions that should inform the various stages of policy decision making. In the first, a concrete example of a technique used to evaluate the effect and sustainability of a situational crime prevention measure implemented at the individual household level is discussed. The method used differs from traditional approaches in that a *Monte Carlo simulation re-sampling* procedure is used to estimate what would have been expected in the absence of intervention and to estimate the statistical significance of observed effects. This type of approach is very different from the simulation methods discussed in the remainder of the chapter, and is used to provide an example of a type of analysis used to answer a very simple "what if" question.

In the second section, discussion moves to the evaluation of area (rather than individual) level interventions. The potential use of *microanalytical simulation* in the estimation of expected area-level crime rates (in the absence of intervention) is discussed, with a particular focus on how this type of simulation can be used to model data-generating processes not explicitly considered in traditional types of analysis. The aim of this section is to discuss some of the relevant issues rather than to present the results of an actual evaluation. However, an empirical illustration is provided to show how levels of crime may vary in an area even in the absence of intervention under different "what if" conditions.

In the third section, issues regarding the implementation of interventions are considered. Evaluations of place-based crime reduction initiatives generally indicate that implementation is gradual rather than abrupt, and that for successful interventions there is a relationship between the timing and intensity of implementation and the volume of crime prevented (e.g., Bowers et al., 2004). However, rarely are the likely effects of different implementation schedules explicitly considered prior to implementation. Consequently, in this section, using an extension of the methodology discussed in section two, examples are provided of how simulations might be used to estimate the possible effects of different implementation plans prior to the inception of crime reduction activity.

In the final section, the potential use of computer simulation to test theoretical models of crime reduction strategies before they are piloted in an operational context will be discussed. A simple example is provided to illustrate some of the concepts and to provide a focus for discussion.

The material covered in the different sections varies in a number of ways. First, the examples selected consider different units of analysis. In the initial section, the research discussed concerns a micro-level analysis of an intervention implemented at the individual household level. In the second and third, the discussion moves to the evaluation of area-based interventions, and in the final section, the example considered focuses on more general policies that may have no specific geographical boundaries.

Second, the computational methods considered are quite different. I start with a simple example similar to the types of methods with which most readers will be familiar and that can be applied right now. The discussion then moves to methods of simulation that are yet to be used in the evaluation of interventions, or in the testing of crime prevention models but that with a little work could be used at this time. I conclude with a discussion of simulation methods that could possibly be used in the future but that require considerable development before that possibility becomes a reality. To make the chapter as accessible as possible, the use of equations and technical vocabulary is avoided where possible.

1. ESTIMATING THE IMPACT AND SUSTAINABILITY OF INTERVENTION

The first example considers how one might evaluate the impact on domestic burglary risk of a traditional target hardening scheme, where individual households (rather than areas) most at risk of victimisation are targeted for intervention. This particular example is used to illustrate a series of issues associated with this type of evaluation and how the flexibility afforded by computational methods can help reduce threats to internal validity (i.e., rule out other explanations for observed changes).

This type of situational crime prevention intervention usually involves the upgrading of physical security measures at households with identified vulnerabilities (e.g., Forrester et al., 1988). Implementation strategies for this type of intervention vary. For example, individual household surveys may be conducted within high crime neighbourhoods to identify homes with inadequate physical security features which may be vulnerable to victimisation. Alternatively, vulnerability may be identified through an analysis of recorded crime data; research consistently demonstrates that prior victimisation is an excellent predictor of future risk (e.g., Budd, 1999) and thus the prevention of repeat victimisation may represent an efficient burglary reduction strategy (e.g., Farrell, 2005; Pease, 1998). In the example discussed below, I consider how one might evaluate an intervention for which the latter strategy is adopted, but this will be discussed only so far as it serves current purposes. A full discussion of the data used and the implications of the findings of this type of evaluation are provided elsewhere (Bowers, Lab and Johnson, 2008) and so only the main points will be covered here.

Approaches to Evaluation

If implemented in a particular area, one approach to evaluation would be to examine changes observed at the area level using an experimental or quasi-experimental design. For both types of design, the counterfactual – what is likely to have happened in the absence of intervention – is estimated by contrasting the crime rates before and after intervention for a treatment and control group, the latter being matched as closely as possible with the former (for an overview of evaluation methods, see Campbell and Stanley, 1963). Where the change observed for the treatment group is preferable to and different from that experienced by the control group by a meaningful amount, the intervention is deemed to have been a success. Some form of statistical significance testing is also typically used to establish whether the size of the effect could have occurred on a chance basis, or is more likely to be attributable to intervention.

Experimental designs allocate target units (people, places or whatever is being studied) randomly to treatment and control groups. This approach is generally preferred because as well as producing matched samples,[1] it eliminates any selection bias[2] that might result from the use of other allocation strategies (Campbell and Stanley, 1963; Shadish et al., 2002). However, when an intervention is implemented in only one or two areas – which is often the case for new types of intervention – (complete) randomization may not produce adequately matched samples. In such cases, either block randomisation[3] or a quasi-experimental design – whereby the control group is selected because of its similarity to the treatment group in as many respects as possible apart from the assignment to the treatment condition (for a further discussion, see the chapter by Henry in this volume) – will be more appropriate.

While this may seem fitting, for an intervention such as target hardening, attempting to estimate the effect of intervention at the area level would be insensitive to the unit of analysis at which implementation occurs. This is so for at least two reasons. First, how does the evaluator define what the geographic area of intervention actually is? One approach would be to use an existing administrative boundary (such as a police beat) which generally encapsulated the area of interest. Even better, a bespoke boundary could be generated using a Geographical Information System (GIS). However, in both cases modifying the boundary used could lead to different results. Referred to as the Modifiable Areal Unit Problem (MAUP; Openshaw, 1984), this is a well documented problem which occurs when data are aggregated at the area level.

Second, unless all homes receive intervention, the evaluation design will be insensitive to expected variation in the change in crime risk to homes that do and do not receive intervention. That is, if measured at the area level, any observable effect of intervention may be diluted as the effect will be measured using data aggregated across two different populations (those that did and did not receive treatment) with different expected outcomes. The extent to which this is a problem will, of course, depend on the dosage of intervention; being more of a problem when relatively few homes receive the intervention. In any event, by not taking account of this, even for an intervention that actually works, the evaluator may underestimate the size of the effect of intervention or make a type II statistical error by assuming that there was no effect where in fact this was simply lost in the aggregation.

Aggregation of the kind discussed also applies to the dimension of time. In the current context, a simple but generally invalid assumption would be that all homes in receipt of intervention were treated on the same day (e.g., the first day of the "after period"). Rarely will this be the case, and implementation may take weeks or even years to complete. However, for the standard before and after design discussed above, the evaluator essentially makes this assumption as crime rates are aggregated for the periods before and after intervention and the effect of intervention is estimated by dividing one by the other.[4] Assuming that the effect of intervention is cumulative, such a design is likely to underestimate any treatment effect.

Additionally, such analysis provides no indication of the longevity of the effect of intervention. Understanding the sustainability of an intervention's effect is important for at least two reasons. First, from a cost effectiveness perspective, the best interventions are those that have a lasting impact on crime. Second, if the probable lifetime of an intervention effect is known, then crime reduction agencies can plan accordingly, timetabling further activity to reinforce intervention.

Survival Analysis

An alternative method would be to see how the risk of crime varies for homes that do and do not receive the treatment before and after intervention. If the intervention is successful then relative to those that do not receive it (the control group), the burglary rate for the treatment group should reduce over time. However, while this approach would deal with the problem of spatial aggregation discussed, it would not address the temporal aggregation problem.

A different approach that could be used, and one that is used frequently in research concerned with recidivism (e.g., Visher and Linster, 1990), is survival analysis. For this type of analysis, the question of interest concerns the typical time to failure, however defined. In the context of studies of recidivism, this is the elapsed time between the start of a rehabilitation programme (for example) and the first offence committed following the start of treatment. For a situational crime prevention intervention, this would be the elapsed time between the treatment and the first victimisation post-intervention. A problem may arise with this type of analysis when the evaluation period covers an insufficient interval of time to allow the time to failure to be identified for all experimental units. For example, consider a household that received an intervention just before the end of the evaluation period. In this case, the likelihood of estimating the true survival time for that home would be low as the data set would essentially be truncated. However, as this problem of what is known as *censoring* is well understood (Tabachnick and Fidell, 2001) and can be corrected for it will be discussed no further here.

The usual approach taken to analysis is to compute a survival distribution (presented as a curve) for those in receipt of treatment and to compare this with those for a suitably matched control group, controlling for the problem of censoring discussed above. In the case of offender rehabilitation, assignment to conditions can often (though not always) be achieved using random allocation. For other types of intervention, random allocation to treatment and control groups is not always possible or even appropriate (for a general discussion, see Sherman, 2007), and hence an alternative matching procedure will be required.

Despite its popularity in the evaluation of medical treatments and offender based programs, hitherto survival analysis has not been used for the evaluation of situational crime prevention measures and so an example of how this method could be used for this type of intervention will be presented along with a discussion of how a suitable control group might be constructed when random allocation is not possible.

Monte Carlo Simulation

As discussed, in the case of survival analysis, the approach to analysis is very similar to the experimental logic discussed at the beginning of this section. Survival curves, which show the cumulative percentage of households unvictimised per unit of elapsed time, are computed for both the treatment and control groups and the patterns compared. To identify a control group, the basic approach would be to describe the treatment group and identify a control group which comprises a set of homes with similar characteristics.

However, for the example discussed here it is possible that for some homes subject to intervention, there will be more than one household that could serve as a control, meaning that the sample sizes would vary across groups if all possible controls were used in the analysis. This may not be problem and one could include all of the potential control households in the analysis. However, as there may be more potential control households for some homes than others, this could lead to a control group for which the overall profile is quite dissimilar to that for the treatment group. The implications of such an aggregation effect for causal inference should require no articulation.

An alternative approach would be to pick a random sample of control households from those available, one for each home in receipt of treatment. The survival curves for the two groups could then be compared and the statistical significance of any differences tested in the usual way. However, the problem with this approach is that any differences observed could be due to the control sample selected: a control sample selection effect.

A different solution is to use a Monte Carlo (MC) re-sampling technique. Here, rather than selecting one control group, a sample of control groups – with each home matched with a treatment household on a one-to-one basis – may be drawn from all permutations possible. For each sample selected, a comparison can be made with the results for the treatment group. Where a large number of samples are drawn (say 99), the average survival curve may be computed along with the standard error. The statistical significance of any observed differences can also be easily estimated, either using the standard errors computed, or more directly by counting for how many of the control samples the survival curve exceeds that for the treatment group (see North, 2002).

An Empirical Example

To illustrate the approach in a more concrete way, the results presented in a recent paper are summarised (Bowers et al., 2008) here. In that study, the effectiveness of the target hardening of individual households was examined for one area on Merseyside (U.K.). The treatment group consisted of 318 households for which intervention had been triggered as a consequence of victimisation experience.

The data available for analysis included the following:

a) The location of all homes within the area that had received target hardening (see Bowers et al., 2008);

b) recorded burglary data for a six year interval; and,

c) Ordnance Survey (OS) data that indicated the address points of every house in the area.

Software was written to identify every home within the area (of which there were 71,500) that did not receive the intervention but that had a similar victimisation profile to those that did. In so doing, the potential problem of regression to the mean (RTM) was reduced (see Campbell and Stanley, 1963). To elaborate, the problem of RTM would occur if homes were assigned to the treatment condition on the basis of an extreme score on a variable (e.g., the number of victimisations experienced in the recent past) that was atypical for that household. The issue is that even in the absence of intervention, over time the risk to such homes would be expected to regress back to the "normal" level generally experienced by them. Where such homes are allocated to the treatment group this may create the illusion

Figure 1. Survival Times for Target Hardened and Non-Target Hardened Homes. (Adapted from Bowers et al., 2008.)

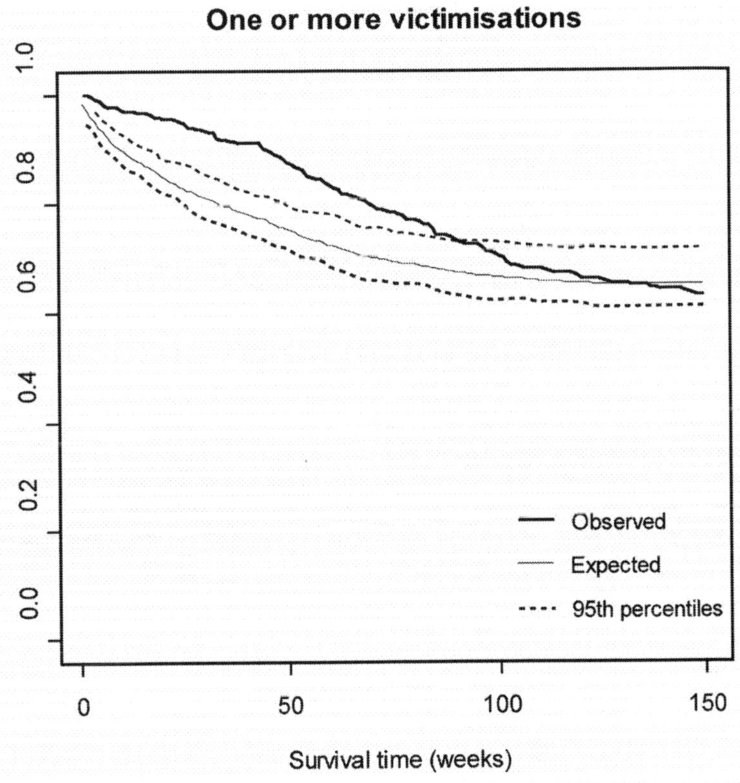

of a treatment effect. However, for the current methodology, as homes were matched on the very variables that could lead to RTM being mistaken for something more than it is, the patterns observed for both groups are equally likely to be caused by RTM. Thus, any difference observed between groups should be attributable to an intervention effect (or at the very least something other than RTM).

On average, for each treatment household, there were around 97 homes that fitted the criteria applied, meaning that a large number of control groups could be identified. A MC simulation was used to (re)sample from the universe of control groups possible, and a distribution of survival curves generated. Figure 1 shows the results of the analysis and indicates that relative to the control group(s), homes that received target hardening were typically less likely to be victimised for a period of around two years. The dotted lines shown in Figure 1 show the 5th and 95th percentiles of the MC simulation. Where the observed values exceed the upper dotted line, this indicates that the treatment group exceeded chance expectation for that point in time. The maximum value on the x-axis is 150 weeks, which represents the maximum interval of time for which any of the households were protected by target hardening for the period of time for which data were available.

For the current analysis, the results show that the difference in the survival curves was statistically significant for a period of about 18 months. Thereafter, the proportion of homes victimised was roughly equivalent between groups. Thus, for these data at least, target hardening appears to have an immediate crime reductive effect that was sustained for around two years.

Observations and Limitations

Re-sampling from all households using a computational approach and recorded crime data has the clear advantage that unlike other research designs that use surveys, the time frame for analysis need not be limited; analyses can be conducted using as many or as few homes as necessary; construction of the control sample is inexpensive; and, the criteria used to identify the control group(s) can be varied in as many ways as the data permit. Thus, the researcher can ask whether the result obtained is likely to be statistically significant for control groups configured in different ways. In the current example, only simple criteria were used but other specifications are possible. Such flexibility would be impossible to achieve without intensive computation for anything other than very small sample sizes, and data collection would be expensive where surveys were required.

However, it is important to note that the approach will only be as good as the data available. For example, one disadvantage with the data used above is that only limited information was available about each home. For those victimised, information may be available regarding the type of home, who owns it (and so on), but such data are unlikely to be found in police data for the remainder of the population. This may pose a problem if one wishes to match households (treatment and controls) on a range of characteristics that may be observable to the would-be offender.

It is possible that this issue may be minimised by using alternative data such as those collected as part of a government census. For example, in the U.K., although unavailable at the individual household level, data are available at a fairly high level of resolution, the most precise being the census Output Area (OA). Each OA contains around 125 homes, and areas are defined to maximise within area homogeneity; that is, as far as possible the geographical boundaries derived delineate areas that maximise the likelihood that similar people live within the same OAs. Thus, although this would not completely resolve the issue, using the OA geography it would be possible to estimate the probability that any particular household shared characteristics with those with which they are to be matched.

As further issue that re-sampling does not entirely resolve is that of selection bias and the related omitted variable problem. For example, in the current example it is possible that there was something systematically different about those homes that did and did not receive treatment, but that this was not apparent from the available data. It may be that this difference explains the variation in the survival curves. This is difficult to overcome in the absence of random allocation or where the data required to more precisely match the two groups – treatment and control – are unavailable. Where more extensive data are available it would be possible to refine the procedure using the propensity score matching approach to sample construction. The aim of the approach would be to ensure that the homes in the two conditions would both be equally likely to have been assigned to the treatment group based on the inclusion criteria adopted (for more details, see the chapter by Henry in this volume). In this case, any observed differences between groups could be attributed to the intervention with increased confidence.

For these reasons, the results generated by techniques such as that described should be interpreted in a sensitive way and used in studies that are carefully designed to minimise as many threats to internal validity as possible. However, it is also important to recapitulate the advantage of using a re-sampling methodology and how this can help to minimise bias. First, as the construction of the control groups is iterative, any observed effects are unlikely to be attributable to peculiarities in the samples identified. Second, as this approach to hypothesis testing enables p-values to be calculated directly using the re-sampling methodology, the data need not conform to a particular statistical distribution, which is a requirement of most statistical tests. Finally, as the approach essentially involves the use of many control groups, there is no risk of making errors of inference that could arise from using only one control group. Consider that if one control group were selected from all those possible, the conclusions drawn would be affected by this selection. If the control group used represented an extreme case (e.g., if it was below the 5th percentile of MC Simulation) and standard statistical tests were used this would lead to an error of inference.

2. ESTIMATING THE IMPACT OF INTERVENTION AT THE AREA LEVEL

There are at least three types of policy question for which computer simulation may be useful. First, simulation may be used to estimate what patterns of crime would be expected in a given area (or for a given population) in the absence of intervention. These estimates may then be compared to patterns observed to determine if an intervention is likely to have had any effect. Second, simulation may be used as a tool for testing the likely effects of an intervention for a range of implementation scenarios in which the timing and intensity of activity is varied. Third, simulation may be used to systematically test theoretical models of interventions before expensive field trials are conducted. In this section the first possibility will be discussed, while the others will be considered in subsequent sections.

Before continuing it is worth outlining some of the main differences between simulation as method and more traditional approaches. Many analytic approaches to theory testing employ a top-down methodology; patterns are observed in the real world and the data generating processes or mechanisms for them inferred. Using simulation, a bottom-up approach is adopted. That is, a data generating process is specified *a-priori* and the simulated phenomena that emerge (e.g., simulated patterns of crime) observed. Put another way, a computer simulation is an implementation of a theory. Thus, much like a thought experiment, one can ask simple "what if" questions under conditions where variables of interest can be manipulated and their effects – along with those of chance – assessed.

A range of simulation methodologies exist (for a general review, see Gilbert and Troitzsch, 2003) and some of these have already been applied to the study of crime (for a review, see Alimadad et al., 2008; and for a collection of examples, Liu and Eck, 2008; Groff and Mazerolle, 2008). For example, McAllister et al. (1991) use a Queing simulation model to examine case processing within the court system in the U.S. and estimate the impact of policy changes on the efficiency of the system. Johnson (2008) uses microanalytical simulation to test theories of crime concentration. A number of researchers (e.g., Groff, 2007a; Birks et al., 2008) have used agent-based models to examine routine activity theory (Cohen and Felson,

Box 1: Microanalytical Simulation

Microanalytical simulation is used to model how the characteristics of a population might change over time under different conditions. Gilbert and Troitzsch (2003) provide a number of examples of how this approach may be used to answer different types of policy questions. One example considers how a researcher might estimate the likely future demands on the nursing sector by computing the likely population of those aged 60 or more with and without support networks (e.g. close relatives). For example, for a given (real) population, this type of model can be used to simulate how the composition of the overall population, and people's support networks, will change when one takes account of factors such as likely variation in rates of births, deaths, divorce, the effects of chance, and so on.

For this type of model, patterns can be measured at the level of the individual or at the aggregate level of the population. This approach requires detailed data on the population considered as well as the specification of those processes that may affect the population concerned.

1979) and the effects of police patrols on offender activity (e.g., Dray et al., 2008). However, before getting too excited about advanced methods of simulation (see Box 1), I will discuss a simple example that uses microanalytical simulation.

Estimating the Counterfactual

Techniques for estimating the statistical significance of experimental manipulations conducted in the laboratory (or medical trials) are quite simple. In the simplest case, a group of people may be randomly assigned to one of two different conditions (experimental and control), and their performance on a test observed. As already discussed, random allocation to conditions will generally lead to the formation of two groups with similar characteristics. This minimises the problem of selection bias, meaning that the results obtained are unlikely to be due to the way in which participants were allocated to conditions.

The types of statistical tests used to determine whether between group differences observed are meaningful generally involve the estimation and consideration of the standard error of the sample means. The larger the sample sizes, the more reliable the estimates. The difficulties of using this paradigm and these types of statistical test in studies of crime prevention implemented at the *area* (rather than person- or household-) level are numerous, but three of the main points are listed below:

- The randomization of allocation of areas to conditions will rarely be possible or, given the highly skewed distribution of crime risk (e.g., Sherman, 2007) and the variation in context across locations (e.g., Tilley, 1993), even appropriate.
- Many studies involve only **one** treatment and control group and these will often be implemented across geographic areas (e.g., studies of street lighting) rather than targeting particular individuals or buildings.
- And, for problem-oriented policing projects, the crime reduction strategy should be designed to interfere with the specific conditions that facilitate crime in the area selected for intervention. It is assumed that these conditions will vary across locations and so the same solution would not be expected to work across all or any conditions. Thus, for problem-oriented projects, the random allocation of areas to conditions would be incongruent with the philosophy of the approach.

A number of alternative approaches have thus been used for the evaluation of area-based interventions (Ekblom and Pease, 1995; Johnson et al., 2004; for a classic overview, see Campbell and Stanley, 1963). For most, the basic assumption is that the crime rate in an area post-intervention will be a function of the crime rate before intervention multiplied by a coefficient of expected change plus some degree of chance fluctuation. The expected change is usually estimated by examining observed changes in similar areas (e.g., Farrington and Welsh, 2006), or the wider area within which the intervention area is located. The statistical significance of a result obtained is then estimated by computing a standard error for the estimate derived. Thus, where a change is observed in an intervention area, the evaluator attempts to rule out threats to internal validity (alternative explanations) for the change by seeing how things changed in similar areas not subject to intervention. Where the change in the intervention area exceeds those in other areas by a substantial amount, the change observed *may* be attributed to the intervention with more confidence.

In addition, if the evaluator wants to understand how the intervention may (or may not) have worked, and to strengthen conclusion validity, he will usually want to identify the likely crime reduction mechanisms (see

Pawson and Tilley, 1997) through which the intervention could have worked and, through the collection of the relevant data regarding intermediate outcomes (e.g., change in the number of residents that have noticed new street lighting), see if these mechanisms were triggered. Where they are not, causal inferences will be challenged or at the very least the mechanisms through which the intervention may have had an impact will need to be revised. The importance of conducting such hypothesis testing and identifying signatures that bespeak mechanism is difficult to overstate (for a detailed discussion, see Pawson and Tilley, 1997 and the chapter by Eck and Madenson in this volume), but for reasons of space will not be discussed further here.

Returning to the estimation of the impact of intervention, using the basic logic discussed above, one simple statistic that may be calculated is the odds ratio (see Farrington and Welsh, 2004). This is computed by comparing the ratio of change (before versus after) in an intervention area to that in a comparator. An odds ratio of 1 so derived would indicate that the changes observed were equivalent across areas. A value above one would indicate a reduction in the treatment area relative to that observed in the comparator. The standard error of the estimate is computed by assuming that the number of crimes in an area conforms to a Poisson distribution, and hence that the variance will be equal to the mean. A potential problem with this approach is that Poisson models are susceptible to the problem of overdispersion whereby estimates so computed may underestimate the variability observed in the real world (e.g., see Agresti, 2002).

Reasons for simple Poisson models underestimating variability relate to the fact that they do not model all of the processes likely to affect the dependent variable. The assumption of independence of events is potentially problematic (see Marchant, 2005; but see Farrington and Welsh, 2004). For example, research demonstrates a dependency in the timing and location of crime events such as burglary (Townsley et al., 2003; Johnson and Bowers, 2004a, b; Bowers and Johnson, 2005; Johnson et al., 2007), vehicle crime (Johnson et al., 2008) and gun crime (Ratcliffe and Rengert, 2007). Theoretical (e.g., Johnson and Bowers, 2004b) and empirical work (Bernasco, 2007; Johnson et al., 2008) suggests that the reason crimes cluster in space *and* time in this way, and do so more than would be expected on the basis of area-level variation in risk, is that the patterns observed reflect the use of optimal foraging strategies by offenders. Simply put, analyses of crimes detected by the police (Bernasco, 2008;

Johnson et al., 2008) demonstrate that having victimized one home, offenders often target the same home again and others nearby within a short space of time. There is dependency in the data.

A potential advantage of microanalytical simulation over standard statistical methods is that space-time processes (where they are known to the researcher and can be formally expressed) can be incorporated into the models enabling their effects on the dependent variable to be estimated. The need to do this was actually discussed some time ago by Barr and Pease (1992), who highlighted the importance of understanding and taking into account normal patterns of crime placement in evaluation research. However, as far as I am aware, such models have not been developed or discussed in any detail hitherto.

An Earlier Experiment Conducted Using Microanalytical Simulation

To illustrate how this might be done, an example of a microanalytical simulation model will be discussed and the results of a simulation experiment presented. The model was originally developed (see Johnson, 2008) for the purposes of theory testing and falsification, with a focus on patterns of repeat burglary victimisation. Over three decades of research demonstrate that prior victimisation is an excellent predictor of future risk for all crime types so far studied (for reviews, see Pease, 1998; Farrell, 2005). However, while the ubiquity of such findings is largely uncontested, debate still exists regarding the theoretical mechanisms that generate the phenomenon. Some argue that patterns of repeat victimisation may be explained by enduring heterogeneity of crime risk across homes; some homes are simply more vulnerable than others and consequently are repeatedly victimised. Others (e.g., Pease, 1998) suggest that a first offence increases the probability of future victimisation, either because the victim's behaviour changes in response to the first offence, or because the offender's newly acquired knowledge of that home increases the attractiveness of it relative to those that remain unknown.

I will not rehearse the findings of the substantial research literature concerned with repeat victimisation any further, but instead discuss how the model was developed to test the two theories, and how it could be used for the purposes of estimating the counterfactual. In the earlier study, patterns of crime were simulated for a virtual population of homes under a range of conditions. The central question was whether patterns of repeat victimization as observed in the real world could be generated by a microanalytical simulation where the risk to individual homes was the product of time-stable risk factors and the roll of a virtual dice, or whether a further mechanism was required.

To test the first question, every home in the simulation, generated using point data for a whole county in the U.K., was allocated a particular risk of victimization. The latter was estimated using police recorded burglary data for a period of four years. Over a simulated interval of four years, on each virtual day some homes were selected as burglary victims while others were not. The selection of which homes were victimized each day was determined by the risk allocated to each home and the output of a uniform random number generator (RNG). Homes with the highest risks were selected more frequently than those with the lowest, but the model was not deterministic and as would be expected the results varied across runs.

In addition to modeling time-stable risks, an element of what I will refer to (for the sake of simplicity) as "contagion"[5] was included in some of the models whereby the probability of victimization at each home increased as a function of the (virtual) burglaries experienced at that home. In addition to modeling these factors, seasonality was included in the models by varying the risk of crime according to the variation observed in the police recorded crime data.

More precise details of the model and the procedures used will not be discussed here (see, Johnson, 2008), but it is worth noting that the risk to each home was estimated using the police recorded crime data and the U.K.OA census geography discussed above. Other methods of deriving the estimates of risk exist, and the use of a particular method may, of course, affect any results generated. In this case, the most significant threat to ecological validity is the Modifiable Areal Unit Problem (Openshaw, 1984), whereby changing the boundaries used in the analysis may affect the estimates derived (for a discussion of other issues, see Johnson, 2008).

Model Validation

An important aspect of simulation research concerns model validation. Townsley and Johnson (2008) discuss a framework for analysis which draws upon the validity typology conceived by Campbell (1957). A lengthy discussion will be avoided here, but some of the questions to be asked include whether constructs formalized as part of the model accurately reflect the intended definition; if threats to internal validity could have evolved from coding or other errors; and whether the results approximate those in the real world (empirical validity). Threats to validity are likely to increase with the complexity of the simulation.

In the case of the Johnson (2008) study, the model was very simple and so only the results generated will be discussed. Simply put, these suggested that whilst area-level crime rates explain some of the variance in crime concentration at the household level, they far from exhaust it. Indeed, only when an element of contagion was introduced did the models generate patterns of victimization that resemble those to be found in police data. A particularly important finding was that time-stable population heterogeneity failed to explain the ubiquitous time course of repeat victimization whereby the risk of revictimization decays exponentially with elapsed time (e.g., Polvi et al., 1991).

For those particularly interested in this type of simulation and how varying the model parameters may affect the results, a variant of it was produced for this chapter. The model was developed in the NetLogo programming language (Wilensky, 1999), which is a cross-platform multi-agent programmable modeling environment which readers can download (http://ccl.northwestern.edu/netlogo/) free of charge.[6]

Using Microanalytical Simulation to Estimate the Counterfactual

If computer simulations can be developed that represent reasonable approximations of how patterns of crime vary in the absence of particular interventions, then such models could be used to estimate the counterfactual. To illustrate, the model described above was here used to explore the potential effects of the space-time dependency of crime placement on the estimation of the counterfactual. To do this, a geographic area was selected from the virtual world at random, and estimates of the volume of crime expected in it generated for a fictional one year period. The area selected, shown as Figure 2, had a total of 5,583 homes within it.

Estimates of the expected volume of crime in the selected area and the associated variance were computed for three conditions, as follows:

1) Where the occurrence of crime at each home depended only on an estimate of time-stable risk at the neighbourhood level for a notional pre-intervention period. The period used to calibrate the model was the same four-year interval used by Johnson (2008).

Figure 2. Area Selected for Microanalytical Simulation Experiment. (Ordnance Survey © Crown Copyright. All Rights reserved.)

2) As per model #1, but with a contagious repeat victimisation process; the risk of victimisation at each victimised home was elevated by a factor of 5 for a period of 1-16 weeks (selected using a uniform RNG). The contribution of time-stable area-level variation in risk was scaled to ensure that the mean count was equal to that for model #1.

Figure 3. Examples of Kernel Density Maps to Show the Patterns Generated for a Fragment of the Virtual World for Two Realisations of the Simulation Experiment. (Ordnance Survey © Crown Copyright. All Rights reserved.)

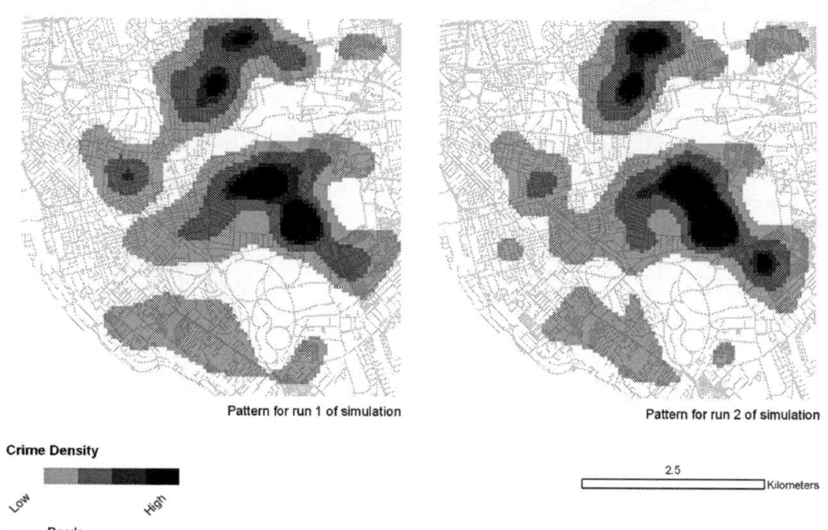

3) And, as per model #2, but with the inclusion of a more general space-time process, whereby the risk to homes within 50 meters of previously victimised locations was temporarily elevated by a factor of 1.1 and for those within 50-100 meters, by 1.05. As with model #2 the elevation in risk was temporary.

For each model, the simulation was run 100 times. For the purposes of illustration, hotspot maps produced from the data generated by the first two realisations of model #3 (for the wider area within which the study area was located) are shown in Figure 3. It should be evident that similarities exist between the two maps but the precise patterns vary. As the patterns are generated for a fictional period, differences in the patterns observed reflect only the effects of the data generating processes specified, nothing more.

Table 1 shows the average volume of crime for the study area for each model. The results indicate that the variance of the estimates is a function of the processes modelled. This suggests that modelling the factors

Table 1. Estimates of the Volume of Crime for Three Different Models (generated from 100 iterations of the simulation)

	Mean	Variance	SD
Area-level model (1)	218.9	229.6	15.2
RV model (2)	218.2	279.0	16.7
Space-Time model (3)	218.3	371.9	19.3

(1) Mixed Poisson model.
(2) As for (1) but the risk to victimised homes is temporarily elevated.
(3) As for (2) but the risk to nearby homes is also temporarily elevated.

which influence crime placement is important in the evaluation of crime prevention schemes. Failing to do so will mean that the expected variance will be underestimated and errors of inference will be more likely. A further advantage of using simple simulation models is that where hypotheses are tested, p-values can be calculated directly without the use of statistical tables, meaning that there is no requirement that the data fit a particular distribution (see above).

In addition to estimating the direct effect of intervention, a simulation of this kind could be used to estimate the extent of any geographic displacement or diffusion of benefit (see Eck, 1993) that may have occurred. The advantage of so doing is that where Space-Time processes are modeled, these would be less likely to be mistaken for spatial displacement, or target switch.

A final benefit of using simulation in this context is that the possible influences of other changes that may occur at the area-level can be modelled. For example, it is possible that during an intervention period the population at risk may change. New homes may be built or old ones demolished. This too can be modelled by adding or removing homes from the simulation. It is also possible that the residential population may change in a way that might be expected to affect area-level crime rates. For instance, over the period of intervention, the population of residents aged 13-17 years – the peak age in offending (Farrington et al., 2006) – may increase. The model could be calibrated to estimate the effect of this, but with the understanding that results obtained would be dependent upon the assumptions made. Other possibilities exist.

Before getting too excited, a note of caution is necessary. In the above examples, models (2) and (3) were a combination of a mixed Poisson and space-time process. Before these types of model can be used for the purposes of evaluation, we need to better understand the influence of the two processes on area- (and individual household-) level crime rates. What should the contribution of each process be? Does this vary by area? How do we calibrate the models? These are questions that require answers. At the very least, the use of the simulation model highlights the need to identify the relevant parameter values and how these might be modeled and validated. Again this requirement of specificity is a benefit of simulation in that it helps to inform the agenda for basic research and understanding.

It is worth noting that for the models tested, the difference in the variance observed across the models tested is perhaps not as dramatic as one might expect. It may be that this is will not be true for other models in which thc Space-Time (or other) processes are more accentuated (or other factors modelled), but one interpretation of this finding is that simple approaches such as the odds ratio method (particularly where conservative estimates are used, e.g., Farrington and Welsh, 2006) may not be as problematic as has been suggested (Marchant, 2005). It is beyond the scope (and aim) of this chapter to explore this further, but this could be investigated more systematically using simulation models.

3. EXAMINING THE LIKELY EFFECTS OF DIFFERENT IMPLEMENTATION STRATEGIES

A second type of question that the above simulation may be useful in helping to address concerns the *dosage* of an intervention and the timing of implementation required to deliver a desired effect. Consider a scenario where an intervention has been selected for implementation and there is a desire to achieve a particular reduction in crime by a given date. Simulation might be used to help determine whether this degree of reduction is plausible and to determine what model of implementation would be required to achieve it.

For a burglary reduction intervention, some of the factors that will influence the impact on crime are the effect of the intervention at the individual household level and the dosage of implementation; the more homes that are treated the greater the expected effect (e.g., Ekblom et al., 1996). Simulation may be used to model different scenarios for a variety of assumptions. For example, if we believe that an intervention will reduce the risk of crime by 20% (or within some range of it) for those in receipt of treatment then this effect can be modelled for different levels of implementation, and the effect on area-level crime rates observed.

Implementation can vary in ways other than dosage. For example, homes could be selected for intervention randomly, or those with the highest risks could be given priority; implementation could be done relatively abruptly within a short space of time, or it could be more gradual, taking months or even years to complete. Simulations could be used to examine the potential impact on crime of a range of models of implementation. Assumptions would need to be made, but across a series of runs, parameters of the model could be varied to examine the effect of intervention for different sets of assumptions.

To illustrate the potential use of this method, two simulation experiments were conducted. In the first, the dosage of intervention was varied and, in the second, the timing of intervention considered. For both experiments, as the aim was one of illustration alone, the simplest model of crime placement discussed above (model 1) was used as a baseline model.

Modeling the Effect of Varying the Dosage of Intervention

In the first simulation experiment, different fractions of homes located within the area used above were selected for intervention on the first day of the simulation. Two different levels of dosage are considered: 50 and 100%. Where the dosage is 50%, two different models of allocation were used to identify homes that received the "intervention." In the first, homes with the highest "pre-intervention" risk were selected. In the second, those with the lowest risks were chosen.

At the individual household level, for the sake of simplicity the intervention is assumed to reduce the risk of crime to those selected by a factor of 50%. Varying this parameter will, of course, affect the results considerably and it is possible that in the real world the effect of intervention (or even the precise intervention implemented) will vary across homes. However, for simplicity a fixed effect is assumed.

Table 2 shows the results observed across 20 runs of the simulation. The first column shows the average effect of changing the risk to a given fraction of homes by 50%. This is derived by dividing the average count of crime in the treatment area for the intervention model by that for the baseline model (for which the effect of intervention is excluded). The second column shows the worst case scenario. To calculate this, the maximum count of crime generated for the intervention model is divided by the mean for the baseline model. This is not strictly the worst case scenario of course.[7] The final column shows the best case scenario for which the

Table 2. Simulated Effects of Using Different Dosages of Implementation Assuming a 50% Crime Reductive Effect at the Individual Level and Only Chance Variation in Risk Over Time (generated from 100 iterations of the simulation)

	Mean % Reduction	Min % Reduction	Max % Reduction
Abrupt Implementation			
100% of homes	49.0	38.5	63.3
50% of homes – Low Risk	14.6	–3.6	28.9
50% of homes – High Risk	34.5	22.0	47.7
Gradual Implementation			
100% of homes	30.6	16.9	44.0

lowest count of crime for the intervention model is compared with the mean count of crime for the baseline model.

Thus, where 100% of homes are selected for intervention this reduces the risk to them by 50%. The results of the simulation suggest that average effect of so doing is a reduction in crime of around 49%.[8] However, when we take account of random fluctuation (excluding Space-Time processes), the results suggest that the effect measured could actually vary between 38-63%. Thus, on the basis of the simulation results, it is plausible that in the real world if the risk to homes was actually reduced by 50%, the effect observed could be as low as 38%, or as high as 63%.

The minimum and maximum effect sizes vary considerably, particularly when only 50% of homes are selected for intervention. This is due to the fact that there is considerable variation in risk across the area. Thus, if a practitioner were to assume that randomly selecting homes for intervention was as good a strategy as any, he would commit the ecological fallacy (e.g., Bowers et al., 2005) by assuming that all homes within the area experience the same risk of victimization. If the assumptions of the model tested are correct, the outcome of such a strategy would be a smaller reduction than could be achieved, and in the worst case, no effect at all.

Estimating the Effect of Using Different Implementation Timelines

In the second experiment, the dosage of intervention is held constant at 50% across simulations, but the timing of intervention varied. For the first model, the simulated implementation phase was abrupt with all homes being treated on day 1. The results for this model are the same as those shown in row 1 of Table 2. For the second model, the rate of implementation was decreased to 17 homes per day, which generated an implementation period of one year.

Unsurprisingly, the results shown in Table 2 indicate that a smaller crime reductive effect is likely to be observed in the one year period when a gradual implementation schedule is used. Of course, the value of the simulation approach is that it can provide an idea of exactly what the effect of intervention might be for a range of different implementation schedules (and assumptions). A simulation of this kind could also be used to estimate how many homes would need to be treated if an effect of X% was required, but only one particular implementation schedule possible (e.g., gradual implementation).

This general approach could also be used to try to better understand the impact of an intervention where an observable effect is produced. For example, if an intervention is believed to reduce crime, and the timing and dosage of intervention are known, then the parameters of a simulation model could be tuned using this information and the other parameters of the model (e.g., the size and sustainability of the effect, possible diffusion of benefit and so on) varied until the model produced results similar to those observed at the area level in the real world. If the results of the model approximate (or do not) those observed, this could help the evaluator test a range of hypotheses.

Additionally, simulation models might be produced to generate "signatures" that bespeak mechanism so that the emergent patterns could be looked for in real world data. For example, instead of assuming that the effect of intervention is permanent, models could be produced to estimate the effect of intervention where the effect decays over time. Models could be produced to show the impact of intervention where a diffusion of benefit occurs, reducing the risk of crime to homes nearby not subject to treatment.

One obvious limitation of the approach described is that it applies to crimes committed at individual properties. Consequently, the application of the approach will be meaningful for some crimes such as burglary (domestic and commercial), shoplifting, and possibly criminal damage, but may be of less utility for crimes such as street robbery. For the latter it is possible that the same approach could be used if a different unit of analysis were employed. For example, in an analysis of police recorded crime data which included a range of crime types, Weisburd et al. (2004) illustrate the value of using street segments as the unit of analysis. Thus, instead of using homes, other simulations could use street segments.

A further limitation of the approach is that the results are only of value if the assumptions made are valid. This is a general issue with evaluation research where the impact of intervention is to be estimated, but something to which I will return in the next section.

4. SIMULATION FOR POLICY THEORY TESTING

> . . . . consider the scenario of a child at the beach letting sand trickle down to form a pile. In the beginning, the pile is flat, and the individual grains remain close to where they land. Their motion can be understood in terms of their physical properties. As the process continues, the pile becomes steeper, and there will be little sand slides. As time goes on, the sand slides become bigger and bigger. Eventually, some of the sand slides may even span all or most of the pile. At some point, the system is far out of balance, and its behavior can no longer be understood in terms of the behavior of the individual grains. The avalanches form a dynamic of their own, which can be understood only from a holistic description of the properties of the entire pile rather than a reductionist description of the individual grains: the sandpile is a complex system.
>
> (Per Bak, 1997, p. 2).

Some of the complexity associated with patterns of crime was alluded to in a previous section in our discussion of offender as forager (see also, the chapter by Ekblom in this volume). In this section, the ecology[9] of crime (for an extended discussion, see Felson, 2005) is considered in more detail and one form of simulation method that may be used to capture the associated complexity and how this might inform policy decisions discussed.

When thinking about solutions to crime problems, the general approach is to consider the problem as currently conceived and attempt to identify points for intervention that might interrupt the cycle. Ideas may focus on different approaches including forms of offender rehabilitation, sentencing policy, changes in the number of police on the street, or situational crime prevention measures. Whatever the approach considered, those involved in making decisions typically do so by reviewing the available evidence (where it exists), and contemplating the crime reduction mechanisms (Pawson and Tilley, 1997) through which a particular intervention might work. Where a particular intervention is likely to have a fairly simple crime reduction mechanism, this approach may work well, helping policy makers to sift through contending approaches to crime reduction.

However, where the effect of an intervention may be influenced by the reactions of a variety of interacting actors (e.g., offenders, police, and victims) thought experiments may be insufficient. Moreover, because the behaviour of the system may not be understood in reductionist terms, thought experiments may be prone to error. To illustrate, consider the example of police patrols. Changes in the location and timing of police patrols may affect offender targeting choices; offenders may prefer to avoid areas when police patrols are visible (or anticipated), or they may simply wait for patrols to leave before resuming their activities. Whatever their decisions, the actions of offenders may influence the plans made by the police and vice versa. This process is iterative and the patterns that emerge may quickly become too complex for a simple thought experiment. Now imagine what happens when other actors who might influence the probability of crime occurrence are considered, and what happens when we acknowledge that the different actors (offenders, victims and guardians) may not represent mutually exclusive populations.

The modelling of complexity of this kind requires a different kind of simulation than has been so far discussed. *Agent based* methods generally describe simulations in which "agents" are represented by self-contained programs that control how they perceive their "world," what actions they will take and how they interact with their environment and each other (for a discussion, see Gilbert and Troitzsch, 2003). Agents are usually autonomous so that their "decisions" are not directed by others, but they may communicate with other agents and their interactions with them may influence their behaviour. Different *classes* of agents can be used to represent a range of populations (e.g., offenders and victims), and models can easily be programmed to incorporate population heterogeneity (e.g., offenders with different rates of offending, victims with different risks).

Returning to our crime prevention example, rather than simply trying to think through what might happen under a given set of conditions (which will require considerable mental gymnastics), agent-based simulations may be implemented to systematically test possible outcomes (see Box 2). Simulations may be run many times to see if the results vary as a consequence of chance effects or starting conditions, and to help identify the conditions under which and the mechanisms through which (optimum) impacts are most probable, and where little or no impact is likely to be observed,

Box 2: Agent Based Simulation

Agent based models (sometimes also referred to as Individual based models) have been used to study a range of phenomenon including the spread of epidemics, consumer behavior, and pedestrian movement. For social science applications, agents, which may be thought of simple representations of people (or whatever is being simulated), are programmed with simple rules about how to behave in a simulated environment. When a simulation is running, agents make decisions based on the rules specified but their choices are not pre-determined, and are instead influenced by the decisions of other agents as well as the effects of chance. Thus, even though the rules provided may be simple, when agents interact with each other or adapt to the impacts that other agents have had on the environment, the behaviour that *emerges* can be complex and unanticipated by the researcher. Such complexity cannot easily be modeled (if at all) using other methods.

Those interested in playing with a range of agent based models may do so by downloading the NetLogo program, available at: http://ccl.northwestern.edu/netlogo/.

For those interested in reading about how such models can be used in a policy context, Batty (2007) provides a fascinating example of how an Agent based simulation was used to examine the likely influence of changes in pedestrian routes on levels of over-crowding at the Notting Hill carnival in London.

or where intervention might lead to unintended consequences (positive or negative).

Of course, to do this the simulator needs to have a fairly good model of how the world works in the absence of intervention (but so too does the practitioner who relies on the thought experiment). This illustrates an important possible limitation of simulation at this time; the utility of the simulation will be a function of how well the model is specified and the extent to which this reflects the way the world might be. Ecological theories of crime (Cohen and Felson, 1979; Ekblom, 2000) provide a useful framework for analysis but, as will be discussed below, more empirical work is required before simulation models can be sufficiently specified.

Nevertheless, simulation offers the potential to improve upon the thought experiment considerably, and to generate results concerning what an intervention might achieve, given a set of clearly specified assumptions. Rather than a weakness this may be considered a further benefit of simulation. That is, the requirement to precisely specify a computer model, which incorporates the decision making processes of all agents, requires the researcher to carefully define the theoretical model used, and to specify the crime reduction mechanisms or logic of the intervention, something that they should always do.

The algorithms used in agent based models are mathematical formalisms intended to mimic or "model" human decision making processes. The basic idea of studying offender decision making is not new. It is central to rational choice theory (Clarke and Cornish, 1985) and has been explored in detail in the context of crime scripts (e.g., Cornish and Clarke, 2003; Lacoste and Tremblay, 2003; see also, Brantingham and Brantingham, 1993). In the case of the latter, the generation of crime scripts involves the identification of templates of behaviour that describe the individual actions (and their sequence) of the various actors (offenders, victims, guardians and so on) involved in crime events. The difference between the approaches is that agent based models can be used to see what patterns emerge when these types of model are implemented in-silico. The generation of crime scripts is a top down analysis, whereas agent based simulation is a bottom-up form of analysis for which crime scripts, or their mathematical analogues define a data generating process.

It is important to note that the algorithms used in agent based simulation are not intended to represent a general theory of cognition, but are instead used to focus on a limited set of decision making processes thought to be important in the behaviour to be understood. While it has limitations, agent based simulation offers the potential to examine models of crime causation and prevention in a more systematic and flexible way than has been possible hitherto.

An Example of an Agent Based Simulation Model

To illustrate some of the issues with agent based simulation, both positive and negative, a concrete example is provided. The example concerns the potential impact of different police patrol strategies on the crime of burglary (see also Birks et al., 2008; Groff and Birks, 2008). Burglary is chosen as an example for two reasons. First, with Henk Elffers and other members of an international collaboration, I am currently developing and testing models of burglar targeting strategies. One of the simpler models under development is used as an example here.

Second, for the crime of burglary the targets are fixed and hence the model is simpler than it would be for crimes such as robbery. For robbery, victimisation occurs when a victim and offender converge in space and time, in the absence of a capable guardian (Cohen and Felson, 1979). Thus, to model patterns of robbery, not only must the behaviour of offenders and guardians against crime be simulated, but we must also model the routine activities of the remainder of the population. To generate such a simulation that has an acceptable level of ecological validity will require considerable work. Thus, a simple model is used here to illustrate the points of central importance.

A picture tells a thousand words. Watching and playing with a simulation tells considerably more. Thus, rather than just describing the model developed and the results generated, the simulation was developed in the NetLogo programming language (Wilensky, 1999) discussed above to allow readers to download and play with it. The model developed for this section is also free to download.[10]

The simulation is made up of two basic elements; the world and two classes of agents (police and offenders) that move around it. The virtual world is made up of a grid of regular sized cells or, to use the nomenclature of NetLogo, patches which represent crime opportunities; homes in this model. Each home is assigned a crime attractiveness value to represent its risk of victimisation. A choice of different models are available that simulate different patterns in the variation in risk across homes. These range from a homogeneous surface where every home has the same risk; a binary risk surface where homes in the East and West side of the grid have different risks; a quad in which risk varies in the four corners of the surface; and, a surface over which the variation in risk is generated using a combination of a uniform RNG and a smoothing function. Figure 4 shows examples of two of the types of surface discussed. The user with a little programming knowledge can easily generate more, and real data on the spatial variation in crime risk could be imported.

Agents are used to model the activity of offenders and police officers. Each agent can traverse the virtual world according to a set of predefined rules. For example, agents have vision for up to *n* cells ahead (this parameter is currently homogeneous within each agent set and selected by the user). Where an agent is at the edge of the grid, they see only as many cells ahead as exist. The number of agents, the number of time steps, how far the agents can see and many other variables can be varied. In the following sections a little more detail is provided about each class of agent.

Figure 4. Example Risk Surfaces (Left: binary surface; Right: random variation).

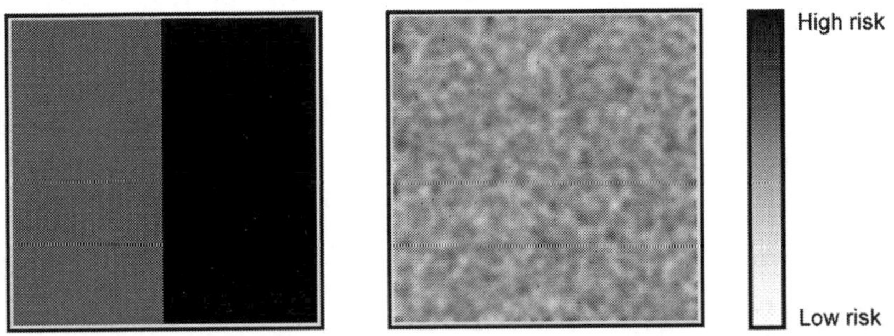

Offender Agents

For every time step, each offender agent turns in the optimal direction, moves and then decides whether or not to commit an offence. The decision to commit a crime is a function of a number of factors which will be discussed below but also of the proximity of police agents. If a police agent is within five cells (this may of course be varied but is held constant here) of an offender agent, the offender agent will not commit a crime. This is used to model the preventive effect of police patrols.

Offender agent movement is determined in the following way:

1. Each agent looks directly ahead in all directions in its Von Neuman neighbourhood (North, East, South and West) and calculates a value to represent the cumulative opportunities in that direction. For example, when looking North, the agent will look at the *n* cells North of it, and add the attractiveness values for each cell together.

   This evaluation has two important additional features. First, every agent's vision is locally weighted so that greater importance is given to proximate locations. Second, rather than being a purely objective calculation, to generate a degree of bounded rationality (see Cornish and Clarke, 1985), a random number is added (or subtracted) to the cumulative value for each direction considered. The maximum value of the random number generated is a function of the risk ahead; the random number will tend to be largest when the attractiveness of the opportunities ahead is greatest.

2. The agent also considers how much crime has been committed in each direction with a view to avoiding areas that have been over-foraged (see Johnson and Bowers et al., 2008) and hence may be subject to police attention.

3. To determine the vector of travel, the agent turns in the direction that offers the optimal balance between the highest estimated cumulative opportunity value and the risk of encountering a police patrol at that time.

The agent then moves one cell and decides whether or not to commit a crime at that location. This is a two stage process, as follows:

a) The agent's state of readiness to offend (e.g., Clarke and Cornish, 1985) at each moment is modelled as a function of an RNG and the individual offending rate for that offender (lambda). For the current model the value of lambda is held constant across agents and time, but this may be varied to examine the effect(s) of population heterogeneity or desistance decisions (Clarke and Cornish, 1985).

b) If the agent is in a state of readiness to offend, and there are no police agents nearby, the attractiveness of the cell in which the agent is located is evaluated. The higher the attractiveness of the particular cell, the higher the likelihood that the agent will offend at that location. Whether an offence occurs or not is thus determined by the attractiveness of the location, the output of an RNG and the agent's interaction with the police agents. When an offence takes place at a particular location, the number of crimes recorded at that cell is updated.

Thus, the offender agents' behaviour is a function of a series of simple rules. As discussed, the model here used is deliberately simple to illustrate the main points. However, the interesting thing is that the emergent behaviour need not be so simple and the local interactions between the different classes of agents and their environment can generate patterns that readers may expect would require more complex models.

Police Agents

Two types of patrolling strategy are modelled. For the first, police agents move randomly. In this case, for each time step, every police agent randomly selects a direction of travel from its Von Neuman neighbourhood and then (on the basis of the output of an RNG) moves one or two cells in that direction. The police agents could of course be limited to moving only one cell per time cycle, but they are not in this model.

In the second model, police agents decide where to patrol based on the volume of crime they "see" in front of them. This is essentially a hotspot policing model. Each police agent looks *m* cells ahead in each direction of its Von Neuman neighbourhood and evaluates the volume of crime in every direction. The value of *m* is selected by the user. Different values are likely to affect the performance of the model but here *m* is set to a constant value of 40 across simulations. The parameter *m* was set in this way so that the police agents would be able to "see" further than the offender agents. This was to reflect the fact that in the real world, the police may be advised about crime locations by other officers or by a command and control centre. Having evaluated the volume of crime in each direction, the police agent moves one or two cells in the direction in which most crime has occurred. The agents act independently and do not communicate with each other. Nor do they attempt to avoid directions where there are other police agents.

Initial Conditions

At the start of the simulation, each agent is placed at a random location on the grid. For the offenders this may thought of as their home location. Considering the variation in victimisation risk across homes, for the current model, the grid is divided into four quadrants across which (but not within) the attractiveness of targets vary.

Results of the Policing Simulation

The results of a simulation may be analysed in much the same way as data generated in the real world. For example, Figure 5 shows an example of a hotspot map generated by one run of a simulation.

To provide a more systematic analysis, for each model described, the effect of increasing the number of police agents is tested on the dependent variable – the volume of offences committed. Specifically, models are tested with 0, 10, 20, 40 and 80 police agents. Every model is executed 20 times and for 1,000 time steps. The reason for running the model a number of times is that the initial conditions of the model (where the agents are initially located) will influence the outcome of the simulation.

Figure 6 shows the mean number of crimes committed for each model tested. With the exception of the model for which there are zero police

Figure 5. An Example of a Kernel Density Map Generated by an Agent Based Simulation.

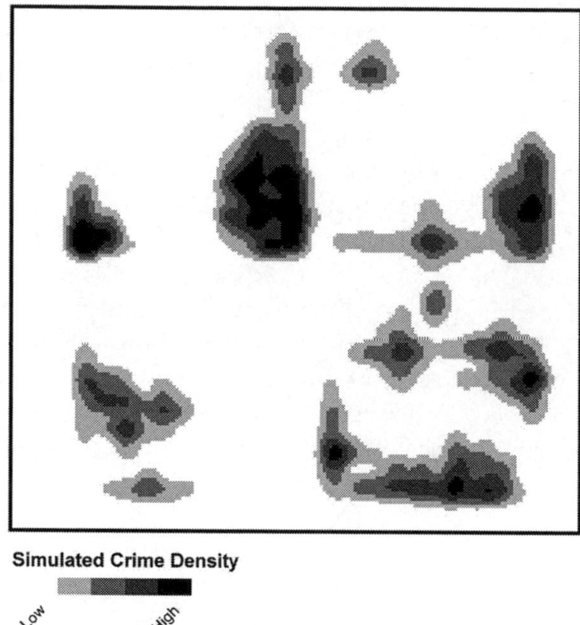

Figure 6. Impact on Crime of Two Patrolling Strategies and Changes in the Number of Police Agents (20 simulations per model, 1000 time cycles per simulation).

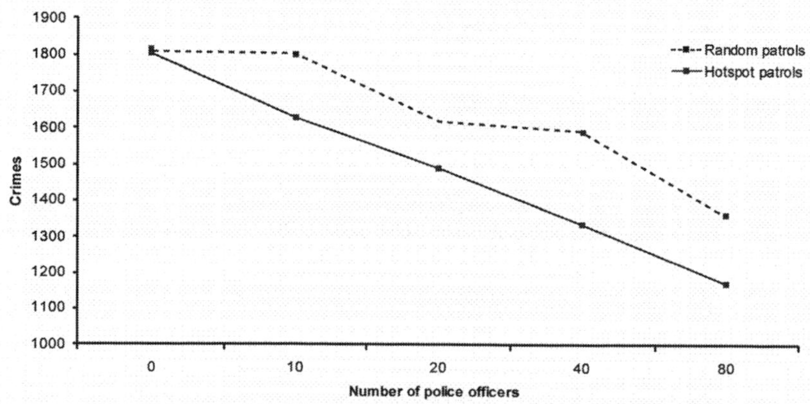

agents ($p=0.79$), less crime is committed for the hotspot policing model (all $ps<0.01$). For the hotspot policing model, increasing the number of police officers has a roughly linear effect on the volume of crime committed. For the random patrol model, the effect is more variable.

Assumptions and Parameter Sweeps

It should be obvious from the above discussion that many decisions regarding parameter settings and the formalisation of decision rules are required to produce a working simulation. On the one hand, this is useful as it forces the researcher to explicitly formalise rules and consider issues that they otherwise might not. On the other, this reminds us of one of the potential problems with simulation. When so many parameters can be manipulated and processes implemented in a range of ways, each permutation will require evaluation if conclusion validity is to be established in any meaningful way.

Fortunately, modelling platforms such as Netlogo have tools which enable the testing of different permutations of parameter values. Running each configuration of parameter settings also enables the effects of chance and initial conditions to be examined on the output of a model.

For the above results, the findings are of course only of any utility if the underlying model reflects the way the world is. There is no suggestion here that the model does. However, whilst considerable caution is clearly necessary regarding the ecological validity of simulation models, the promise is equally exciting. Even at this stage of maturity, simulation can be used for theory testing and falsification and, in the context of policy simulation, could (with some degree of caution) be used to identify those conditions under which certain types of intervention – with simple crime reduction mechanisms – might work. Thus, simulation models could be used as tools to help researchers and practitioners think through how an intervention might work in a systematic way.

What Else Might be Included in the Simulation Model?

The simulation described above was quite simple. Further models could easily be developed to generate a more realistic simulation. The possibilities are considerable, but some examples include:

1) The incorporation of a street network which would affect agent mobility in different directions (Birks et al., 2008; Groff, 2007ab);

2) The inclusion of an algorithm to allow the agents to navigate the world in a more deliberate way (see, Groff, 2008). This could draw on findings from research concerned with space syntax (e.g., Hiller, 2004) which suggest that the geometry of the street network can affect navigation in subtle ways. For example, as a consequence of variation in sight lines due to street network configuration, the route taken from two locations A and B, is often different from the route taken from B to A by the same person;
3) Barriers to offender movement, physical or social (e.g., Bernasco and Nieuwbeerta, 2005), could be included;
4) Offenders could form individual mental maps of their world based on their learning experiences in it, and perhaps choose to offend with a higher probability in those areas they know best;
5) A range of routine activity nodes (e.g., home, friends' homes, shops) could be generated for each agent (e.g., Groff, 2007a) and they could be encouraged to travel to them on certain days and at particular times. More detailed insights into human mobility patterns, routine activities and the anisotropy of human movement could also be incorporated into the models (Gonzalez et al., 2008);
6) A form of gravity could be used to encourage offender agents to avoid travelling too far from their home location or routine activity nodes;
7) The offender agent's readiness to offend could be varied over time, perhaps as a function of recent success; and,
8) The activity and visibility of the police could be modelled in a more realistic way, drawing upon research extant (e.g., Clarke and Hough, 1984).

Other Types of Intervention?

This type of approach could, of course, be used to look at other types of crime prevention strategies, such as street lighting. However, in some cases there may be a risk of producing models that generate nothing more than pre-supposed emergence. To illustrate, consider that if we produce a model in which we say that street lighting reduces the risk of victimization by 20% and then run the model and examine the impact of intervention, the problem will be that the model is tautological. The results of the simulation will only tell us what we put into it; it will not test a causal mechanism.

As an alternative, we could test the effects of increased illumination on crime reduction mechanisms. For example, we could see what the effect of increasing an offender's visible range has on their foraging strategies and rate of offending given the possible changes in attendant risks. Likewise, the effects of increased illumination on the potential victims' visible range, and hence potential avoidance strategies, could be tested. However, it is worth noting that such a mechanism assumes that the effect of street lighting is produced as a consequence of the increase in luminescence generated. In relation to this, an illuminating finding is provided by Farrington and Welsh (2002, p. 36) who examined the effects of street lighting on crime during the day and night. Similar effects were observed at both times of the day, suggesting that the mechanism of change was not simply the change in illumination.

CONCLUSION

The potential benefits of using computational methods for theory testing and evaluation are numerous. The examples provided in this chapter were intended to illustrate some of the possibilities and how they might be used to inform the sequenced decision making processes that policy actors routinely engage in. It is important to realize that other types of simulation methodology exist and that the types of questions considered here represent the tip of the iceberg. However, it is also important to remember that care needs to be taken when using simulations. The results of a model do not tell us what will happen in the real world, only what might happen if the assumptions of the model are valid. They may not be, but numbers can be seductive and so one risk is that the output of simulation models may inspire confidence where caution would be more appropriate. Before policy simulation is pursued in earnest, the way forward requires considerable effort in testing and maximizing the validity of models designed to simulate normal patterns of crime, perhaps along the lines suggested by Townsley and Johnson (2008). For individual studies, it will be important to conduct sensitivity analyses by sweeping the parameter space of models used and summarizing the effect of changes made on the outcomes generated. Moreover, replication is the cornerstone of good science and so the independent verification of findings from research which involves simulation will be important (Townsley and Johnson, 2008).

Despite the obvious need for caution, as other authors have concluded (e.g., Groff and Birks, 2008) simulation methods offer researchers exciting new tools for research. If appropriately specified, simulations could allow the systematic testing of ideas before fieldwork begins, as well as providing tools to help decision makers better understand the likely impacts of tested interventions.

Address for Correspondence: UCL Jill Dando Institute of Crime Science, University College London , Second Floor Brook House, 2- 16 Torrington Place, London WC1E 7HN, UK; e-mail: shane.johnson @ucl.ac.uk

Acknowledgments: This work was supported by a British Academy research grant, award number LRG-45507. I would like to thank the editors and the other contributors to this book each of whom provided helpful comments on an earlier draft of this paper. In particular I would like to thank Gary Henry, Paul Ekblom and Elizabeth Groff for detailed comments and suggestions. Thanks also go to Ken Pease and Henk Elffers.

NOTES

1. Matched samples may not be generated using random allocation where the sample sizes are small or where the population is non-homogenous.
2. Where a selection bias exists, the treatment effect may be confounded with the allocation strategy employed.
3. Block randomisation is a two-stage process. In the first stage, pairs of candidates (e.g. areas for intervention) are identified that are matched on a range of variables that might influence the dependent variable. In the second stage, one member of each pair is randomly allocated to the treatment condition. For an example in a criminological context, see Braga and Bond, 2008.
4. Time series analyses (e.g. Bowers et al., 2005) do not suffer from this problem. However, such analysis will only be appropriate where data are available for an interval of time which allows adequate diagnosis of ARIMA model parameters and where the volume of crime per unit time satisfies basic requirements. For example, it would be inappropriate to analyse time series data for a small area for which many of the

observations (e.g. monthly crime counts) were zero values (a statistical floor effect).

5. There is no suggestion here that changes in the risk of victimisation are likely to be the consequence of a biological or similar mechanism. The simile is merely useful as a mental shortcut.
6. To use the model, the reader should first open the NetLogo program. Once running, the user can load the simulation model using the File command. Details of what the simulation does and how to use it can be found in the "information" tab. The simulation model may be downloaded from: http://www.jdi.ucl.ac.uk/british_academy_network/history/index.php
7. We could divide the highest count of crime for the treatment area by the lowest count for the baseline model. However, the mean represents what would be typically expected in the absence of intervention and is thus the denominator used here. For the estimation of the treatment effect, in reality time only flows one way and so we will observe only one outcome. For this reason, I use the highest and lowest estimates in this case (there will actually be no average in reality).
8. This is an estimate of the mean effect, generated over 20 simulations. The true value of 50% would be observed if a larger number of simulation runs was used.
9. Although the use of simulation is relatively new in the field of criminology, it has been used for decades in the field of ecology to study behaviour not dissimilar to that discussed here. For example, Pyke (1981) describes a computer simulation used to test theories of optimal foraging in Honeyeaters.
10. http://www.jdi.ucl.ac.uk/british_academy_network/history/index.php.

REFERENCES

Agresti, A. (2002). *Categorical Data Analysis (2nd Edition)*. Florida: Wiley.

Alimadad, A., Borwein, P., Brantingham, P., Brantingham, P., Dabbaghian-Abdoly, V., Ferguson, R., Fowler, E., Ghaseminejad, C. G., Li, J., Pollard, N., Rutherford, A., & Waall, A. (2008). Using varieties of simulation modelling for criminal justice system analysis. In L. Liu & J. Eck (Eds.), *Artificial crime analysis systems: Using computer simulations and geographic information systems*. New York: Information Science Reference.

Bak, P. (1996). *How nature works: The science of self organized criticality*. New York: Springer-Verlag.

Barr, R., & Pease, K. (1992). A place for every crime and every crime in its place: An alternative perspective on crime displacement. In D. J. Evans, N. R. Fyfe, & D. J. Herbert (Eds.), *Crime policing and place: Essays in environmental criminology*. London: Routledge.

Batty, M. (2007). *Cities and complexity*. Cambridge, MA: MIT Press.

Bernasco W. (2007). Them again? Same-offender involvement in repeat and near repeat burglaries. *European Journal of Criminology*, *5*, 411–431.

Bernasco, W., & Nieuwbeerta, P. (2005). How do residential burglars select target areas? *British Journal of Criminology*, *45*, 295–315.

Birks, D. J., Donkin, S., & Wellsmith, M. (2008). Synthesis over analysis: Towards an ontology for volume crime simulation. In L. Liu & J. Eck (Eds.), *Artificial crime analysis systems: Using computer simulations and geographic information systems*. New York: Information Science Reference.

Bowers, K. J., & Johnson, S. D. (2005). Domestic burglary repeats and space-time clusters: The dimensions of risk. *European Journal Criminology*, *2*, 67–92.

Bowers, K. J., Lab, S., & Johnson, S. D. (2008). Evaluating crime prevention using survival analysis. *Policing: A Journal of Policy and Practice*, *2*, 218–225.

Bowers, K. J., Johnson, S. D., & Hirschfield, A. F. G. (2005). Closing off opportunities for crime: An evaluation of alley-gating. *European Journal on Criminal Policy and Research*, *10*(4), 285–308.

Bowers, K. J., & Johnson, S. D. (2005). Domestic burglary repeats and space-time clusters: the dimensions of risk. *European Journal of Criminology*, *2*(1), 67–92.

Bowers, K. J., Johnson, S. D., & Pease, K. (2005). Victimisation risk, housing type and area: The ecological fallacy lives! *Crime Prevention and Community Safety: An International Journal*, 7(1), 7–18.

Bowers, K. J., Johnson, S. D., & Hirschfield, A. F. G. (2004). The measurement of crime prevention intensity and its impact on levels of crime. *British Journal of Criminology*, *44*,(3), 1–22.

Braga, A. A. (2001). The effects of hot spots policing on crime. *Annals of the American Academy of Political and Social Sciences*, *578*, 104–125.

Braga, A. A., & Bond, B. J. (2008). Policing crime and disorder hot spots: A randomized controlled trial. *Criminology*, *46*(3), 577–607.

Brantingham, P., & Brantingham, P. (1993). Environment, routine, and situation: Toward a pattern theory of crime. In R.V. Clarke & M. Felson (Eds.), *Routine activity and rational choice*. New Brunswick, NJ: Transaction Publishers.

Budd, T. (1999). Burglary of domestic dwellings: Findings from the British Crime Survey. *Home Office Statistical Bulletin*, 4/99. London: Home Office.

Campbell, D. T. (1957) Factors relevant to the validity of experiments in social settings, *Psychological Bulletin*, *54*,297–312.

Campbell, D. T., & Stanley, J. C. (1963). *Experimental and quasi-experimental designs for research*. Boston: Houghton Mifflin.

Clarke, R. V., & Cornish, D. B. (1985). Modelling offenders' decisions: A framework for research and policy. In M. Tonry & N. Morris (Eds.), *Crime and justice: An annual review of research*, 6. Chicago: University of Chicago Press.

Clarke, R. V., & Hough, M. (1984). Crime and police effectiveness. *Home Office research study 79*. London: Home Office.

Cornish, D., & Clarke, R. V. (2003). Opportunities, precipitators and criminal decisions: A reply to Wortley's critique of situational crime prevention. In M. J. Smith & D. B. Cornish (Eds.), *Crime prevention studies*, Vol. 16. Monsey, NY: Criminal Justice Press.

Dray, A., Mazerolle, L., Perez, P., & Ritter, A. (2008). Drug law enforcement in an agent-based model: Simulating the disruption. In L. Liu & J. Eck (Eds.), *Artificial crime analysis systems: Using computer simulations and geographic information systems*. New York: Information Science Reference.

Eck, J. (1993). The threat of crime displacement. *Criminal Justice Abstracts, 25*, 527–546.

Ekblom, P. (2000). The conjunction of criminal opportunity – A tool for clear "joined-up" thinking about community safety and crime reduction. In S. Ballintyre, K. Pease, & V. McLaren (Eds.), *Secure foundations: Key issues in crime prevention, crime prevention and community safety*. London: Institute for Public Policy Research.

Ekblom, P., Law, H., & Sutton, M. (1996). Safer cities and domestic burglary. *Home Office study 164*. London: Home Office.

Ekblom, P., & Pease, K. (1995). Evaluating crime prevention. In M. Tonry & D Farrington (Eds.), *Building a safer society: Strategic approaches to crime prevention, crime and justice: A review of research*, 19. Chicago: University of Chicago Press.

Farrell, G. (2005). Progress and prospects in the prevention of repeat victimization. In N. Tilley (Ed.), *Handbook of crime prevention and community safety*. Cullompton, UK: Willan.

Farrington, D. P., & Welsh, B. C. (2006). How important is "regression to the mean" in area-based crime prevention research. *Crime Prevention and Community Safety, 8*,, 50–60.

Farrington, D. P., & Welsh, D. C. (2002). *Effects of improved street lighting: A systematic review*. Home Office research study 215. London: Home Office.

Farrington, D. P., Coid, J. W., Harnett, L., Jolliffe, D., Soteriuo, N., Turner, R., & West, D.J. (2006). Criminal careers up to age 50 and life success up to age 48: New findings from the Cambridge study in delinquent development. *Home Office research study 299*. London: Home Office.

Felson, M. (2005). *Crime and nature*.Thousand Oaks, CA: Sage.

Forrester, D., Chatterton, M., & Pease, K. (1988). *The Kirkolt burglary prevention project, Rochdale*. Crime prevention unit paper 13. London: Home Office.

Gilbert, N., & Troitzsch, K. G. (2005) *Simulation for the social scientist* (2nd ed). Maidenhead, UK: Open University Press

Gonzalez, M. C., Hidalgo, C. A., & Barabasi, A.-L. (2008). Understanding individual human mobility patterns. *Nature, 453*, 779–782.

Groff,E. R. (2007a). Simulation for theory testing and experimentation: An example using routine activity theory and street robbery. *Journal of Quantitative Criminology, 23*(2), 75–103.

Groff, E. R. (2007b). 'Situating' simulation to model human spatio-temporal interactions: An example using crime events. *Transactions in GIS, 11*(4), 507–530.

Groff, E. R. (2008). Spatio-temporal aspects of routine activities and the distribution of street robbery. In L. Liu & J. Eck (Eds.), *Artificial crime analysis systems:*

Using computer simulations and geographic information systems(pp. 226–251). Hershey, PA: Idea Group.
Groff, E., & Birks, D. (2008). Simulating crime prevention strategies: A look at the possibilities. *Policing: A Journal of Policy and Practice*, *2*,, 175–184.
Groff, E. R., & Mazerolle, L. (2008). Special issue: Simulated experiments in criminology and criminal justice. *Journal of Experimental Criminology*, *4*(3), 187–333.
Hillier, B. (2004). Can streets be made safe? *Urban Design International*, *9*, 31–45.
Johnson, S. D. (2008). Repeat burglary victimization: A tale of two theories. *Journal of Experimental Criminology*, *4*, 215–240.
Johnson, S. D., & Bowers, K. J. (2004a). The burglary as clue to the future: The beginnings of prospective hot-spotting. *European Journal of Criminology*, *1*,(2), 237–255.
Johnson, S. D., & Bowers, K. J. (2004b). The stability of space-time clusters of burglary. *British Journal of Criminology*, *44*(1), 55–65.
Johnson, S. D., Summers, L., & Pease, K. (2008). Offender as forager: A direct test of the boost account of victimization. *Journal of Quantitative Criminology*, online first DOI 10.1007/s10940-008-9060-8
Johnson, S. D., Bowers, K. J., Birks, D., & Pease, K. (2008). Predictive mapping of crime by ProMap: Accuracy, units of analysis and the environmental. In D. Backcloth, W. Weisburd, W. Bernasco, & G. Bruinsma (Eds.), *Putting crime in its place: Units of analysis in spatial crime research*. New York: Springer.
Johnson, S. D., Bernasco, W., Bowers, K. J., Elffers, H., Ratcliffe, J., Rengert, G., & Townsley, M. T. (2007). Near repeats: A cross-national assessment of residential burglary. *Journal of Quantitative Criminology*, *23*(3), 201–219.
Johnson, S. D., Bowers, K. J., Jordan, P., Mallender, J., Davidson, N., & Hirschfield, A. F. G. (2004). Estimating crime reduction outcomes: How many crimes were prevented? *Evaluation: The International Journal of Research and Practice*, *10*, 327–348.
Lacoste, J., & Tremblay, P. (2003). Crime and innovation: A script analysis of patterns in check forgery. In M. J. Smith & D.B. Cornish (Eds.), *Crime prevention studies*, Vol 16. Monsey,NY: Criminal Justice Press.
Liang, J., Liu, L., & Eck, J. (2001). *Simulating crimes and crime patterns using cellular automata and GIS*. Presentation to the 2001 UCGIS Summer Assembly, Buffalo, NY.
Liu, L., & Eck, J. (2008). *Artificial crime analysis systems*. New York: Information Science Reference.
Marchant, P. (2005). What works? A critical note on the evaluation of crime reduction initiatives. *Crime Prevention and Community Safety*, 7, 7–13.
North, B. V., Curtis, D., & Sham, P. C. (2002). A note on the calculation of empirical *p* values from Monte Carlo procedures. *American Journal of Human Genetics*, *71*, 439–441.
Openshaw, S. (1984). *The modifiable areal unit problem*. Norwich: Geo books.
Pawson, R., & Tilley, N. (1997). *Realistic evaluation*. London: Sage.
Pease, K. (1998). *Repeat victimization: Taking stock*. Home Office police research group, crime detection and prevention series, paper 90. London: Home Office.

Polvi, N., Looman, T., Humphries, C., & Pease, K. (1991). The time course of repeat burglary victimization. *British Journal of Criminology, 31*, 411–414.

Pyke, G. H. (1981). Honeyeater foraging: A test of optimal foraging theory. *Animal Behaviour, 29*, 878–888.

Ratcliffe, J. H., & Rengert, G. F. (2008) Near repeat patterns in Philadelphia shootings. *Security Journal, 21*, 58–76.

Shadish, W. R., Cook, D., & Campbell, D. T. (2002). *Experimental and quasi-experimental designs for generalized causal inference*. Boston: Houghton Mifflin.

Sherman, L. (2007). The power few: Experimental criminology and the reduction of harm. *Journal of Experimental Criminology, 3*, 299–321.

Summers, L. Johnson, S. D., & Pease, K. (2007). El Robo de (Objetos en) Vehículos y su Contagio a través del Espacio y el Tiempo: Aplicaciones de técnicas epidemiológicas. *Revista Electronica de Investigacion Criminologica, 5*, 1–22.

Tabachnick, B. G., & Fidell, L. S. (2001). *Using multivariate statistics*. Boston: Allyn and Bacon.

Tilley, N. (1993). After Kirkholt — Theory, method and results of replication evaluations. *Police research group crime prevention unit series paper 47*. London: Home Office.

Townsley, M., & Johnson, S. D. (2008). The need for systematic replication and tests of validity in simulation. In L. Liu & J. Eck (Eds.), *Artificial crime analysis systems: Using computer simulations and geographic information systems*. New York: Information Science Reference.

Townsley, M., Homel, R., & Chaseling, J. (2003). Infectious burglaries: A test of the near repeat hypothesis. *British Journal of Criminology, 43*, 615–633.

Visher, C., & Linster, R. (1990) A survival mdel of pretrial failure. *Journal of Quantitative Criminology, 6*, 153–184.

Willensky, U. (1999). *Netlogo* (http://ccl.northwestern.edu/netlogo). Center for Connected Learning and Computer-Based Modelling, Northwestern University. Evanston, IL.

Weisburd, D., Bushway, S., Lum, C., & Yang, S.-M. (2004). The trajectories or crime at places: A longitudinal study of street segments in the city of Seattle. *Criminology, 2*, 283–321.